Dr Peter Oakes is Greenwood Lecturer in the
versity of Manchester and he has also taug
University of Liverpool. He is editor of the
the New Testament Booklist and his publications include *Philippians:
From People to Letter* (Cambridge University Press, 2001), and, as editor,
Rome in the Bible and the Early Church (Baker/Paternoster, 2002).

READING ROMANS IN POMPEII

Paul's letter at ground level

PETER OAKES

Fortress Press
Minneapolis

First published in Great Britain in 2009 by
Society for Promoting Christian Knowledge
36 Causton Street
London SW1P 4ST
www.spckpublishing.co.uk

and in the United States of America in 2009 by
Fortress Press, an imprint of
Augsburg Fortress
Box 1209
Minneapolis, MN 55440

Research for this project was supported by the Arts and Humanities
Research Council.

Cover design: Laurie Ingram

British Library Cataloguing-in-Publication Data
A catalogue record for this book is available from the British Library

SPCK ISBN 978–0–281–05931–7
eBook ISBN 978–0–281–06296–6

Library of Congress Cataloging-in-Publication Data is available

Fortress Press ISBN 978–0–8006–6359–9

Typeset by Graphicraft Limited, Hong Kong
First printed in Great Britain by MPG
Subsequently digitally printed in Great Britain

Produced on paper from sustainable forests

Contents

Contents

Tables

Figures

Preface and acknowledgements

It was not so much the details of the Pompeian evidence. It was the experiencing of Pompeii. The sense of many different first-century lives, lived cheek by jowl in this mass of houses, apartments, shops and workshops. How could we still read first-century Christian texts as though they were addressed to generalities such as 'gentile Christians'? Life was full of many, varied people, then as now. Surely these texts were written for such people rather than for the somewhat abstract entities that inhabit the pages of most academic books?

The detailed evidence from Pompeii did, of course, overwhelm me, as it will have overwhelmed many of you who have visited the town. Twice I had the delight of spending the best part of a week visiting a single block of houses, the Insula of the Menander, equipped with Roger Ling's history of the structures and Penelope Allison's list of what was found in each room. This block of houses, apartments, workshops and bars shows evidence of a kaleidoscopic range of social situations, from a senator to several dozen slaves; from a cabinet-maker, who owned a surprising range of surgical tools, to a barmaid called Iris who was the object of a graffiti slanging match between two rival lovers.

This book attempts two tasks. First, it seeks to show that, among the first-century non-elite, there was a diversity that involved social stratification. It uses evidence from Pompeian housing to demonstrate this and to offer some sort of shape for the stratification. Second, it explores what it might mean to read New Testament texts in relation to such social diversity. It tries out this approach in readings of aspects of Paul's letter to the Romans.

To make its case, the book begins with a row of four houses in Pompeii (Chapter 1). The layout, decoration and loose finds are considered. They demonstrate the existence of a widely differentiated set of non-elite social locations. In particular, three of the houses had non-elite householders and, on every economic indicator, the wealthiest of these must have had several times the resources of the middle one who, in turn, must have had several times the resources of the poorest one. We then give these observations more shape by putting them in the context of a survey of Pompeian housing (Chapter 2). This leads to a model that seeks to give some shape to the non-elite social structure in Pompeii. This model is then discussed in relation to other suggested models of first-century society. Next, we explore what all this means in terms of the types of social differentiation there would have been in the kind of group of people that we would expect to have belonged to a craftworker-led house church (Chapter 3). We consider who were the expected hearers of Paul's letter to the Romans and we develop models to represent craftworker house churches in a town such as Pompeii and in Rome (meeting mainly in apartment blocks).

We then attempt some initial exploration of what this social framework could mean for the interpretation of NT texts. We first consider how Romans 12 would relate to issues faced by a craftworker house church of the kind in our model (Chapter 4). Our second reading exercise takes four model individual hearers of differing social types: a slave bath-stoker, a poor stoneworker, a sexually exploited slave, and a craftworking house-church host (Chapters 5–6). The four are representative of social situations in our four Pompeian houses. We consider how Paul's language about salvation in Romans relates to issues faced in each type of social situation. Finally, we reflect briefly on some possible implications of our study for the interpretation of Romans (Chapter 7).

Thanks are due to many people over the past nine years. To Roger Ling, for conversations in 1999 and since, and for kind permission to reproduce his plans. To all the other members of the project on the Insula of the Menander, above all to Penelope Allison for her monumental work on the loose finds. To the governors of Northern College, Manchester for sabbatical leave that autumn. To Andrew Wallace-Hadrill, Maria Pia Malvezzi and the other staff of the British School of Art and Archaeology at Rome, for help and hospitality from 1999 onward. To the Soprintendenza Archeologica di Pompei for their great kindness in granting access to houses on the site in 1999 and 2007, and also for granting permission to reproduce photographs that Janet, my wife, took on each visit.

To Philip Law, for a helpful discussion in 2000 of a sketch of part of this book. To John Davies, for the opportunity to teach a Roman History course at the University of Liverpool based on my study of the Insula of the Menander, in 2002 and 2004. To the many groups of students and scholars who have patiently sat through videos and slide shows of the Insula and engaged in helpful discussion about the block and about house-church life in relation to it. I would particularly mention the international meeting of the Context Group for Biblical Research, generously hosted by Santiago Guijarro and others at the Pontifical University of Salamanca in 2006. To Nils Aksel Røsag for interesting discussion on Pompeii and Pauline studies.

To the University of Manchester, for granting research leave in spring 2008. To George Brooke, Todd Klutz, Kent Brower, Gerald Downing and all my other colleagues there, for their continuing support. To Harold Attridge, Paul Stuehrenberg, Adela Collins, Dale Martin and others at Yale Divinity School for the granting of a Visiting Fellowship during the spring. To Jonathan Bonk, Judy Stebbins, Pam Huffman, and David and Natalie Eastman for their hospitality at the Overseas Ministries Study Center during that time. To the Arts and Humanities Research Council, for awarding a research leave grant to bring this book to completion. To Eddie Adams for kindly reading through a draft of the book. To Rebecca Mulhearn and Neil Elliott, for taking the project on at SPCK and Fortress, and to them and many of their colleagues for help in bringing it successfully into print. Last, but far from least, to my wife, Janet, for photography, preparation of the typescript, and patient support throughout.

1

Craftworkers' houses, a bar and a mansion

The House of the Stoneworkers (I.10.6)

We are standing in a street in Pompeii, looking into the doorway of Region I, Block 10, House 6 (according to the numbering system devised by the archaeologists), flanked by the narrower entrances to Houses 5 and 7 (Figure 1.1). 'House' is a misnomer for 5 and 6. House 5 is an upstairs apartment. The beginning of the staircase can be seen behind the safety gate. The Italian *casa*, the term the archaeologists originally used, has a different range of meaning from its common translation, 'house'. In any case, all that the archaeologists could see, when they first unearthed the street, was a row of doorways. The 'houses' were assigned numbers, months before anyone knew what each 'house' was. As we will see, doorways 2 and 3 in the block turned out to be entrances to the same bar/house, leaving it with the odd label House 2–3. As we will also see (in Chapter 3), the semantic arbitrariness of people's use of the word 'house' spills over into the study of early Christianity in the issue of how to use the term 'house church'.

The wide entrance of House 6 is typical of shops and workshops. The main room is a fairly plain space (*c*. 3.5 m × 4.6 m).[1] Slots in the door-posts show that it was closed by wooden shutters with a locking bar. Where plaster remains on the walls, the lower half is painted plainly in pink. The floor too is very plain. The only sign of a structure is something vague in the back right-hand corner. Unlike most Roman shops, there are no signs of joist holes that would support the steps of a wooden stair-case leading up to some sort of upstairs space (although ladders could also be used in the same way). In the back left-hand corner of the room, there is a doorway.

---

[1] Roger Ling, *The Insula of the Menander at Pompeii. I: The Structures* (Oxford: Clarendon Press, 1997), p. 282. The block of houses is named after a picture of the Greek poet Menander, painted on a wall inside the largest house.

Figure 1.1 Entrance to House I.10.6, flanked by the entrances to I.10.5 and I.10.7

The doorway leads through to a small side room, about 2.5 m × 4.5 m (Figure 1.2).[2] At the extreme left of the photograph is a patch of white plasterwork. The plasterwork was decorated simply but attractively in the Pompeian 'Fourth Style' (current from about the middle of the first century CE: see below), including a depiction of a pair of birds. Clearly overlaying this plasterwork is the back end of the lower portion of the stairs leading up from doorway 5 to its separate apartment. The over-laying shows that this stairway was added later, maybe in the early 60s, reducing the space in the room. The birds were in one of two deep arched recesses created under the stairs. The section of staircase above the birds collapsed sometime between 1986 and 1992.[3] The low recess is visible in the picture. A small niche was also created above the lower recess. In Pompeii, this kind of niche was usually a *lararium*, a shrine to the household gods. In the middle of the north wall is a window, lighting the room. At the right-hand side is a terracotta pipe, enclosed in plaster. Out of the picture, above this, is a slot that probably held a seat for a latrine in the upstairs apartment.[4] I imagine that this arrangement engendered some-thing of a smell in the downstairs room, not improved by the inhabitants knowing that it was caused by a facility they did not themselves have.

The presence of the painted birds suggests that, when House 6 was created, the side room was used as a living space. Although the side room then shrank with the building of the stairs to I.10.5, it was probably still a living space. In any case, someone was likely to have to sleep in House 6, after barring the shop door. Even if we had no further information, House 6 would provide a window into what was a typical kind of existence for low-level craftworkers or traders. Thousands occupied such limited spaces, which were workshop, shop and living accommodation. Such archaeological remains are found right across the Roman empire. If we think of typical early Christians as members of craftworking families, as most scholars do, we need to realize that this was the most common kind of setting for such people. We could stop our archaeological and historical work at this point and start reading New Testament texts, such as Romans, in relation to such

---

[2] Ling, *Menander* I, p. 282.

[3] Ling, *Menander* I, p. 282.

[4] Ling, *Menander* I, p. 145. Penelope Allison suggests, rather less excitingly, that the pipe could alternatively have been for roof drainage: Penelope M. Allison, *The Insula of the Menander at Pompeii. III: The Finds: A Contextual Study* (Oxford: Clarendon Press, 2007), p. 335. It would seem rather perverse to bring the sometimes torrential rain of the region down a pipe through a house, when the pipe is right next to an external wall and the water is not being collected for use. However, there may be a similar feature in room 5 of House 2–3.

Figure 1.2 Side room of I.10.6, looking north

lives. Already, the issues that would seem likely to be of most relevance to the hearers of the texts would look rather different from those that fill the commentaries.

However, there is more to be learned, even about House 6. We can be a bit more specific about the lives of the people there. As soon as we are, the monochrome picture of first-century craftworkers dissolves, to be replaced by a more colourful one – even before we go next door to look at an astonishingly different craftworking social situation. To the idea of reading the NT texts in relation to the reality of poor craftworking lives, we need to add the fact of considerable social diversity, even among craftworkers.

For House 6, as for the rest of the block, we know a considerable amount about the structural situation at the time of excavation, the structural history of the building, and what was found in each room.

Three structural points from the excavation reports supplement the observations that can be made by walking round the house today. First, the reports state that the structure in the south-west corner of the main room was a pair of basins (*c.* 1 m × 0.6 m each, with 0.88 m-high walls between them and on their east side).[5] In the side room, the excavators record the presence of a cesspit below the downpipe. This caused the floor to sag,[6] which offers some support to the theory that the room had an unappealing smell. Finally, Roger Ling notes a possible breach in the workshop wall, about 1.25 m above the floor.[7]

Penelope Allison lists the items found in House 6 in a way that can be approximately set out as in Table 1.1. Allison also notes that a small bronze buckle was found, but in the upper layers of the volcanic deposit, so it was possibly from the apartment above.[8]

What are the social implications of all these pieces of evidence? Two types of evidence give clues about the work going on in House 6: the built-in basins and the pieces of stone. The basins led early interpreters to think that the workshop was used for fulling cloth.[9] However, the basins are rather small for that, as Elia noted even in 1934, and the whole space is rather limited for such an activity. Moreover, the objects found in the

---

[5] Olga Elia, 'Pompei: Relazione sullo scavo dell'Insula X della Regio I', *Notizie degli scavi* 12 (1934), p. 276; Ling, *Menander* I, p. 147 n. 3, quoting *Giornale degli Scavi*, 24 December 1932.

[6] Based on *Giornale degli scavi*, 28 December 1932, as quoted in Ling, *Menander* I, p. 145.

[7] Ling, *Menander* I, p. 282.

[8] Allison, *Menander* III, no. 1014, pl. 68.8.

[9] Elia, 'Relazione', p. 276; M. Della Corte, *Case ed abitanti di Pompei* (Naples: Faustino Fiorentino, 3rd edn, 1965), p. 299, cited by Ling, *Menander* I, p. 147.

Table 1.1 Loose finds in House I.10.6

Workshop	*Side room*
Along east wall, on floor[1]	*Along north wall, on floor*
4 marble bases	2 marble bases
3 marble supports (diameter *c.* 230 mm, height *c.* 300 mm)	marble support (height 550 mm)
	travertine base[3]
2 travertine (hard white limestone) bases	6 strips of bronze
travertine capital (fluted Doric, height 200 mm)	clay lamp (found with above)[4]
Entrance, in volcanic deposit	*Along north wall, on floor, or in recesses*[5]
clay lamp (double nozzle, decorated with crescent, discus, eagle and hare)[2]	4 plates (*c.* 230 mm)
	3 pots (diameter *c.* 250 mm), for cooking or storage
	3 lids (100–150 mm)
	jar (height 190 mm)
	jug (height 450 mm), probably originally for *garum* (the ubiquitous Roman fish sauce)
	3 amphorae (heights 320–480 mm); size suggests for domestic storage
	a mortar, and another possible fragment[6]
	Entrance, in volcanic deposit
	dish (diameter 179 mm), *terra sigillata* (about half remaining)
	bowl, *terra sigillata* (fragment)
	bowl (diameter 250 mm)
	2 lids (110 mm)
	jug (height 200 mm)
	bronze lock plate for piece of furniture[7]
	Unknown location
	bronze lamp (max. length 210 mm), chains for hanging[8]

[1] Allison, *Menander* III, nos 985–92. Size of bases ranges from 130 × 130 × 50 mm to 350 × 320 × 120 mm.
[2] Allison, *Menander* III, no. 984. The lamp and many other finds were destroyed in one of the most pointless bombing raids of the Second World War.
[3] Allison, *Menander* III, nos 999–1002, with photos, pls 68.1–2.
[4] Allison, *Menander* III, nos 999, 1012, pl. 68.6.
[5] Elia, 'Relazione', p. 277, puts the finds in the recesses but Allison follows the *Giornale degli scavi* in putting them elsewhere. Since the recesses were the most obvious storage area, I would be surprised if Elia was not correct for at least some of these items.
[6] Allison, *Menander* III, nos 1003–11.
[7] Allison, *Menander* III, nos 993–8, pls 68.3–5.
[8] Allison, *Menander* III, no. 1013, pl. 68.7.

room suggest that, in 79 CE at least, it was being used for another purpose. In 79 CE, the occupants of House 6 possessed (or looked after) a collection of minor, miscellaneous pieces of decorative stone, most of which were on view in the shop. Their trade presumably related to that. No stone-carving tools were found. That is not a huge surprise. No bodies were found in the house and anyone fleeing the volcano would probably have taken tools with them. On the other hand, we might have expected the odd discarded broken tool and would also have expected stone chippings to be around (unless the excavators were careless and missed them). Probably something less creative than sculpture was going on.[10] We cannot be sure that there were no better pieces of stonework in the shop at some point. Small statues might have been taken at the time of escape or, remembering the possible breach in the wall, they could have been looted in the years or centuries following the eruption. However, it looks most likely that the occupants of House 6 were engaged in some sort of low-value craftworking or trading activity to do with decorative stone. One can imagine them trading in reused stonework: acquiring it somewhere, maybe cleaning it up (in the basins), carrying out minor repairs or remodelling, then selling it on. Given the damage caused by earthquakes in Pompeii from 62 CE onwards, with the subsequent abandonment or downgrading of some buildings and the refurbishment of many others, such stone recycling would seem a reasonable business idea, albeit a rather marginal one when conducted on such a small scale as this.

If we only had the finds from the workshop, we would probably assume that House 6 had been abandoned quite a while before the eruption. The only item that rather suggests habitation is the clay lamp. Of course, the workshop could have been full of objects that have not survived the passage of time (e.g. textiles, wood, foodstuffs). However, many such objects use durable items such as metal catches. As noted above, pieces could also have been removed from the workshop at the time of the eruption or afterwards. However, extremely few objects were found in the workshop. It is the side room that gives better evidence of habitation in 79 CE, especially the domestic pottery. Allison suggests that, despite the house's tiny size compared with others in the block, House 6 'shows the most significant pattern of . . . food-preparation and eating equipment'.[11] Looking at the list, the quantity and range suggests to me that there were about two people living there. They had four plates, maybe one or two good-quality *terra*

---

[10] Although Ling does suggest specialist stone-carving: *Menander* I, p. 147.
[11] Allison, *Menander* III, p. 386.

sigillata dishes (although the fact that neither dish was found entire makes one cautious), and various pots and jugs.

The bronze strips probably came from a nice wooden casket (about 235 mm wide, the length of the longest strips). The bronze lock plate could have been from a cupboard in the room, though we might then have expected some hinges or nails. There was one nice, though quite plainly decorated, bronze lamp to hang up and give light to the room. However, the room also included some of the stone pieces. The inhabitants lived among their work. They probably could not afford, or had no space for, substantial wooden furniture with metal fittings, such as a couch – although we must be cautious about arguments from gaps in the evidence, given the possibilities of removal. They could have slept on something like a straw-filled mattress.[12] Despite the range of cookware, no cooking-stove was found. This sounds rather odd, but such a lack of cooking facilities was quite common in the Roman world, particularly in places such as the apartment blocks of Ostia and Rome (to which, of course, this book will return).[13] If the stoneworkers really did not have facilities for cooking, then they might have bought hot food from a bar such as House 2–3, a pattern of behaviour that seems to have been prevalent in places such as Ostia. Alternatively, they might have acquired it from House 4 next door, the lavish House of the Menander.

As Ling argues, House 6 was cut out from the corners of Houses 4 and 7 (in about 50 CE).[14] House 7 was once linked to House 4 and was likely still to have been the property of the owner of House 4. Thus it is almost certain that House 6 was created, and still owned, by the owner of the House of the Menander. He may have rented it out to someone unconnected with House 4. However, this would also be a typical situation in which the owner would set up a business to be run either by slaves, with almost all the income going to the owner, or by freed slaves. In the latter case, the freedpersons would keep some or all of any profit from the business but probably pay rent to their former owner, who was now their permanent patron (and to whom they might well get in debt). If the occupants of House 6 were slaves or freed slaves of House 4, the continued relationship with House 4 could well have included some food supply. However, the range of domestic

---

[12] As was probably common in Pompeii. See the comments below on House 7, rooms 2, 4 and 5.

[13] James E. Packer, *The Insulae of Imperial Ostia* (American Academy in Rome Memoirs 31; Rome, 1971), p. 73.

[14] Ling, *Menander* I, p. 148.

pottery indicates that, even if they collected their food from House 4 or a bar, the stoneworkers generally ate at home. They were a household in their own right. Further evidence of this point comes from the presence of the niche, which was almost certainly a *lararium*. A shrine of the household gods implies that the side room was for living in, rather than just being a storeroom. It acted as a symbolic focus for the idea that, even though this was just a couple of probably very poor people, they were a household.

Some points in the discussion above have illustrated a general complication that arises in using archaeological evidence. Various pieces of evidence come from different times. Loose finds do not generally date from the time of the decoration of walls, let alone the original construction of a house. Moreover, the final sealing of a building, to await the archaeologists' eventual digging up, is never typical of the life of the people in the building. Usually, a building is covered by earth after decades or centuries of decay. Sometimes that process follows a catastrophe such as fire or flood. If the sealing is gradual, it is obvious that we must ask, of any piece of structural or loose evidence, what period it relates to. For Pompeii, despite the fact that the town was suddenly overwhelmed, this question is still vital. The problem is that people are less likely to realize it.

The situation in Pompeii is, of course, far better than at almost any other archaeological site. Consider House 6. The main structures and the decoration with the birds date from about 50 CE. The intrusive staircase and presumably much of the plainer redecorating date from the 60s. The loose finds were *in situ* on 24 August 79 (though this precise dating of the eruption has sometimes been challenged). The one exception to that could be the lamp in the workshop, which might conceivably have been introduced by a looter. We do not know what, if any, other loose items might later have been removed by looters (or by returning owners), although we can assume that they would be easily portable items of significant value. Similarly, we do not know what items the inhabitants may have removed from the house when they fled the eruption, although the same points about portability and value hold. Pompeii suffered a major earthquake in 62 and various other tremors between then and the day of the eruption. We do not know how these affected the use of this house, although the domestic pottery suggests that it was still inhabited in 79.

The interest of this book is in first-century life in general, particularly as it might relate to the social situations of house-church members. Pompeii

9

is being used as a source for something akin to 'thick description'[15] of some specific situations. Despite the seismic activity, which did lead to the abandonment of some buildings, there is plenty of evidence of normal ways of life going on in the town in 79. The copious graffiti gives evidence of all sorts of activities, from politics to prostitution. The vast quantities of loose finds show thousands of people living their lives in relatively normal ways – although with a lot more repair and redecoration going on than one would expect in an average town. The presence of pieces of stonework in House 6 may, as suggested above, relate to business activity that derives from the collapse and restoration of buildings. That type of specificity is not very interesting for Pauline studies (although, in fact, earthquakes were actually a significant factor in some Pauline cities in the first century). What is interesting for the study of Paul's letters is to find, in House 6, an instance of the social situation of a couple of poor craft-workers. These happen to be craftworkers in an earthquake zone, which is not ideal. But, of course, it is precisely because of the effects of Vesuvius that, for these particular craftworkers, we get to see the contents of their crockery cupboard. Even though we will not make use of the details of the crockery, we can see something of their lives with a degree of rounded-ness that NT scholars have not generally seen before. If we combine this with a number of other instances of actual first-century social situations, we begin to develop a framework which should enable us to understand NT texts in ways that relate them more appropriately to their first-century context.

Sabina the stoneworker

It will be useful to have a shorthand way of referring to the type of social situation evidenced by the remains of House 6. To do so, we will imagine an inhabitant of a description that would fit with the evidence. Others would also fit, but we will focus on one. We have seen that the structural history of House 6 suggests the likelihood of occupation by slaves or freed slaves from the House of the Menander. The degree of independence evidenced by the crockery and the *lararium* makes occupation by freed slaves more likely than slaves. Freed slaves were generally on the older side, their former owners having had the benefit of their work in their

---

[15] Clifford Geertz, 'Thick Description: Toward an Interpretive Theory of Culture', in Clifford Geertz, *The Interpretation of Cultures: Selected Essays* (New York: Basic Books, 1973), pp. 3–30. Cf. Louise J. Lawrence, *An Ethnography of the Gospel of Matthew: A Critical Assessment of the Use of the Honour and Shame Model in Biblical Studies* (WUNT 2.165; Tübingen: Mohr Siebeck, 2003).

youth. Even allowing for removal of valuables before or after the eruption, the stoneworkers appear to have been very poor. The layout of the house, its simple decoration, and its simple contents are evidence of that. Although the freed slaves still had their former owner as their patron, that was no guarantee against poverty.

We will take House 6 to have been inhabited by a freed slave couple in their late thirties or beyond. We do not know the names of the inhabitants. We will call the female freed slave Sabina. She works with her husband on the stonework and also handles the housework and acquisition of food. They have no children, although Sabina may have borne children while she was a slave, in which case they would still be slaves, maybe living in House 4. The primary driver of Sabina's daily life is concern for where tomorrow's meal will come from. They are not far from destitution.

We are ultimately heading towards an exercise in which we reflect on how the letter to the Romans would relate to people in the types of social situation we find in Pompeii (with some thought as to how these situations would be modified by life in Rome). This requires us also to assume that Sabina heard the letter, which more or less means she would have to be a Christian. To put it at its most general, Sabina represents the social type of a very poor, female Christian craftworker. House 6 provides evidence of what being a very poor craftworker could mean in practice.

The Insula of the Menander as a whole

Region I, Block 10, the Insula of the Menander ('insula' here used in the archaeologists' conventional sense of 'a block of houses surrounded by streets'),[16] lies about halfway between Pompeii's forum and its amphitheatre. The block is set one street back from the main, shop-filled artery that links forum and amphitheatre (now called the Via dell'abbondanza). However, the block did contain some shops and is close enough to the heart of the town for there to have been a reasonable amount of traffic along its north side at least. In Figure 1.3, House 6 can be seen at the top of the plan. The large '6' marks the street entrance. The side room is marked 6A. The solid black lines mark boundaries between houses. We will shortly visit House 7, then House 2–3, with its bar marked on the plan below the large '2'. Finally, we will consider the aspects of the vast House 4, the

---

[16] For a discussion of what *insula* meant in antiquity, see A. Wallace-Hadrill, '*Domus* and *Insulae* in Rome: Families and Housefuls', in David L. Balch and Carolyn Osiek (eds), *Early Christian Families in Context: An Interdisciplinary Dialogue* (Grand Rapids: Eerdmans, 2003), p. 9.

Figure 1.3 The Insula of the Menander

Source: Ling, *Menander* I, fig. 24, drawn by S. Gibson, J. S. Gregory, R. J. Ling and D. Murdoch, with thanks to Roger Ling for permission to reproduce the plan.

House of the Menander, that relate to the lives of the non-elite people who were the great majority of its inhabitants.

The Insula of the Menander was unusually well published in the imme-diate aftermath of its excavation in the late 1920s and early 1930s. Olga Elia wrote an excellent, detailed article on each house except the House of the Menander.[17] That house was published in an extensive book by the great Pompeian archaeologist of the period, Amadeo Maiuri, who led the

---

[17] Elia, 'Relazione'.

12

dig.[18] The graffiti and inscriptions from the block were published by Matteo Della Corte.[19] Many other studies have included consideration of the House of the Menander (or, occasionally, others in the block).[20] In the late 1970s and early 1980s a team was invited by the Soprintendenza Archeologica at Pompeii to conduct a detailed survey of the Insula. This has led to a full-scale series publishing the Insula, under the editorship of my colleague Roger Ling. He contributed Volume I, on the structures and their history.[21] He and Lesley Ling wrote Volume II, on the paintings and mosaics.[22] In Volume III, Penelope Allison covers the loose finds.[23] Volume IV, by Kenneth Painter, looks at the silverware discovered in a cellar under the bathhouse of the House of the Menander.[24] A further volume, by Antonio Varone and Joyce Reynolds, is due to deal with the inscriptions and graffiti.

The monumental effort required for Penelope Allison's volume indicates why blocks of houses have not previously been published in this comprehensive way. How do you go about the apparently straightforward task of making a list of which moveable objects, large or small, were found in each room? Apart from some broad indications in the publications of Elia and Maiuri, Allison had two main sources to work with: the *Giornali degli scavi* – the handwritten daily reports made by the excavators – and the vast collections of material kept in various places, such as the drawers in the storage warehouses. The daily diaries recorded some things and not others (imagine trying to record all the pieces of broken pottery or roof tile if you were coming across it in large quantities!). The contents of the drawers then might or might not match what was listed. Moreover, the excavators gave various names to objects which might or might not describe their actual function, and which might or might not make it easy

---

[18] Amadeo Maiuri, *La Casa del Menandro e il suo tesoro di argenteria* (Rome: La Libreria dello Stato, 1933).

[19] M. Della Corte, 'Epigrafi della via fra le isole VI e X della Reg. I', *Notizie degli scavi* (1929), pp. 455–76; 'Pompei: Iscrizioni dell'isola X della Regione I', *Notizie degli scavi* (1933), pp. 277–331; M. Della Corte (ed.), *Corpus Inscriptionum Latinarum* (*CIL*) (Berlin: Königlich Preussische Akademie der Wissenschaften zu Berlin, 1952), IV.3.I.

[20] For example, John R. Clarke, *The Houses of Roman Italy, 100 BC–AD 250: Ritual, Space and Decoration* (Berkeley: University of California Press, 1991), pp. 14–16, 170–93, etc.

[21] Ling, *Menander* I.

[22] Roger and Lesley Ling, *The Insula of the Menander at Pompeii. II: The Decorations* (Oxford: Clarendon Press, 2004).

[23] Allison, *Menander* III.

[24] Kenneth S. Painter, *The Insula of the Menander at Pompeii. IV: The Silver Treasure* (Oxford: Clarendon Press, 2001).

to tell what the object looked like. It took years of work for Allison to get the evidence sorted into publishable form.[25]

Ling's study of the structures in the Insula, based on analysis of building techniques and decorative style, helps us to understand the history of the development of the block. Broadly speaking, it is a story of a relatively egalitarian initial layout being progressively taken over by the all-consuming House 4. The houses on the north side of the block began to be built in the late third or very early second century BCE. House 18 did not exist. Its space was part of Houses 1 and 3. The north side of the block consisted of four houses of similar size (1, 3, 7 and 8), on either side of the rather wider, grander and more formal House 4, which was centred around an atrium, probably with a small garden behind. The layout of other parts of the block at this period is unclear.[26]

The so-called 'First Style' of Pompeian decoration was typical from the mid-second to the early first century BCE. Its most recognizable feature is the painting of walls to imitate construction from blocks of various types of stone. During this period House 18 was created, shortening Houses 1 and 3. House 4 gained a peristyle area, although not as big as it eventually became. House 4 probably also became joined to House 7, which itself was extended backwards, as was House 8.[27]

During the period of the 'Second Style' (first century BCE, most notably represented by large *trompe-l'œil* schemes – the ones at the villa at Oplontis are particularly breathtaking), the Casa degli Amanti was built. The peristyle of the House of the Menander was enlarged to its full extent. A bath suite (rooms 46–49) was also added. More radically, a house that had roughly lined up with door 15 was destroyed to make space for new rooms on the peristyle's east side.[28]

The 'Third Style' period (in which decoration generally lost three-dimensional extravagance and favoured a 'picture gallery' scheme on the walls) ran from the late first century BCE to the middle of the first century CE. The kink in the north-east corner of the block represents the arrival of publicly provided drinking water in a fountain just outside House 1. Early in the period the garden of House 7 was reshaped to form corridor M–M2 as a hidden service link between that house and House 4. Near the

---

[25] Her first major study of material from Houses 4 and 7 was as part of her Ph.D. thesis, now published as *Pompeian Households: An Analysis of the Material Culture* (Monograph 42; Los Angeles: Cotsen Institute of Archaeology at UCLA, 2004).

[26] Ling, *Menander* I, pp. 223–5.

[27] Ling, *Menander* I, pp. 225–7.

[28] Ling, *Menander* I, pp. 227–30.

end of the period, the two houses were separated. Corridor M2 was blocked and the kitchen (room 11) and back staircase of House 7 were created.[29]

The 'Fourth Style' period covers the final 30 years of Pompeii's life. Wall pictures generally became smaller and the borders between wall panels regained a three-dimensional flamboyance. In about 50 CE, House 6 was cut out from the corners of Houses 4 and 7. The space lost from House 4 was replaced by creating an upper apartment at the front of the atrium. Over the following years, probably straddling the time of the earthquake in 62 CE, the development of the south-east quarter of the House of the Menander took place, resulting in its grandest room (18), its stable court-yard (29–34) and its other service quarters (35–40).[30] The earthquake caused a considerable amount of damage. Some walls collapsed, including several of those in the bath suite of House 4. Paintings on various remaining walls were damaged. This probably led to the redecoration of the atrium of House 4. The upstairs apartment that was accessed from doorway 5 was put in, further reducing the limited space in House 6. Doorway 2 and the food-and-drink shop behind it were created at about this time. The period after 62 CE saw some further damage to the Insula. Pieces of the recent decoration of room 18 of House 4 fell off and ended up as fill in an abandoned cellar. At several places in the Insula (Houses 1, 4, 8 and 18), piles of building material attest to repair and redecoration work continuing up to the time of the eruption.[31]

The House of the Cabinet-Maker (I.10.7)

One odd effect of the looting that took place over the centuries after the eruption is that the most complete sets of finds tend to be from open areas such as atria and gardens. The volcanic *lapilli* (small stones) filled these up while leaving many enclosed rooms clear for looters to reach (once they had dug through a ceiling or wall). As can be seen from the Insula plan, in House 7, the atrium, the garden (at the back of the house) and the portico (10) occupy most of the space (Figure 1.4). This left scope for an abundance of finds.

The excavators called House 7 the Casa del Fabbro. This really means 'House of the Blacksmith', which is not at all a good representation of the

[29] Ling, *Menander* I, pp. 230–2.
[30] Ling, *Menander* I, pp. 232–4.
[31] Ling, *Menander* I, pp. 237–7.

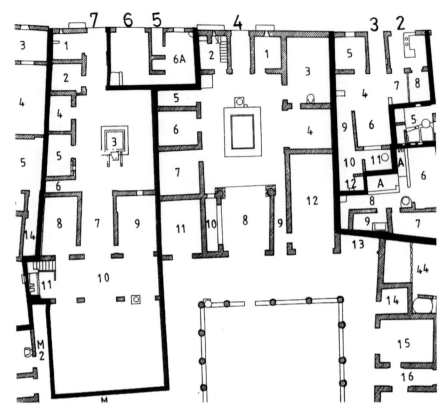

Figure 1.4 Part of north side of Insula of the Menander, from House 2–3 to House 7

types of tools found there. At a stretch, maybe one could translate it as 'House of the Craftsman', which would be reasonable. However, for our study, we want to differentiate between different craftworkers. For reasons that will become evident, we will call I.10.7 the 'House of the Cabinet-Maker'.

With a ground-floor area of 310 m², this is a much larger house than the House of the Stoneworkers, which, at 40 m², is too small to have previously been dignified with a name. On the other hand, House 7 is still very small in comparison with the House of the Menander, at 1,700 m². Beside doorway 7 is a stone bench, traditionally a place for clients waiting to see a patron.[32] Inside the door is a *fauces* (entrance corridor). Figure 1.5 looks back towards it across the atrium.

---

[32] Elia, 'Relazione', p. 278.

Figure 1.5 I.10.7: view from south side of atrium

In the *fauces*, a 150 mm key with six teeth was found, together with a large lock, two handles, another key, a latch, many nails and many studs of the kind that might decorate a door.[33] The final occupiers of the house had presumably left the front door locked, with the key on the inside. A simple bronze finger ring had also been dropped in the entrance corridor.[34] Room 1, just inside the front door, contained a wooden staircase. Behind the staircase was a latrine. A stone channel ran from this along the north wall of the room to join the atrium water-storage overflow in a drain below the pavement outside the front door.[35] Running diagonally across the room, from the south-east corner to the latrine, was a channel made out of roof tiles, which seems to have been used to flush the latrine. All this plumbing was covered by a raised wooden floor.[36] Neither the *fauces* nor room 1 was decorated.

Rooms 2, 4 and 5 are three small rooms opening off the west side of the *fauces* (2) or the atrium (4, 5). Each is simply decorated in the Fourth Style. Room 2 has a tiny window overlooking the atrium. Room 4 and 5 each include a recess, probably to take the end of a bed (see Figure 1.6). All these rooms had breaches in their walls, so they have probably been looted. However, rooms 2 and 5 still yielded a fair number of loose finds. These could generally be described as personal domestic objects: a button-and-loop fastener; several small glass bottles; part of a mirror; a spoon made of bone; a spindle; a clay lamp; a bronze jug; the foot of a glass; six bronze needles and a bone one, all probably for sewing. A rather spade-like hoe was also found in room 2, although it could have been moved there by looters (or escapees) who broke through the walls.[37] There are no identifiable bed fittings. However, both the decoration and (for rooms 2 and 4) the finds suggest these were personal spaces (insofar as there was privacy in such a house), such as bedrooms. The general scarcity of remains of beds in Pompeii leads Allison to argue that 'Beds and bedding in Pompeii were probably normally made purely of organic material (for example, wood and cloth) and so were not recorded'.[38] Elia suggested that room 2 could have been for a doorkeeper, able to keep an eye on the atrium too through the little window. Many of the finds in the room seem to me to be rather too feminine for a typical hulking

---

[33] Allison, *Menander* III, nos 1015–23 and p. 336.
[34] Allison, *Menander* III, no. 1024, pl. 69.1.
[35] Ling, *Menander* I, p. 152, citing excavations by S. C. Nappo.
[36] Ling, *Menander* I, p. 152, Elia, 'Relazione', p. 278.
[37] Allison, *Menander* III, nos 1034–51, 1146–54, pp. 337–8, 340, pls 70.1–10, 76.5–11.
[38] Allison, *Menander* III, p. 392.

Figure 1.6 I.10.7, room 4: bed recess (left), simple Fourth Style wall decoration, loose finds including lion's head drainage tile from rim of *compluvium*[1] and, possibly, base and capital from House 6[2]

[1] cf. Ling, *Menander* I, pl. 82.
[2] cf. Allison, *Menander* III, pls 68.1, 2.

doorkeeping slave. However, the proximity to the latrine could suggest that the inhabitants were of low status.

The final room opening off the west side of the atrium, room 6, was a storeroom. Holes in the walls show where shelving was fitted. A few domestic bronze and ceramic objects were found. There was also part of an amphora sold to M. Volusius Iuvencus. Della Corte took this to be the name of the householder[39] but a single amphora is not a strong basis for such an identification, especially of a non-elite householder, who would seem unlikely to place an order sufficiently substantial to get his name painted on amphorae. Above rooms 1, 2, 4, 5 and 6 ran a further set of small rooms, reached by the staircase in room 1. A few areas of Fourth Style decoration remain, although not enough for Ling and Ling to offer a comment on where these rooms stood in the house's 'hierarchy of space', except to say that the use of solid colours upstairs shows that the painting was a little more expensive than that in the rooms below.[40] The listing of finds from upstairs rooms is complex when, as in these cases, the floor has collapsed. It can be particularly difficult to distinguish material originating upstairs from material that was stored off the ground in downstairs cupboards. However, from the upper levels of volcanic deposit above rooms 1, 2, 4, 5 and 6, or from above the nearby western edge of the atrium, came a veterinary clamp, a lead weight, a ceramic basin, a cylindrical lead container (450 mm in diameter; 550 mm high) with some decoration, a bronze lamp, and some bronze ring handles.[41] This is not a very informative group of objects. Allison cites Adamo Muscettola as seeing the above type of lead vessel as a water container.[42] The ceramic basin is of a size for washing or mixing.[43]

And so to the atrium. Allison's catalogue for House 7 contains over 500 entries, many describing multiple items. More than a hundred of the finds were in the atrium. Contrary to the traditional picture of an atrium, the walls were coated in plain plaster and, along three of them, stood chests or cupboards filled with a host of objects. In the centre of the atrium was an *impluvium*, the traditional sunken basin that collected the rain water from the *compluvium*, the corresponding gap in the roof above. The water

---

[39] Della Corte, *Case ed abitanti*, no. 599, cited by Allison, *Menander* III, p. 348.

[40] Ling and Ling, *Menander* II, p. 145.

[41] Allison, *Menander* III, nos 1386–90, 1414–16, pls 91.1–4, 92.8–10.

[42] Adamo Muscettola, 'Le ciste di piombo decorate', *La regione sotterrata del Vesuvio: studi e prospettive* (Naples: Università di studi di Napoli, 1982), pp. 701–34, here p. 730, cited by Allison, *Menander* III, p. 195.

[43] Allison, *Menander* III, p. 345.

Table 1.2 House I.10.7, atrium: selected loose finds, with approximate categorization

Personal	several silver and bronze coins
	gold necklace (quite substantial) with pendant of Isis-Fortuna
	pair of gold and pearl earrings
	gold finger ring
Domestic	bronze incense burner
	several ceramic jugs
	bronze inkpot containing ink
	six stones, possibly for gaming[1]
	lead bowl containing pumice stone
	bronze strigils (scrapers for use in bathing)
	glass vase
	ceramic vase
	glass cup
Work-related	bronze tongs for metalworking
	bronze ruler, with clamping arm
	bronze surgical forceps (length 98 mm)[2]
Uncertain use	many glass flasks and bottles
	small ceramic jars
	iron knife (length 210 mm)
	marble mortar
	marble pestle, with handle shaped like finger (with nail)
	bronze ointment scoop or medical probe[3]
	bone needle
	bronze musical instrument (horn, but missing its bell)[4]
	bronze saucepan-shaped vessel (diameter 219 mm)

[1] Elia, 'Relazione', p. 296.
[2] Allison, *Menander* III, no. 1090, pl. 73.10; cf. no. 41 and comment attributed to Ralph Jackson.
[3] A *ligula*: Allison, *Menander* III, no. 1122, and discussion, p. 20.
[4] Elia, 'Relazione', p. 295.
Source: Selected from Allison, *Menander* III, nos 1052–1145, pp. 338–40, pls 71.1–76.4.

was fed down into a cistern and drawn out from an opening beside the *impluvium*. Oddly, this had been rendered almost unusable by the presence of a nicely decorated marble table, fixed above the cistern head cover. Presumably the house was relying on other cisterns in the back garden.[44] Maybe the atrium cistern was damaged in one of the earthquakes. Among the finds from the atrium are those listed in Table 1.2.

[44] Ling, *Menander* I, pp. 151, 161.

What is immediately clear from this collection is that the inhabitants had some quite valuable possessions, especially the jewellery. Combining this with the reasonable but fairly inexpensive decoration of the rooms we have seen so far, and with the plain-plastered atrium given over to storage rather than show, we begin to get an impression of a household that is some way from being either abjectly poor or elite. This is clearly of significant interest for Roman social history and Pauline studies. We need to look for further aspects of this social location as we consider further aspects of the house.

A range of personal and domestic activities are attested by these finds: from bathing (strigils and possibly the pumice) to writing and maybe entertainment or religious activities. We also begin to get work-related evidence, with a metalworking tool and a surgical instrument. The many glass flasks, bottles and small ceramic jars also suggest that some particular activity is going on, but there are various domestic or work-related possibilities. Allison suggests paint, food essences, cosmetics or medical supplies as possible contents of the containers.[45]

Overall, the finds in the atrium are an interesting mix. The cupboards do not contain the main collection of domestic pots, pans, plates, etc. Nor do they contain a set of tools for a particular trade. However, it looks a reasonably functional collection rather than a scavenged hoard. Turning the question on its head, there are some six wooden chests or cupboards in the atrium. We will shortly see evidence of woodworking activity in the house. Could it be that some of this furniture had been made for sale?[46] This could explain the somewhat opportunistic appearance of the contents of some of the cupboards.

The location of room 7 would traditionally be that of a *tablinum*, the classic space for a patron to receive his clients. However, it is extremely unlikely that in 79 CE, room 7 functioned in this way. Like the atrium, it had little decoration. Among various stored items found here, the most notable are two bronze balances, a bronze *patera* (shallow pan), two bronze basins and a very heavy marble weight (295 mm diameter, 190 mm high), presumably used in a work process.[47] At the south side of room 7, the remains of a folding wooden door indicate that this room could be shut off from the portico.[48]

---

45 Allison, *Menander* III, p. 339.
46 As Janet Oakes has suggested to me.
47 Allison, *Menander* III, nos 1169–84, pls 77.8–79.2.
48 Allison, *Menander* III, no. 1181, pl. 79.1, p. 341.

Figure 1.7 I.10.7, the portico (10), viewed from the east side of the garden. From left to right: the kitchen, the rear staircase, and the entrances to rooms 8, 7 and 9. In front of room 9 is the tube for access to a water cistern

Table 1.3 House I.10.7, room 8: selected loose finds, with approximate categorization

Bone-working	dozens of bone plaques, various sizes: many *c.* 125 × 35 mm but up to 85 mm wide; many decorated, including some with paint or gold leaf 4 small bone wedges 2 bone discs bone piece with teeth, as though being worked for comb
Woodworking	iron furniture leg with bone decoration nails bronze bands for chest (could be chest in use rather than in production) 3 bronze furniture feet
Other uses	iron shovel iron ladle/trowel
Uncertain use	iron wedges iron hook iron point

Source: Allison, *Menander* III, nos 1185–1229, pls 79.3–82.4.

The main craftwork in the house seems to have taken place in the portico (10) and in room 8 (Figure 1.7). Room 8 is expensively decorated in the late Third Style (*c.* 50 CE). It includes a picture of a banquet scene in which a woman and a man recline on a couch surrounded by various attendants and a child. As Ling and Ling argue, a particular (probably mythological) couple might be intended but it is hard to tell who. Earlier theories involving the deaths of Sophonisba or Cleopatra seem very unlikely in terms of the normal range of Pompeian paintings.[49] The scene, as a generic one, would seem very suitable for a room intended for eating or as a bedroom. The ceiling is somewhat lowered at the back, which favours the latter idea.[50] In any case, a glance at the list of loose finds (Table 1.3) shows that it was being used differently in 79 CE.

Some of the bone pieces were completed, but some appear only partially worked. This room was clearly used for storing, and quite likely also for working, bone pieces, particularly of types used for applying to furniture. This fits quite well with the evidence given by the loose finds from the

---

[49] Ling and Ling, *Menander* II, pp. 140–1.
[50] Ling, *Menander* I, p. 152.

Table 1.4 House I.10.7, portico 10: selected loose finds, with approximate categorization

Bone-working	bone pommel
	bone plaques
	bone strips
Woodworking	iron axe/hammer
	nails
	various bronze fittings
	studs
	4 pumice stones for sharpening tools
	2 bronze dividers
	iron compass
	19+ iron chisels
	iron gouge
	iron blades
	iron saw
	iron hammer
Metalworking	tool for cutting hot metal
	7 iron files
	iron tongs
Medical	bronze spatula (possibly surgical)
	bronze scalpel handle and dissector
Other uses	4-wheeled wooden cart (1.3 m × 0.79 m, wheel diameter 0.56 m)
	cupboard
	2 iron braziers
	iron shears for cloth, etc.
	stone handmill
	bronze weight
	iron jugs
	bronze jars
	ceramic vases (one containing 6 bronze coins)
	bronze needles
	glass beads
Uncertain use	3 marble weights with iron handles

Source: Allison, *Menander* III, nos 1252–1360, pls 84.3–89.1.

portico (Table 1.4). This collection reinforces the impression that the main commercial activity in the house was woodworking, probably mainly producing furniture. Elia described the householder as 'una *faber arcarius*, un costruttore di casse e di mobili' ('a maker of chests and furniture').[51]

---

[51] Elia, 'Relazione', p. 292, n. 1.

'Cabinet-maker' is the usual term for that. However, this can only be an approximation. The nature of the work will undoubtedly have differed from what we think of as cabinet-making.

The presence of some metalworking tools is not a difficulty for this view. Some metalworking would presumably be necessary in furniture-making. What is more of a problem is the absence of planes and drills from the portico and from the rest of the house. It could be that surfaces were levelled in other ways, possibly using files. There is also a question of how much of a wooden plane would survive other than the metal blade, which could then be hard to distinguish from other blades such as the many found here. More fundamentally, there was undoubtedly all sorts of craftwork going on in Pompeii but I would be surprised if more than a handful of complete sets of craftworkers' tools have been discovered. The main alternative to seeing the primary commercial activity of the house as woodworking is to see it as fairly general salvage.[52] However, there seems to be more homogeneity in the house's contents than is implied by the latter suggestion. Some variety of contents would be expected in any house of reasonable size. Craftworkers would also be likely to tackle jobs of types other than their main work. Some degree of hoarding of slightly random items would probably go on too, without that being the main activity. This debate is not crucial for our book, but Elia's impression of the house's main activity does seem reasonable.

The finds in room 9 are very different from those in the adjoining portico. There was a bronze foot from a portable stool, a small bronze amphora, four bronze jugs, a bronze *patera*, a bronze weight and, with its head in a recess, a wooden bed, painted red, with two iron legs and the remains of bone decoration.[53] On the bed was a skeleton with a small wooden casket, two bronze rings, 26 silver coins and 48 bronze ones.[54] At the foot of the bed was another skeleton, of someone younger, with a cloth bag and 26 bronze coins.[55] Sadly, these finds make it no longer any surprise that the street door appears to have been locked from the inside.

The room was finely decorated, in the late Third Style, with much use of the particularly expensive colour black. Figure 1.8 shows part of the east wall. Columns flank a picture of a mainly pastoral scene which is much faded, but includes a column surmounted by a disc or globe, to the right of the *lararium*. The *lararium* niche itself has paintings of two snakes and

---

[52] Allison, *Menander* III, p. 349.
[53] Allison, *Menander* III, nos 1233–7, 1239–40, 1250–1, pls 82.7–11, 13, 83.1, 84.2.
[54] Allison, *Menander* III, nos 1241–6, pls 83.1, 84.1.
[55] Allison, *Menander* III, nos 1247–9.

Figure 1.8 I.10.7, room 9: part of decoration of east wall with *lararium*

a rocky altar.[56] The west wall has a picture of the fall of Icarus, with Icarus seen falling into a rocky landscape with a lake and various spectators. The north wall's picture is of the judgement of Paris. Hermes approaches the seated Paris to draw attention to the three goddesses whose beauty he is to adjudicate. However, the goddesses themselves are omitted. This is not unprecedented in Pompeii. In this case, the omission seems due to the presence of a window. Like the *lararium* on the east wall this was probably not a later disruption but was present when the painting was carried out.[57] The floor is the lone particularly expensive one on the ground floor. It consists of *cocciopesto* (a surface using crushed terracotta), painted red, with patterns of inserted white limestone *tesserae* (small cubes for mosaics). These mark out the spaces to be occupied by the three couches of a *triclinium* dining room.[58]

There was only one couch in the room at the time of the eruption. The finds show that, unlike room 8, this room was still used for domestic life rather than craftwork. Probably it was used for dining, but not in *triclinium* layout. It may well have also been slept in. The items found with skeletons further reinforce our picture of the economic level of the inhabitants. They died holding some money, but not great amounts of it.

The kitchen (11) has the classic masonry cooking bench (Figure 1.9). On top were three small *fornelli*, masonry stoves or ovens. The masonry sides of two of them are still visible at the left side of the bench, under the large broken pot. Also found in the kitchen were a bronze jug, two bronze cooking pots, a bronze lid and various ceramics: two bowls, two mortars, two jugs, a lid, an amphora and a vase.[59] All the finds point to this being in use as a kitchen in 79 CE.

The garden, which was entered through a gate between the middle pillars of the portico (otherwise separated from the garden by wooden fence-bars),[60] was centred on a wooden pergola, which was possibly a location for dining. The other main find from the garden was a 440 mm herm of Hercules, depicted largely from the waist upwards but with genitalia.[61] This garden also yielded a few other finds, including a mortar and handmill, four amphorae (two with Greek inscriptions) and a jug which declared its contents as LIQVAMEN OPTIMVM INFANTIONIS,

---

[56] Ling and Ling, *Menander* II, p. 264, fig. 112.
[57] Ling and Ling, *Menander* II, pp. 142–4, 264–5.
[58] Ling and Ling, *Menander* II, p. 262, fig. 111.
[59] Allison, *Menander* III, nos 1361–71, pls 89.2–4.
[60] Ling, *Menander* I, p. 154.
[61] Allison, *Menander* III, no. 1374, pl. 90.2.

Figure 1.9 I.10.7: kitchen, cooking bench

high-quality fish sauce.[62] Parts of the garden were being used for storage or craftwork but most of it seems to have remained recreational space.

As we have seen before, it is difficult to distinguish finds originating in upstairs rooms, with collapsed floors, from those held off the ground in downstairs rooms, for example in cupboards. Some of the finds attributed to upstairs rooms may therefore actually come from the ground floor (especially those found at about the one-metre level). The rear range of rooms, above rooms 7, 8 and 9, produced a large number of finds: Allison's catalogue has just under 160 entries. Apart from cabinet fittings and so on, they are basically as shown in Table 1.5.

---

[62] Allison, *Menander* III, nos 1375–6, 1380–4, pl. 90.3.

Table 1.5 House I.10.7: selected finds from rooms above rooms 7–10, categorized by material, with most likely work-related items in bold

Glass (mainly in a chest along with much of the ceramic ware)	7 glass bowls 2 tubes with pear/funnel-shaped end and capillary rod (wine siphons)[1] boat-shaped dish (possibly for sauce)[2] jar glass beads cylindrical blue glass box with lid **16 bottles** (60–174 mm high) **5 flasks**
Bronze (excluding medical instruments)	2 cups 2 saucepan-shaped objects 2 bowls 2 basins dish mug jug mirror razor/scraper lampstand 2 bells (22, 30 mm high) **box** (125 × 73 × 20 mm, in four compartments) **box** (105 × 68 × 30 mm, in four compartments) **whetstone cover with whetstone** **bronze and silver bowls**, possibly from scales
Medical instruments (bronze unless noted, all in a wooden casket)	**extractor** **2 spatula probes** **probe** cylindrical container, holding **forceps, needle and probe** cylindrical container, holding **4 scoop probes** **4 scalpel handles and dissectors** **iron scalpel**
Gold and money	2 gold earrings gold ring 14 silver coins 10 bronze coins
Iron	small tripod (possibly a stand for cooking vessels) grill, probably used as fence or in window 2 scrapers/razors **spade** **chisel** **pick**

Table 1.5 (*cont'd*)

Ceramics	7 plates
	6 vases
	6 cups
	2 lids
	6 amphorae
	jar
	9 lamps
Miscellaneous	bone beads
	bone pin (137 mm with pine-cone-shaped terminal)
	collection of beads and amulets
	4 shells
	marble flask
	marble slab (probably from furniture)
	2 whetstones

[1] Allison, *Menander* III, nos 1489–90.
[2] Allison, *Menander* III, no. 1488.
Source: Allison, *Menander* III, nos 1417–1584, pls 93.1–100.5.

The rough division of finds in Table 1.5 into domestic and work-related ones (the latter in bold) shows quickly that there was a fair amount of tableware upstairs: in fact, almost all the tableware in the house. This fits with Ling's suggestion that there was at least one high-quality room up there, citing an excavator's report of some marble pieces.[63] It looks probable that there was an upstairs dining room, overlooking the garden. This concentration of tableware has an important implication for the social structure of the house. It suggests that it contained a single household, rather than being divided into apartments. Much of the use of space in the house in its final years seems fairly clear and rational if it is viewed as a single unit with a latrine right at the front, predominantly sleeping accommodation on the front west side (on both floors), storage in the centre (and rear), kitchen and craftwork at the rear, and dining upstairs at the back and maybe also in the garden or room 9.

Among the work-related items found upstairs, the obvious group is that of medical instruments,[64] to go with the three instruments from downstairs. When the whole house was occupied, there must have been a fair number of people – say, about ten. Despite the tendency of households

---

[63] Ling, *Menander* I, p. 158, citing *Giornali degli scavi*, 23 December 1932.
[64] As noted above, Ling cites Ralph Jackson's comments on the finds as being medical: *Menander* I, p. 162.

to follow single trades, it would not be very surprising if two household members had different occupations. Alternatively, it could be that a cabinet-maker might fancy trying his hand at minor surgery. He would have a steady hand and be used to work that required attention to detail.

Some issues about House 7 are more important for our purposes than others. It is not very significant to us whether the main commercial occupation in the house was woodworking, metalworking, or even the collection and resale of materials. We are interested in the range of social situations of non-elite craftworking, or trading, households. The occupants of this house certainly fall into that category. On the other hand, we do need to be careful about the sequencing of decoration and occupation. The very expensive Third Style decoration of room 8 does not fit the final occupants' usage of the room for craftwork. We should assume that they did not commission the artwork, which would imply the same for room 9. This point is supported by the simpler, though reasonable, Fourth Style decoration that was carried out in rooms 2, 4 and 5 towards the end of the house's life. The occupants could afford to decorate some of the rooms in reasonable but modest style. This fits with other evidence such as the quantities of money and jewellery found in the house.[65] The occupants were far from destitute but also far from elite. In Chapter 3 we will return to discussing the social structure of the household, which clearly included many more people than the two who were trapped by the eruption.

Holconius the cabinet-maker

We could call the householder of I.10.7 Volusius, using the name on the amphora from room 6. However, it would be better to distance ourselves from Della Corte's assumption that that really was his name. Instead, we will steal a well-known Pompeian name to use for our representative figure from the house. We will focus on the householder himself, for three reasons. First, the most interesting aspect of I.10.7 for NT scholars is that it is the house of someone who does not fit the scholarly dichotomy between the rich and the abjectly poor. The inhabitant who most clearly occupies this interesting socio-economic position is the householder. Second, the householder, who rents the house, is the person likely to have the closest relationship with the cultural artefacts in the house, even if he

---

[65] Allison implies that there were three successive social levels of occupation from *c.* 50 to 79 CE, represented by the expensive decoration of rooms 8 and 9, the modest decoration of rooms 2, 4 and 5, and the plain plaster of the atrium (*Menander* III, p. 340). This seems unnecessarily complex, since the quality of the loose finds suggests that the final occupants were at a socio-economic level appropriate to the decoration of rooms 2, 4 and 5.

did not commission all of them. It will be interesting to consider the cultural reference points of this cabinet-maker, and then to reflect how NT texts would sound to someone with such reference points. Third, and again undermining a scholarly dichotomy, I.10.7 would provide a viable setting for a fair-sized house church. Scholars tend to locate early churches in either elite houses or non-elite apartments. House 7 is neither. If a house church were based here, Holconius would be its host. It is interesting to reflect on what that would imply.

Iris's bar (I.10.2–3)

More briefly, we turn to Houses 2–3 and 4. House 2–3 begins not with a picture, but with three pieces of graffiti from the wall between the doorways to Houses 3 and 4:

> Successus the weaver loves the innkeeper's servant girl, whose name is Hiris. But she isn't bothered about him. Yet he propositions her. She pities him. A rival wrote this. Goodbye.

> Jealous! Because you are bursting yourself, don't injure [?] the handsomer man, and who is the most wicked and beautiful.

> I said it. I wrote it. You love Hiris, who isn't bothered about you . . . [becomes largely unreadable but includes the name Successus] . . . Severus[66]

The graffiti begin with a challenging insult to Successus, who may live in House 8, which contained a large weaving loom. The Latin is fairly good. The misspelling of 'Iris' might conceivably be a satire on Successus' pronunciation. Successus provides a riposte, in Latin so bad as to be incomprehensible in places. The counter-riposte repeats the original insult and

---

[66] My translation of the Latin given by Della Corte, *Corpus Inscriptionum Latinarum* IV.3.I, nos 8258–9; 'Epigrafi della via fra le isole VI e X della Reg. I', pp. 457–8, nos 152–3: (1) *Successus textor amat Coponiaes ancilla[m] nomine Hiredem quae quidem illum non curat; sed ille rogat, illa com[m]iseretur. Scribit rivalis. Vale.* (2) *Invidiose, quia rumperes, sedare noli formonsiorem, et qui est homo pravessimus [sic] et bellus.* (3) *Dixi, scripsi. Amas Hiredem quae te non curat. Sev[erus?] Successo ut s . . . . . s . . . . . Severus.* Della Corte suggests that *secare* (injure) or *insectari* (attack) might be intended instead of the surprising *sedare* (calm). N. Lewis and M. Reinhold, *Roman Civilization, Selected Reading. II: The Empire* (New York: Columbia University Press, 3rd edn, 1990), p. 277, offer the following translation: 'The weaver Successus loves the innkeeper's slave girl, Iris by name. She doesn't care for him, but he begs her to take pity on him. Written by his rival. So long!' 'Just because you're bursting with envy, don't pick on a handsome man, a lady-killer and a gallant.' 'There's nothing more to say or write. You love Iris, who doesn't care for you.' This flows very nicely, although maybe more nicely than the state of the Latin warrants.

reveals the challenger's identity. Severus probably ends up ahead in the honour stakes here.[67] I would assume that Successus would try to even things up with a physical challenge.

House 2–3 is a bar linked to a small two-storey house. Of course, it was not really Iris's bar. She was a slave girl belonging to the bar owner (who is also a woman). Iris probably cleaned the house, served at the bar and, given the way in which bars were reputed to operate, was probably compelled to have sex with some of the customers in return for money, to be paid to her owner.[68]

Figure 1.10 shows the front half of House 2–3. On the left-hand side we see room 5, which has traces of some good-quality decoration. Then there is the *fauces* leading to door 3, with a nicely painted *lararium* niche (covered with a plastic protector) on the right of the corridor. Finally there is the bar. We can see door 2 with, just inside it, a very recent reconstruction of the bottom 50 cm or so of the bar counter, which has a stove at the near end. To the right of that is a taller reconstruction of part of the thin wall separating room 8 from room 7. The rest of the house includes a latrine (12), a small courtyard with a water cistern (11) and, on the west side of central space 4 and corridor 9, clear evidence of a staircase to an upper floor and, at the rear of the house, a mezzanine with a very low ceiling. Almost none of the house's decoration has survived. However, traces of reasonably good decoration were found in rooms 5 and 6 and in fragments from upstairs. The bar's back room (8) had some basic decoration and the bar counter was evidently painted red.[69]

Virtually no loose finds were discovered in the bar, just a few bronze coins.[70] The counter itself was typical of Pompeian shops selling food and

---

[67] For the dynamics of challenge-and-riposte encounters as competition for honour, see Bruce J. Malina and John J. Pilch, *Social-Science Commentary on the Letters of Paul* (Minneapolis: Fortress, 2006), pp. 334–5.

[68] Carolyn Osiek and Margaret Y. MacDonald, *A Woman's Place: House Churches in Earliest Christianity* (Minneapolis: Fortress, 2006), p. 276 n. 4, cite the most specific evidence for this: namely, the fact that late Roman jurists exempted female tavern workers, whether slave or hired, from prosecution for adultery, since chastity was not expected or required of them. Osiek and MacDonald cite Thomas A. J. McGinn, 'The Legal Definition of Prostitute in Late Antiquity', in Malcolm Bell III and Caroline Bruzelius (eds), *Memoirs of the American Academy in Rome* 42 (Washington, DC: American Academy in Rome, 1997), pp. 90–1, 94–6, and Thomas A. J. McGinn, *Prostitution, Sexuality and Law in Ancient Rome* (New York: Oxford University Press), p. 196. Justin J. Meggitt, *Paul, Poverty and Survival* (Edinburgh: T. & T. Clark, 1998), pp. 109–11, provides a vivid overview of classical writers' disparaging remarks about the category of back-street bar into which Iris's one presumably fell.

[69] Ling and Ling, *Menander* II, pp. 162–3, 78–9; Elia, 'Relazione', p. 272.

[70] Allison, *Menander* III, nos 53–5.

Figure 1.10 I.10.2–3: view from room 6, looking north

drink: an L-shaped bench with two inset pots and a cooking stove. A graffito from the wall proclaims the bar to be *capella Bacchis*, 'chapel of Bacchus', god of wine.[71] There also appears to be a tally of money or the score of a game, marked on the wall.[72] Within and outside the bar are a few graffiti with names of girls.[73] However, on excavation, one side of the stove was missing. That, and the shortage of loose finds, makes it likely that the bar was not in use at the time of the eruption.[74]

Room 7, at the back of the bar, yielded glassware – five bottles and a flask – perhaps for cosmetics.[75] The rest of the house yielded a general mixture of finds, mainly from upstairs. There was very little that could not fit into a domestic assemblage of material. The finds, including those in rooms 2 and 7, are broadly as set out in Table 1.6.

The differences between the contents of House 6 and House 7 have already revealed to us some of the clear economic differentiation within the non-elite. The structure, decoration and contents of House 2–3 lie somewhere between those of 6 and 7. We can see three distinguishable points on the socio-economic spectrum of the non-elite. The inhabitants of House 2–3 were better off than the stoneworkers but less well off than the cabinet-maker.

We do not know what business, if any, was carried out in House 2–3 in 79 CE. Maybe the bar was still running somehow. In any case, the bar almost certainly ran for a significant period before that. The 'chapel of Bacchus' was then open to devotees and Iris was working for the woman in charge.

Iris the barmaid

Iris will be taken as representing the social situation of a type of sexually exploited slave. We do not know whether the historical Iris was exploited in this way but such prostitution was notoriously common in first-century bars. The fact that Iris's bar may not have been open at the time of the eruption prevents us from drawing inferences about her from the loose finds. However, the presence of Iris in the graffiti, in coordination with the structural evidence of the adjacent bar, alerts us to the exis-

---

[71] Della Corte, *CIL* IV.3.I, no. 8230.
[72] Della Corte, *CIL* IV.3.I, no. 8239.
[73] Della Corte, *CIL* IV.3.I, nos 8241, 8282 etc.
[74] Allison, *Menander* III, p. 293.
[75] Allison, *Menander* III, nos 59–64.

Table 1.6 House I.10.2–3: selected finds, categorized by material

Glass	9 bottles
	flask
	cup
Bronze	buckle
	base of case
	forceps
	scoop probe
	tube, possibly for candleholder
	pendant
	3 rings
Money, jewellery	5 bronze coins
Ceramics	plate
	bowl
	2 vases
	cup
	3 lids
	2 amphorae
	jar
	6 lamps
Miscellaneous	bone discs
	bone spoon
	stone handmill
	3 shells
	2 marble weights
	marble slabs (probably from furniture)
	horn
	various furniture fittings such as locks

Source: Allison, *Menander* III, nos 53–122, pls 4.1–5.10.

tence of such people and encourages us to consider how our biblical texts would, or would not, relate to them.

The non-elite in the House of the Menander (I.10.4)

The House of the Menander, named after a helpfully labelled painting of the poet in one of the beautiful alcoves in the peristyle area, is a classic among elite urban houses. The original, traditional house, centred on the atrium, mushroomed southwards, levelling the ground for a Hellenistic

Figure 1.11 I.10.4: atrium from north-east corner showing *impluvium*, rooms 6 and 7 and view through *tablinum* (8) to peristyle

peristyle and garden, surrounded by beautiful rooms and, in one corner, a private bath suite, to which we shall return. The owner of the house was probably senatorial. However, the inhabitants of the house were mainly slaves. The great majority of people who lived in elite houses were themselves non-elite. The House of the Menander was almost completely disrupted at the time of the eruption and had probably been so for some years. The life for which the house was designed was not being lived. Instead, the house was mainly given over to repair work and, consequently, storage of items moved from their normal locations. We are not interested in the social dynamics of a house under repair. We are interested in how it would have functioned in normal use. This means that the loose finds are of little help to us. They are mainly either elite items in storage or the belongings of the people involved in the repair of the house and the supervision of that. We need instead to concentrate on the layout of the house, with some help from the differences in decoration between various types of room.

Technically, the House of the Menander ought not to be designated simply as I.10.4 but as I.10.4, 14, 15, 16 and 17. All of the south-eastern quarter of the block, with its doorways, belonged to the house, as did the central part of the west side. In normal use, there would be slaves, and probably some freed slaves, in every part of the sprawling house. They would be ever-present in the 'show' areas of the house (in contrast to stately homes in nineteenth-century England, where servants spent most of their time in separate areas, only emerging to perform specific duties). However, there are certain parts of the house that particularly suggest the presence of slaves and other non-elite.

Around the atrium, room 1 (see Figure 1.3) is decorated simply, in contrast to most of the other spaces. That and its proximity to the front door suggest that a doorman lived there. The staircase in room 2 rose to a small apartment built, late on, across the front rooms of the house. Such an apartment would seem likely to be inhabited by someone non-elite: maybe a couple of freed slaves or an impoverished relative of the owner. The smartly decorated rooms around the atrium and elsewhere would need slaves to clean them. The *tablinum* (8), for receiving clients (who might sit on the benches outside the front door), implies the need for one or more secretaries to organize and record the owner's dealings and to organize his seeing (or not seeing) of various clients. In the peristyle, there was a garden, no doubt tended by slaves. There were also a number of dining rooms, including a very large banqueting hall (18), which, as excavation of its floor shows, was built over a previous, smaller house, the rooms of which had been filled with rubble. The dining rooms imply slaves to serve the food, and probably sometimes to be served up as part of the after-dinner entertainment. Also around the peristyle were elite *cubicula*: rooms for sleeping, living and, sometimes, receiving guests. These rooms imply female and male slaves as attendants, hairdressers, and so on.

On the west side of the peristyle, the narrow corridor M led away from the expensively decorated areas of the house to a service area. This included a kitchen (27). In there was a *lararium*,[76] presumably provided by or for the cooks and other slaves who worked there. Next to the kitchen was a latrine (26). The degree of overlap between elite and non-elite areas is suggested by the absence of latrines in the elite areas. Although the elite presumably often used chamber pots, one imagines that they also had occasion to go down the service corridors to use latrines such as this one. Down a flight of steps from corridor M was a garden (R). This was presumably a functional space in which slaves grew food crops. Area S gives access to the spaces behind and beneath a bath suite (46–49). At the time of the eruption, one room of the bath suite, a *laconicum* (dry sweating room, 49), had been dismantled. There was also no boiler in place for the *caldarium* (hot room, 48).[77] However, when it was in place, it will have needed frequent stoking to provide hot water for a bathtub in room 8 and the heating of the suite by a hypocaust. The bathhouse itself will have had a slave attendant and maybe also someone like a masseur.

The other major service area was reached from the south-eastern corner of the peristyle. Corridor P1–P–P2 and a couple of staircases linked the remaining service-related spaces. The social contrast between different areas of the house can be seen by comparing the spacious atrium and peristyle with the narrow corridor P2 (Figure 1.12). Ling suggests that rooms 35–38, and those above them, were either storerooms or staff bedrooms.[78] Although, at the time of the eruption, some of these rooms were undoubtedly being used for storage, even then there were also personal hygiene items in two of them.[79] There are also joist holes for a very large shelf or mezzanine in at least one of them.[80] The division of such small rooms by mezzanine platforms would seem a likely accommodation strategy for sleeping quarters ('bedrooms' dignifies them too much) for

---

[76] Allison, *Menander* III, p. 312; Ling and Ling, *Menander* II, p. 253. Confusingly, Ling and Ling also include room 27 in 'Rooms 26–8' on p. 243, reporting no decoration.

[77] Ling, *Menander* I, pp. 62–6.

[78] Ling, *Menander* I, p. 115.

[79] Allison, *Menander* III, pp. 324–5.

[80] Allison, *Menander* III, pp. 324–5.

Figure 1.12 I.10.4: corridor P2 with possible slave sleeping quarters on right

slaves other than those whose roles meant that they slept in more public areas of the house.[81]

The south-eastern corner of the house largely consisted of a stable yard (34). The stable itself (29) is identified by a low podium on the west side, which supported a wooden manger.[82] Around the yard are store-

---

[81] On slave accommodation see Michele George, '*Servus* and *domus*: The Slave in the Roman House', in R. Laurence and A. Wallace-Hadrill (eds), *Domestic Space in the Roman World: Pompeii and Beyond* (JRASup 22; Portsmouth, RI: Journal of Roman Archaeology, 1997), pp. 15–24.

[82] Ling, *Menander* I, p. 108.

rooms, accommodation and a latrine. A wide doorway (14) allows access for carts such as the two-wheeled one actually found in the yard, a reconstructed version of which was *in situ* when I visited the site. The House of the Menander is on the edge of an area of the town in which some small-scale agriculture took place. Slaves, and possibly freed slaves, based in the stable yard presumably travelled from there to work either in these horticultural plots or in market gardens or other farmland beyond the town walls.

A final set of rooms to consider is the house whose street doors are 16 and 17 (a shop doorway). This house was linked to House 4. Maiuri identified it as the home of a steward in charge of House 4 and its estate. He identified the steward with a skeleton found on a bed in room 43, near a seal carrying the name of Q. Poppaeus Eros, who Maiuri saw as a freedman of the owner of the house, one of the Poppaei, the family of Nero's second wife.[83] It is clearly difficult to verify this. However, the extensive range of finds in this room and the nearby atrium (41)[84] lend support to the idea that the man was indeed some sort of dependant of House 4, storing material from there. The same would then probably be true of a young girl whose skeleton was also found in this room.

Primus the bath-stoker

The social situation of a slave is inherently dreadful. However, even among slaves there would, in a large household such as House 4, be a sharp hierarchy. It would be interesting to consider (as Dale Martin has done) the reading of NT texts in relation to the situation of some of the upper slaves in the hierarchy.[85] However, if our focus is to be more squarely on the slave situation, it is more useful to focus on the lower end of the household. We will take Primus (one of the most common slave names) to be a middle-aged slave in a menial, out-of-the-way job. Keeping the bathhouse boiler going will not get him noticed by his owner, so as to have a chance of being manumitted (freed) as a favour, maybe in a will. Nor will the job earn him tips, allowing the chance of buying his freedom. He will have seen many fellow-slaves younger than him manumitted. He just has to keep on doing this hot, dirty job, without the prospect of release unless his owner

[83] Maiuri, *Menandro*, pp. 15–16, 19–20, 201–2, 212, 225–7.

[84] Allison, *Menander* III, nos 712–93, 796–863.

[85] Dale B. Martin, *Slavery as Salvation: The Metaphor of Slavery in Pauline Christianity* (New Haven: Yale University Press, 1990), ch. 1.

Figure 1.13 I.10.4, room 46: *atriolum* (mini-atrium) of bath suite

is particularly cruel and 'liberates' Primus on to the streets as soon as he becomes too ill or weak to work.

Pompeian houses and the study of Pauline Christianity: some initial reflections

Scholars commonly characterize the members of the Pauline churches – those that Paul founded or wrote to – as typically being craftworkers. As long as we think of craftworking families as a whole, not just a single male artisan, this seems reasonable. It certainly fits well with Paul's injunction to 'work with your hands' in 1 Thessalonians 4.11 and with his own practice as a tent-maker, as characterized by Luke in Acts 18.3.

Awareness of Houses 6 and 7 in the Insula of the Menander cracks apart the category 'craftworker', revealing, in some detail, the breadth of situations that the term can cover. Roman elite writers bracketed craftworkers together, along with the rest of the social 'dregs' of the city.[86] We can now see how badly that misrepresents the situation as it would appear from ground level. The Cabinet-Maker's House occupies eight times as much land as the Stoneworkers' House. If we add in the upstairs rooms, the cabinet-maker and his household occupy at least 12 times as much space as the stoneworkers. The stoneworkers left before the eruption but, even though they would have taken any valuables with them, the impression from the remains is that their possessions were simple and meagre. They certainly could not afford elaborate decoration. Two of the cabinet-maker's household were trapped in their house by the eruption and the wide range of finds includes valuables such as jewellery. The decoration of the rooms also tells an interesting social story, with its mixture of expensive schemes in a few rooms and simpler schemes elsewhere.

Single houses form risky bases for comparison. Our next chapter will be devoted to putting these houses into context. However, even single first-century houses can help twenty-first-century readers think more accurately about the social situation of first-century Christians. The Cabinet-Maker's House shows that someone non-elite, a craftworker, could have space to host a meeting of a fair-sized house church. Forty or so people could fit into the garden, portico and rear-facing dining rooms – as long as they did not mind stepping over boxes of tools and work in progress. The cabinet-maker's household had some disposable assets. If they were Christians and either ran into economic difficulties or wanted to help

---

[86] For example, Cicero, *On Duties* 1.42.

fellow church members or itinerant apostles, they could sell something such as the jewellery. On the other hand, the cabinet-maker held a particular position in society. He was quite likely to have been a client to his elite landlord next door and, informally, patron to some poorer craftworkers and others. This position, balanced in the middle of the non-elite social structure, may have been quite common among house-church hosts. Such a position needed maintaining. If the cabinet-maker's wife stopped wearing her gold necklace on the appropriate occasions, who knows how it might disrupt the family's social position!

More broadly, as more and more houses at Pompeii are published in detail, they offer increasing opportunities to key various early Christian individuals or groups into specific, concrete instances of social situations that the texts indicate for them. This can most easily be done for partic-ular jobs that are ascribed to people in texts, since many Pompeian hous-es yield evidence of their inhabitants' occupations. There are also a range of other social indicators for people in Pauline and other early Christian texts. Each of these could be used to key people (from Graeco-Roman urban contexts) into specific Pompeian houses or sets of houses. The range of accompanying evidence from those houses can then be used to open up potential lines for reflection on the situations and actions of the early Christians in question. This is, of course, a technique that must be han-dled with great caution. If we know of a tent-maker's house in Pompeii, we cannot simply say, 'Prisca and Aquila lived like this' or 'Paul lived like this'. There were a range of experiences and situations in any profession. However, it would be of great value even to be able to say, 'Here is one possibility of how people such as Prisca and Aquila lived', when such a possibility is expressed by detailed, concrete, first-century evidence. In fact, even to be able to say, as we now can, 'Prisca and Aquila were craftwork-ing house-church hosts. Here is the house of a craftworker of the kind who could function as a house-church host', is of considerable value when we can flesh out the statement with the extensive, datable evidence of a building such as House I.10.7.

2

Pompeian houses and first-century society

Readers who are familiar with debates about the structure of first-century society will realize that something which is, potentially, very interesting academically was going on as we looked at the three very different non-elite houses in the previous chapter. Studies of ancient society have had great difficulty in giving any shape at all to differences in socio-economic level among the non-elite. Geza Alföldy is typical in his classic description of Roman society. His social pyramid differentiates between seven socio-economic levels among the elite, who make up only 1% or so of society, but makes no differentiation of level among the other 99%. He does distinguish urban from rural, and slave from free or freed, but makes no distinctions of economic level within any of those categories.[1] In the study of Paul's churches the same has occurred. Most notably, Justin Meggitt, reacting against studies that arguably overestimate the role of members of the social elite in Christian groups, argues that less than 1% of society were elite, that all the non-elite were very poor, and that Pauline Christians came entirely from the non-elite.[2] Even scholars such as Steven Friesen, who have worked hard to try to articulate economic differences among the non-elite, and consequently within Paul's churches, have struggled to find any method for working out an economic profile for the non-elite members of the population. The three Pompeian non-elite houses are clearly telling us something about social differentiation among the non-elite, and thus potentially among the early Christians. But what is it? To make progress on this question, we clearly need to begin by considering a much larger number of houses and looking for evidence of socio-economic patterns. We then need to compare those patterns with some of the previous scholarly models of first-century society and of the social make-up of the Pauline churches. Since our ultimate aim is to read Romans, we will then need to consider (in our next chapter) how the social

---

[1] Geza Alföldy, *The Social History of Rome* (Totowa, NJ: Barnes & Noble, 1985), p. 146.
[2] Justin J. Meggitt, *Paul, Poverty and Survival* (Edinburgh: T. & T. Clark, 1998), chs 3–4.

situation of the inhabitants of our four houses compares with that of the readers Paul had in mind when he wrote Romans.

Wallace-Hadrill's survey of housing in Pompeii and Herculaneum

In 1994, Andrew Wallace-Hadrill published a ground-breaking study, *Houses and Society in Pompeii and Herculaneum*. A central part of this was a survey of 234 houses, gathering information on their size, form (he noted whether a house had an atrium and/or peristyle) and decoration. By comparing the three types of information he was able to draw out many interesting social patterns. The houses were from three areas. Sample I is all the houses (78) in Pompeii region I, blocks 6–12, an area of mixed housing and businesses.[3] Five of the blocks each have one side on a major road, on which there was a certain concentration of shops and bars. Sample II is the houses from Herculaneum, blocks III to VI. Two of the blocks had short sides on the sea wall, which was occupied by elite houses. Wallace-Hadrill sees sample II as comprising 52 houses, a figure that excludes public baths.[4] For my own sample I shall exclude VI.21–24, the Sacello degli Augustali, which is an association meeting hall and shrine. I shall also exclude III.7, a public latrine. This leaves my version of sample II as 50 houses. Sample III covers Pompeii region VI, blocks 9–16. Two sides of this sample are major roads that somewhat favoured shops and bars. This is also the part of Pompeii with the highest concentration of large houses. A major difficulty with this sample is that it was one of the earlier areas of excavation, and so the habitations other than the large 'show' houses tend to be in a poor state of preservation. This was an acute problem for Wallace-Hadrill in trying to survey how far down the socio-economic scale various forms of decoration were used. To a lesser extent, it is also a problem for us, because the question of where one house unit ends and another begins can sometimes be particularly unclear. It is often unclear in any case because dwelling units were probably sometimes separated by wooden partitions that have not survived, or by no physical partition at all. Wallace-Hadrill sees sample III as containing 104 houses.[5] I am unclear how he arrives at this figure and would see sample III as comprising 102 houses.

---

[3] Andrew Wallace-Hadrill, *Houses and Society in Pompeii and Herculaneum* (Princeton: Princeton University Press, 1994), p. 67.

[4] Wallace-Hadrill, *Houses and Society*, p. 68.

[5] Wallace-Hadrill, *Houses and Society*, p. 68.

For each sample, Wallace-Hadrill gathers the data for house plan size into sets of 100 m^2: that is, he counts how many are between 0 and 99 m^2, how many between 100 and 199 m^2, and so on. He then compares the distribution of house sizes in the three samples, showing that, although the distributions vary in detail, they have a broadly similar shape.[6] The average house size in each sample is also surprisingly similar: 266 m^2 for sample I, 241 m^2 in sample II, and 289 m^2 in sample III. He also compares this with standard Greek house sizes calculated by Hoepfner and Schwander from sites ranging from Piraeus to Dura Europos.[7] His Pompeian average of 271 m^2 is very close to the 250 m^2 average of the Greek figures. This is an interesting comparison, especially given the difference between the standardized Greek housing and the widely varying house sizes in Pompeii.

Having shown a reasonable similarity between the results for the three samples, Wallace-Hadrill then aggregates the numbers of houses in the samples to provide an overall pattern of distribution of house sizes.[8] With our amended samples, the numbers of houses, and the percentage distribution of house plan sizes, are as in Table 2.1. In the penultimate column of the table, I have taken the average of the percentages for the three samples. Above 600 m^2, our sample is too small to reach detailed conclusions. The numbers continue to drop off as house size increases, although not in a predictable way. By 900 m^2, all three samples have dropped to zero. However, at 1,000 m^2 or slightly larger, all three samples pick up again, registering a surprising number of bigger houses. In the final column, I have produced a round-number model that tries to represent the trends in the figures. I have put a notional small figure into the model for the 900–999 m^2 range on the assumption that a large enough sample would reveal that the Romans did not systematically avoid ever building houses of that size! The very large houses are scattered over a wide range of sizes, the largest being 2,865 m^2. Trying to model that scatter in any detail would be pointless. I have therefore gathered all the houses above 1,000 m^2 together in the model, as a rounded figure of 5% (rounded from 4.82%).

We need to plot these results on a graph. But what is it a graph of? Moreover, if this represents a socio-economic model, what is it a model of? Focusing on the first question: if we take the combination of the three samples as representative of Pompeii and Herculaneum altogether, then

---

[6] Wallace-Hadrill, *Houses and Society*, p. 77, fig. 4.8.

[7] Wallace-Hadrill, *Houses and Society*, p. 76, citing W. Hoepfner and E.-L. Schwander, *Haus und Stadt in klassischen Griechenland* (Munich: Deutscher Kunstverlag, 1986), p. 257.

[8] Wallace-Hadrill, *Houses and Society*, p. 77, fig. 4.7; p. 79, table 4.1.

Table 2.1 Distribution of house sizes in Wallace-Hadrill survey

Size (m²)	Sample I Pompeii I.6–12		Sample II Herculaneum III–VI		Sample III Pompeii VI.9–16		Average	Model
0–99	21	26.92%	20	40%	38	37.25%	34.72%	34%
100–199	18	23.07%	12	24%	20	19.61%	22.23%	22%
200–299	11	14.10%	8	16%	12	11.76%	13.95%	14%
300–399	9	11.54%	2	4%	7	6.86%	7.47%	8%
400–499	10	12.82%	2	4%	7	6.86%	7.89%	8%
500–599	5	6.41%	2	4%	4	3.92%	4.78%	5%
600–699	1	1.28%	1	2%	5	4.90%	2.73%	2%
700–799	1	1.28%			1	0.98%	0.75%	1%
800–899					2	1.96%	0.65%	0.6%
900–999								0.4%
1,000–1,099					1	0.98%	0.33%	⎫
1,100–1,199			2	4%	1	0.98%	1.66%	⎬ 5%
1,200–1,299	1	1.28%			1	0.98%	0.75%	⎪
1,300+	1	1.28%	1	2%	3	2.94%	2.07%	⎭
Total	78		50		102			

it is a graph of the distribution of house plan sizes in Pompeii and Herculaneum. 'House plan size' is the total area of a distinct housing unit, including any gardens or open work areas such as stable yards. Combining the three samples has its drawbacks. One might argue that it would be better to remove the somewhat more polarized figures from Herculaneum, which have a lower proportion of houses between 300 and 1,000 m² than the Pompeian samples. This consideration is probably outweighed by the advantage of making our overall sample as large as possible, especially since our ultimate interest is not specifically in Pompeian society but in using the Pompeian evidence to improve our understanding of Graeco-Roman urban society in general. However, the variation between the samples must act to keep our feet on the ground. Although the general shape of the graph is similar for the three samples, all the specific figures are subject to a range of variability. For instance, in each sample the largest group of houses is those below 100 m², but the size of this largest group varies between the samples, from 26.9% to 40%.

A space-distribution model and its implications

At its most basic, our model is a model of the distribution of household occupation of urban space in Pompeii and Herculaneum. As a graph, it can be represented as in Figure 2.1. From the minimum-sized houses of

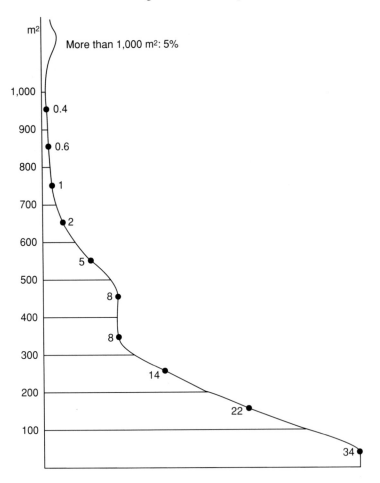

Figure 2.1 A model of the distribution of household occupation of urban space in Pompeii and Herculaneum

10 m², the number of houses in Wallace-Hadrill's samples expands rapidly to reach a maximum for units of 25 m². From that point, the number of houses decreases fairly steadily until 1,000 m², except for an unexpected bulge between 400 m² and 600 m². Beyond 1,000 m², the numbers increase briefly before contracting again.[9]

The key characteristics of the model are:

1 The largest group of households occupy less than 100 m².
2 At least 50% of households occupy less than 200 m².

---

[9] If one breaks down the figures into bands smaller than 100 m², the pattern (inevitably) becomes more erratic, while still following the same general trends.

3 A significant minority of non-elite households occupy between 200 and 800 m².

4 As many households occupy 400–500 m² as occupy 300–400 m².

5 The distribution of space does not tail off at the upper end as it would in a random distribution. Instead, a small group of households (5% in the model) occupy far more space than they would in a random distribution. The houses in this group are of sizes from about 1,000 m² upwards.

These five observations are characteristic of each sample as well as of the average of the three samples. Observation 1 is not surprising. It does, however, represent the combination of two different phenomena. This can be seen by referring back to the plan of the Insula of the Menander (Fig. 1.3). Six of the houses in the Insula are smaller than 100 m². Two of them, House 1 (90 m²) and House 2–3 (80 m²), are of a minimum size for a fairly fully articulated house, although clearly not for one in the classic Roman style. Each house has cooking facilities (the north-west corner of House 1, room 5; the stove in the bar of House 2–3), a latrine (the south-west corner of House 1, room 5 – such proximity to a cooking range was common – and House 2–3, room 12), a small yard and facilities for collecting water (House 1, room 5 again, House 2–3, room 11: the circles represent the covers of water cisterns), and a range of other rooms, some of which were probably decorated professionally, though reasonably simply. Each house also had some upstairs rooms, so the total accommodation exceeded the floor plan size. House 2–3 was, of course, a bar. For a while, House 1 included a shop (in room 2) but the shop entrance was later closed up. The other four 'houses' were simpler work premises with, at most, one additional living space. House 6 (40 m²) was, as we have seen, a workshop with a side space for living and storage. Houses 9, 12 and 13 (10 m², 25 m² and 25 m² respectively) were shops and a bar. Houses 12 and 13 each have signs of stairs leading to upper living spaces, so those houses presumably had a total available space of almost twice their ground-floor area. The houses of less than 100 m² in the Insula are typical of such houses in the survey as a whole, being made up of the smallest articulated houses and a large number of shops, workshops and bars, most of which show signs of living accommodation in or above the ground-floor space. One important implication of this is that the high proportion of very small houses in the Herculaneum sample is not direct evidence of an unusual number of very poor people but of a large number of shops and bars (although the shopkeepers were no doubt generally poor).

A rather laborious and very uncertain attempt could be made to estimate the upstairs living space in the areas of Wallace-Hadrill's samples and to include them in a model. This would increase the average size of the houses in the samples, especially at the lower end, because of shops with mezzanine floors that were almost as large as the ground-floor area. The overall shape of the graph would remain similar to what it now is, but it would be pushed up somewhat, especially at its widest point. If we were considering upstairs floors we would also include upstairs apartments with separate entrances, such as I.10.5. These would almost all be in the 0–100 m^2 bracket, which would pull the widest point of the graph back down a little, and probably make it a little wider.

For Pompeii, given our very limited knowledge about the extent of upstairs living space, and given the relatively small number of entirely separate upstairs apartments, the gains in including estimated upstairs space in our model seem to be outweighed by the sharp increase in uncertainty. There are very few upstairs apartments with separate street entrances in the areas of Wallace-Hadrill's samples (and almost all of these are in Herculaneum). For the rest of the houses, ground-floor area is probably at least as useful an economic indicator as total living area. Urban space was a key scarce resource. The amount that a household occupied was more significant, economically, than whether or not they knocked up a wooden mezzanine platform to provide storage or sleeping quarters for slaves. That would be the bottom end of the range of upstairs accommodation, but it was a very common type and it demonstrates the point that even if we could add up the total quantity of upstairs accommodation, it would be very difficult to handle as an economic variable. If we were considering Rome, rather than Pompeii, the prevalence of apartment blocks would mean that an attempt to produce a model equivalent to our Pompeian space-distribution one would require a very different approach. Our next chapter will consider how to relate our work to the expected hearers of Romans.

Observation 2 is, again, not surprising. Looking again at the Insula of the Menander, a size range of up to 200 m^2 would exclude House 8 (270 m^2) but include House 18, which is 120 m^2 and would still have been below 200 m^2 in its original shape, prior to its evident loss of a corner to House 2–3. A house the size of House 18 is large enough to take a standard Roman form, with an atrium, but would not be large enough to include a significant garden.

House 18 included some upstairs rooms. If about 50% of households occupied a house whose plan size was up to 200 m^2, we would need to add something to this size if we wanted to estimate the total living space controlled by a householder halfway up the space-occupation scale. Upper floors would not be as high a proportion of the space of 100–200 m² houses as they would be of those smaller than 100 m². The slightly larger houses had more open-air space and less motive for cramming in mezzanine floors. If we were to guess that a typical 200 m² house would have had an additional 50% space upstairs, then the majority of the house-holders controlled 0–300 m² in total space, including upstairs rooms. This is quite a high figure by modern standards. However, this comparison is probably somewhat misleading, because the average number of inhabitants per house was undoubtedly higher than it is now and the houses tended also to be places for work and work-related storage, leaving much less space for living than we would expect.

Observation 3 has the potential to disrupt many scholars' picture of first-century social structure and of the Pauline communities. We will deal with it when we consider what kind of socio-economic model the graph presents. Observation 4 may be a statistical anomaly that happens to occur in all three samples. Alternatively, there could be a systemic factor elevating the numbers between 400 m² and 500 m².[10]

Observation 5 offers an interesting way to define the elite. We could say that a society has an economic elite if, instead of resources being distributed in a random pattern that tails off steadily at the upper end, there is a group that monopolizes more resources than we would expect. In definitional terms, this would mean that an economic elite is a wealthy group that controls a larger share of scarce resources than would be expected in a random distribution. In this case, the scarce resource in question is urban space. The existence of an elite is attested by the 'bump' at the top end of the distribution. Given that the bump begins at about 1000 m², it seems reasonable to say that, in our model, the elite are those who control households that occupy more than 1,000 m².

The advantage of this definition of the term 'elite' is that it is properly economic. There are, of course, many perfectly proper definitions of 'elite' that are not economic. Politically, in Roman society the elite were men who were eligible for appointment to at least the local senate, the decuri-ate. This required being free-born, wealthy and, usually, connected to existing powerful families. First-century politics in places with other forms of governance has been less studied but, given the Roman imperial practice

---

[10] Plotting on a logarithmic graph suggests that the depression of the 300–400 m² group is much less marked than the elevation of the 400–500 m² group.

of effectively governing through strong local elites, the general characteristics of non-Roman political elites will have been similar to the Roman
ones. As well as being free-born, well connected and wealthy, these men
would have had education through to adulthood, including training in
a gymnasium and something like a rhetorical school. This political elite
would also be what Graeco-Roman writers thought of as society's elite in
general terms. The system was encapsulated in the three *ordines* (ranks)
of the Roman empire: the decurions (town councillors), the equestrians
and the senators.

Membership of the *ordines* was dependent on wealth. However, it is not
right to see the *ordines* as being the economic elite per se as, for instance,
Steven Friesen effectively does in his important and influential 'poverty
scale for the Roman empire'.[11] Although membership of the *ordines* was
dependent on wealth, the possession of wealth did not always result in membership of the *ordines*. The clearest counter-examples to this were wealthy
freedmen. Most visitors to Pompeii will have visited the unforgettable House
of the Vettii. Many others will have seen pictures of the marvellous frieze
of cupids, engaged in various trades, which is painted around the walls of
one of many magnificent rooms. The Vettius brothers were undoubtedly
part of the economic elite even though, as freedmen, they were ineligible
for decurial status. Willem Jongman offers another neat example of this
phenomenon, in an inscription which says that the decuriate of Pompeii
elected a six-year-old to their ranks in return for his great generosity in
paying for the restoration of the temple of Isis. The explanation of this
oddity is that the boy's father was very wealthy but was a freedman and
thus ineligible for the town council: a member of the economic elite but
not of the political elite.[12]

If we try to estimate the percentage of the population of Pompeii that
were members of the elite, there is a very sharp difference between an
ordines-based calculation and one based on an economic variable such as
occupation of urban space. The *ordines*-based calculation starts from
the Pompeian decuriate typically having 100 members, a notional figure
that was fairly commonly used in Roman towns.[13] It then multiplies that

---

[11] Steven J. Friesen, 'Poverty in Pauline Studies: Beyond the So-called New Consensus', *JSNT* 26 (2004), pp. 337–47.

[12] Willem Jongman, 'The Loss of Innocence: Pompeian Economy and Society between Past and Present', in John J. Dobbins and Pedar W. Foss (eds), *The World of Pompeii* (London: Routledge, 2007), p. 511.

[13] A. N. Sherwin-White, A. H. M. Jones and T. Honoré, 'decuriones', in Hornblower and Spawforth (eds), *Oxford Classical Dictionary* (Oxford: Oxford University Press, 3rd edn, 1996), pp. 437–8.

by, say, four to cover immediate family members, and concludes that the number of elite in Pompeii was about 400 (about 2% of a population of about 10,000).[14] The calculation produces the same number of elite at all times and in all towns with a Roman system of governance! In contrast, the urban space method uses Pompeian evidence to measure a variable. It produces an estimate that 5% of households occupied a disproportionate amount of urban space (over 1,000 m^2). We will see below that house-holders and their immediate families (spouse and children) constituted about half of the population. This means that if elite families were 5% of the families of householders, they would be 2.5% of the population as a whole.

One complication in this calculation is that some elite families may have occupied more than one house, in which case the percentage for the elite would need to be reduced somewhat. However, although elite families would indeed have typically had two or three residences, only one of them would tend to appear in our samples. In addition to a house in town, they would usually have had one or more villas in the countryside, and, if they were very wealthy, a house or large apartment in Rome. It is also important to note that, in our survey, we are talking not about ownership but about occupation. The elite probably owned almost every scrap of land in Pompeii. Our model is about who occupied various houses, not who owned them. The non-elite will usually have been tenants, not owners. We will need to take this into account in thinking about what our model represents in socio-economic terms.

It would be useful if we could produce a definition of poverty that was some sort of reverse of our definition of the economic elite. However,

---

[14] Friesen estimates that there were 172,850 decurions in the Roman empire, and divides them up among the urban centres. He is interested in urban centres with a population of over 10,000, which he sees as sufficient to be the kind of place where Paul's churches were founded. He uses an estimate that one-fifth of urban centres with decuriates were of this size. He then infers that one-fifth of decurions will have lived in these towns ('Poverty in Pauline Studies', pp. 340–3, 360–1). Even if two of the implicit assumptions of this argument were true – that all the relevant towns in the empire had decuriates (which ignores the varying forms of governance in the large towns of the eastern half of the empire) and the decuriates were all the same size – this calculation would be wrong in principle. Friesen is trying to estimate the size of level 3 on his poverty scale, an economic scale. For him, the decurial level is essentially a level of wealth. If one is arguing that the number of people at a certain level of wealth is the same in Pompeii (pop. *c.* 10,000) and Ephesus (pop. well over 100,000), one would have to posit very strange behaviour on the part of the wealthy and a very unusual socio-economic structure for Ephesus. Friesen is aware that not all the wealthy were actually decurions or members of their immediate families ('Poverty in Pauline Studies', p. 360, n. 113, p. 361, n. 114), but he effectively assumes that the exceptions were too limited to affect the calculations seriously.

there are two reasons why this is not possible: one in principle and one in relation to these statistics. The reason in principle is that 'poor' is not a term of the same kind as 'elite'. 'Elite' is a term of separation from the usual socio-economic spectrum. Even though 'poor' can helpfully be defined in terms of inability to participate in the normal activities of society,[15] people can be in that category because of a random distribution of wealth. Someone can be poor without their poverty being exceptional in statistical terms. Indeed the whole of a society could be poor if, for example, a marauding army robbed everyone of the necessities for normal existence. Second, from our particular set of statistics we cannot produce a definition of poverty, because there is no obvious size of house below which we can say that all households are poor. We could try choosing such a point but it would require other kinds of argument. For example, we could estimate a typical family size and consider what would be a reasonable minimum floor plan area per person for normal life. However, I suspect that this approach would not succeed because the total floor area in even the smallest houses could fit in several people. More complex questions would have to be asked about how the space was used. Moreover, there are very many poor people who do not appear in our model at all, either because they did not occupy the archaeologically attested spaces but lived in the street or in temporary structures, or because their poverty was a function of relative deprivation within a household: the householder might have controlled plenty of space but some occupants of the house could still have starved.

A socio-economic model

In Willem Jongman's classic study, *The Economy and Society of Pompeii*, he uses house size as an indicator of wealth. He considers lists of names of witnesses to transactions conducted by the Pompeian auctioneer Caecilius Iucundus. He wants to test a number of variables that might affect the order in which the witnesses sign. He tests for whether wealth affects signing order by using the sizes of known houses of witnesses as an indicator of their wealth. Wealth, measured in this way, turns out not to correlate with high places on the lists, which turn out to relate more closely to status of certain kinds[16] (which reinforces our conclusion that the economic elite is not identical with the status elite).

---

[15] See Peter Oakes, 'Constructing Poverty Scales for Graeco-Roman Society: A Response to Steven Friesen's "Poverty in Pauline Studies"', *JSNT* 26 (2004), pp. 367–71.

[16] Willem M. Jongman, *The Economy and Society of Pompeii* (Dutch Monographs on Ancient History and Archaeology 4; Amsterdam: Gieben, 1988), pp. 239–41, 247–64.

The economic elite will generally have owned their houses, so the size of their residence in Pompeii is a reasonable indicator of their wealth. It is not, however, a perfect indicator. The cost of houses would also vary depending on their location in town. The mode of use of the space would also be significant. A substantial corner of the House of the Menander is a stable yard. Another house of the same size, in which all the space was given over to more showy forms of use, would tend to indicate greater wealth.

Unlike Jongman's work, our own study is primarily interested in the economic non-elite. Most of those would have rented, rather than owned, their accommodation. In general terms, most property in pre-industrial societies is owned by the elite. In the Roman empire, this was reinforced by various factors, including the fact that qualification for membership of the *ordines* depended on ownership of property. In the Insula of the Menander, two particularly likely examples of tenancy are Houses 6 and 7. As we noted in Chapter 1, House 6 was cut out from the corner of the House of the Menander. The same process also removed space from House 7 – a change that would have been unlikely unless the owner of House 4 also owned House 7. Further evidence of this lies in the blocked-up doorways that earlier connected the two houses.

If non-elite householders were generally tenants, not owners, then the space they occupied will tend to be an indicator of the householder's income, rather than their wealth. Again, rentals must have varied between locations. Many other factors will also have affected the degree to which ground-floor space related to rental, and rental related to income. However, in general terms, a graph of distribution of house-plan size seems likely to correlate reasonably well with distribution of income among householders. We can therefore suggest that in a broad sense, with a significant margin of error, Figure 2.1 represents a model of income distribution among householders in Pompeii and Herculaneum, as indicated by occupation of urban space. The elite, for whom one might see it as a model of wealth distribution rather than income distribution, are only loosely plotted in the graph. In any case, their income would relate to their wealth.

Although there is likely a reasonable correlation between amount of space occupied and level of income, income would not be directly proportional to space. The householder occupying 400 m^2 does not, even on average, have exactly twice the income of one occupying 200 m^2. Rentals are not generally directly proportional to space. In most markets, rental cost per m^2 is higher for smaller properties than for larger ones. Also, the proportion of income that is spent on rental will vary. The poorer the householder, the higher the proportion of income that is likely to go on rental. In addition to these systemic tendencies, there would also be many random factors. Any graph of income against house size would produce a wide scatter of points. However, undoubtedly there would be a clear trend that the larger the house the higher the average income of the householder.

If we somehow knew the income of a large number of people such as the cabinet-maker (310 m² house), the bar tenant (80 m²) and the stoneworkers (40 m²), then we could calibrate our model, with a scale of incomes on the vertical axis. However, the scraps of evidence we have about first-century incomes seem far from sufficient to do such a thing in a worthwhile manner. Wallace-Hadrill has shown an interesting correlation between house size and the prevalence of various decorative features.[17] However, this is unlikely to offer a route that gets us closer to income, especially given the sporadic occurrence of decorative activity. It seems better to stick to talking of the figures in our model in terms of urban space, but with awareness of space having some relation to income. So, for instance, it seems safe to suggest that the bar tenant (80 m²) probably has a significantly higher income than the stoneworkers (40 m²), and that the cabinet-maker (310 m²) probably has a considerably higher income than either of the other householders. We can also say that the stoneworkers and bar tenant are probably in the bottom third of incomes (34% of houses are up to 100 m²), while the cabinet-maker probably has a higher income than 70% of other householders (34 + 22 + 14). Our model does not give specific figures for income distribution but it does articulate the pattern of income distribution in interesting ways.

Our model primarily covers only about one-eighth of the population of Pompeii. Wallace-Hadrill extrapolates from the *c.* 1,000 excavated habitable units on the site to a total of between 1,200 and 1,300 for the whole site, including unexcavated areas.[18] Estimating the population of Pompeii is a rather contested scholarly field but Wallace-Hadrill sees scholars as tending towards a consensus of about 10,000.[19] The exact figures are unimportant but it seems safe to see the proportion of habitable units, hence households, and hence householders, as about one in eight of the population (1,250 ÷ 10,000). The figure could be as low as about one in ten, or as high as about one in six, but one in eight gives a good general idea of the likely proportion.

---

[17] Wallace-Hadrill, *Houses and Society*, p. 154 and fig. 7.6.
[18] Wallace-Hadrill, *Houses and Society*, p. 99.
[19] Wallace-Hadrill, *Houses and Society*, p. 99.

A crucial point about this figure is that if we multiply it by four, the average urban family size in Bagnall and Frier's demographic studies based on censuses from Roman Egypt,[20] we come up well short of the total population. Although Bagnall and Frier's work has elicited some critique,[21] and Roman Egypt is clearly not entirely representative of the first-century world in general, the family-size figure of four is probably close enough to sustain the assertion that householders and their immediate families (spouses and children) made up something like half the population of Pompeii.

The point of all this is that our income model strictly covers only about an eighth of the population, that is, householders. Even if we blur the sharp economic differentiation within each family and describe our model as a family income model, we still only cover about half the town's population. The other half are slaves (Ramsay MacMullen estimates slaves as 25% of the population of Roman Italy),[22] or are dependants of other kinds living in someone else's house, or are homeless or living in marginal accommodation that is not part of the main archaeological record. Our model says nothing about the income of this other half of the town's population. On average it would, of course, be less than that of householders. In the case of slaves it would technically be zero although, in practice, they were able to hold money as what was called a *peculium*.[23] Even so, their income, from tips or, sometimes, from sharing their owner's income generated by a business that the slave ran (such as a workshop), would usually tend to be very low. If we were to put the 'missing half' of the population into a position in our model equivalent to their income, the great majority should no doubt be placed in the lowest section. If the poorest group of householders and their families are 34% of the total number of householders and their families, then they will be about 17% of the total population. If we included just about all of the 'missing half' of the population in this category too, we would end up with 67% of the population in the lowest category. It may seem unreasonable to include more or less all of the 'missing half' in the lowest category. What about senior

---

[20] Roger S. Bagnall and Bruce W. Frier, *The Demography of Roman Egypt* (Cambridge: Cambridge University Press, 1994 edn), p. 68, table 3.3. Their exact survey figure is 4.04.

[21] Tim G. Parkin, *Demography and Roman Society* (Baltimore: Johns Hopkins University Press, 1992); April Pudsey, 'Sex, Statistics and Soldiers: New Approaches to the Demography of Roman Egypt', *28 BC–259 AD* (Manchester: unpublished PhD thesis, 2007).

[22] Ramsay MacMullen, *Roman Social Relations: 50 BC to AD 284* (New Haven: Yale University Press, 1974), p. 92.

[23] A. F. Rodger, 'peculium', in *Oxford Classical Dictionary*, p. 1130.

slaves and other dependants who might effectively be relatively wealthy? The answer is that, as a percentage of the total number of slaves, dependants and homeless people, the proportion of the 'missing half' who had income equivalent to renting a house larger than House 1 (90 m^2) in the Insula of the Menander would surely have been extremely small. In any case, even if we did move 1 or 2% of the population into a higher category it would not change the overall shape of our model.

If we incorporate the 'missing half' into our model in the above way, and regard the families of householders as sharing in the householders' income (as beneficiaries), this produces the very tentative model in Table 2.2. Two-thirds of the population are in the lowest category. Our cabinet-maker and his family, in a house of 310 m^2, are in a better economic position than 85% of the population (67 + 11 + 7). I am very wary of this version of the model. So many disparate factors have been combined to create it that its figures are subject to very wide margins of error. However, it does securely make the point that a householder such as the cabinet-maker, who is 70% of the way up the economic scale of Pompeian householders in terms of occupation of urban space, is much higher on an economic scale that includes all the population.

Pompeii and Herculaneum are two small towns in southern Italy. To what extent is a model based on distribution of urban space in these towns of value for understanding socio-economic structure elsewhere? In the next chapter, we will consider the special case of Rome. More generally, the archaeological evidence shows an astonishing degree of repetition of patterns of building across most of the Roman empire. Inscriptions and other finds reinforce this point by indicating a high degree of commonality in social and political structures. Although no town apart from Pompeii was a previously Samnite, river-port Roman colony with a strongly Etruscan distant past, historically pervasive influence from Greek neighbouring towns, and an economy fuelled to a great degree by the particular richness of volcanic soil but undermined towards the end by seismic activity, yet there are endless features of Pompeii that are replicated in the more fragmentary archaeological evidence from other sites around the Mediterranean.

Consider Philippi, for instance. This was a country town of similar size to Pompeii. It too drew on a fertile agricultural hinterland and was (for reasons different from Pompeii) also involved in trade. It too was a Roman colony with heavy prior Greek influence. Almost all the pre-Christian excavated buildings in Philippi have equivalents in Pompeii. Many of the honorific and funerary inscriptions are also very similar. Although

Table 2.2 A very tentative model of income distribution in Pompeii and Herculaneum, based on equivalent urban space occupied

Equivalent space occupied (m²)	*Percentage of population*
above 1,000	2.5
900–999	0.2
800–899	0.3
700–799	0.5
600–699	1
500–599	2.5
400–499	4
300–399	4
200–299	7
100–199	11.0
0–99	67

Philippi had a different ethnic mix from that of Pompeii, I would be surprised if the overall socio-economic structure was radically different from our model for Pompeii. Maybe at Philippi there would be a bit more social polarization because of the ethnic situation, so perhaps the pattern would look more like the Herculaneum sample (sample II, although with different reasons for the pattern) than like the overall average. However, our Pompeian model would still seem a good starting point for thinking about issues of social structure in another Graeco-Roman town of similar size, such as Philippi.

Evidence from Pompeii is in the same category as the census returns from Roman Egypt: preserved by local conditions to a degree of detail that is more than ten times as great as for similar material elsewhere in the Roman empire. Patterns drawn from the Pompeian and Egyptian evidence must offer key starting points for construction of social models with any useable level of numerical detail. To anticipate an argument below: statistics from first-century Pompeii are more likely to be of use for constructing models of Graeco-Roman society than are statistics from medieval Florence. Of course we need to adjust or, if necessary, abandon our Pompeian model where other contexts are systemically different, such as in very large cities. However, for the bulk of the urban population, living in small towns across the Roman empire, a Pompeian model provides a reasonable starting point for reflection on socio-economic structure.[24] The

---

[24] For an attempt at working out a Pompeian model and comparing it with Pauline towns, see Peter Oakes, 'Contours of the Urban Environment', in Todd Still and David Horrell (eds), *After the First Urban Christians* (London: T. & T. Clark, 2009).

value of this approach can be seen by comparing our model with others that are currently in use.

Comparison with other models

One weakness we have seen in our model is that it is essentially focused on householders – only about one-eighth of society. However, the same is true of almost all the other available models of first-century social structure. To an extent, Alföldy's structure is, in principle, an exception in that he divides the non-elite into free, freed and slave, thus including a group of whom extremely few were, in any sense, householders.[25] However, his work is of very limited help in analysing non-elite social structure because he makes no attempt to depict differences of economic or status level within any of these three categories, except for separating out the imperial household and rich freedmen, whom he sees as straddling the boundary between elite and non-elite.

Gerhard Lenski's model of advanced agrarian societies offers some differentiation among the non-elite in terms of power, linked with privilege and prestige. He divides the non-elite into retainers, merchants, peasants, artisans and 'expendables'. Members of each group cover something of a socio-economic range, with retainers and merchants towards the upper end, expendables at the bottom, artisans towards the bottom, and peasants, by far the largest group, in the middle.[26] The outline shape of Lenski's population distribution is not entirely dissimilar to our model, although he does not offer a statistical analysis. This approach of dividing the non-elite into categories of job is an attractive one. There is plenty of evidence of types of work that were done by people in ancient societies. There is also enough evidence to produce a rough socio-economic ranking of typical holders of such jobs (although one must be careful to avoid thinking in terms of mass paid employment, as is the pattern today: most free ancient workers were self-employed, working in family units). I followed this approach in constructing a model of society in Philippi in the middle of the first century, dividing the population up into a landowning elite, commuting colonist farmers, 'service groups' (retainers, traders and craftworkers) and 'poor' (non-viable service groups), with slaves

---

[25] Alföldy, *The Social History of Rome*, p. 146.

[26] Gerhard Lenski, *Power and Privilege: A Theory of Social Stratification* (New York: McGraw-Hill, 1966), p. 82. For the use of this model in NT interpretation see Dennis C. Duling, 'Matthew as Marginal Scribe in an Advanced Agrarian Society', *Hervormde Teologiese Studies* 58 (2002), pp. 520–75.

indicated with their owners of various types. In principle, the groups were primarily categorized by relationship to the means of (agricultural) production: landowners; farmers; those providing goods and services to landowners and farmers. I also categorized the population ethnically and offered estimated percentage ranges for the various groups.[27] The specific categorizations differ from those of Lenski, as does the urban context, contrasting with Lenski's predominantly agricultural picture. However, the basic route to modelling social structure is similar: divide society into groups by job, etc.; consider the relative proportions of the groups; rank the jobs socio-economically.

Although such an investigative process yields a useful picture of social structure, it only really gives a relative ranking of social groups, without saying much about how far apart they are in economic terms. This limitation is particularly evident in my Philippi model, in which the colonist farmers are depicted as being in some social sense 'above' the service groups, but it is unclear how and to what extent. It is also unconvincing to have the whole of one group 'above' the whole of the other. Lenski avoids this problem by having the socio-economic range of 'merchants', for instance, overlapping that of 'peasants'. However, this immediately raises questions about how the extent of the overlap can be detected and measured. Ultimately, such a model lacks a vertical scale on which any coherent set of figures could be put. The model ranks groups but does not measure the relative value of each rank (in terms of whatever key variable is being used, such as 'power').

Ekkehard and Wolfgang Stegemann, in their study of the social history of the early Jesus movement, produce a model of social structure that, like Lenski's, in principle uses power as its primary variable.[28] However, they also introduce some differentiation into the non-elite by use of an economic variable, namely, relationship to 'minimum existence'. In outline, their model is as in Figure 2.2. They calculate 'minimum existence' with reference to the amount of wheat needed for the calorific intake of a family of four. They then convert that into a minimum farm size and a minimum annual income, which they calculate as 250–300 denarii in the countryside and 600–700 denarii in a town, including rental. The extra costs of living in Rome put their figure for that city up to 900–1,000

---

[27] Peter Oakes, *Philippians: From People to Letter* (SNTSMS 110; Cambridge: Cambridge University Press, 2001), pp. 14–50.

[28] Ekkehard W. Stegemann and Wolfgang Stegemann, *The Jesus Movement: A Social History of its First Century*, tr. O. C. Dean Jr (Minneapolis: Fortress, 1999), pp. 60–5.

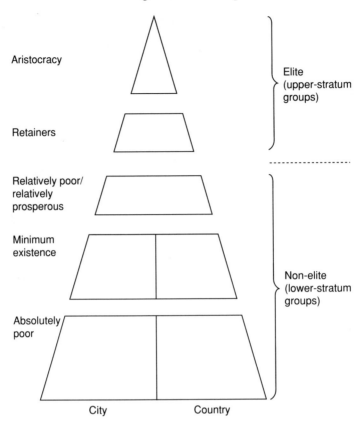

Figure 2.2 The Stegemann and Stegemann social pyramid

Source: Stegemann and Stegemann, *The Jesus Movement*, p. 72, social pyramid I.

denarii.[29] The Stegemanns then categorize the non-elite as being at, above or below the minimum level. This three-fold scheme is helpful in that it focuses analysis of the non-elite on a key issue: survival. Relative comfort means simply being a discernible distance above subsistence level. Most would not have managed that. They were either living on the knife-edge of just making ends meet, with periodic slides below that, or they were constantly below what they needed for healthy life. They were in fact gradually dying from the diseases brought on by hunger.

However, the Stegemanns' differentiation among the non-elite is very limited. In particular, the uniform characterization of those living above subsistence offers little help for understanding the social dynamics of early house churches. Also, the boundaries between the Stegemanns' social levels are undefined. In principle, 'minimum existence' is a specific level,

---

[29] Stegemann and Stegemann, *The Jesus Movement*, pp. 79–85.

Table 2.3 Friesen's poverty scale for the Roman empire

PS1	Imperial elites (including a few retainers, local royalty)	0.04%
PS2	Regional or provincial elites	1.00%
PS3	Municipal elites (including some merchants)	1.76%
PS4	Moderate surplus resources (some merchants, some traders, some freedpersons, some artisans, military veterans)	7%?
PS5	Stable near-subsistence (many merchants and traders, regular wage earners, artisans, large shopowners, freedpersons, some farm families)	22%?
PS6	At subsistence level (small farmers, labourers, artisans, wage earners, most merchants/traders, small shopowners)	40%
PS7	Below subsistence level (some farm families, unattached widows, orphans, beggars, disabled, unskilled day labourers, prisoners)	28%

rather than a band. If one does represent it as a band, it is not easy to come to a decision about where the edges of the band should be placed. This makes a third limitation inevitable: the model is not suitable for estimating the relative size of the various groups.[30]

Steven Friesen tackles head on the problem of estimating the size of the various groups in a model of social structure. In his 'poverty scale for the Roman empire', he divides society into seven 'poverty scale' (PS) levels and estimates the percentage of the population in each (Table 2.3). Despite my criticism above of Friesen's calculation of the numbers in his PS3 category, his overall figure of 2.8% for the total proportion of elite in larger cities (population 10,000 and above) is reasonably in line with our own model and with other scholars' estimates. In any case, the exact figure for the elite makes little difference to the percentage of non-elite, where our main interest lies. To divide up this remaining 97.2% of the population (rounded to 97%), Friesen draws on C. R. Whittaker's use of figures from pre-industrial European cities in a classic article, 'The Poor in the City of Rome'. Whittaker notes, from a study of thirteenth-century Florence, that 70% of households were recorded as having 'needs greater than their incomes'.[31] Friesen follows Whittaker in arguing for structural similarity between such a city and large ancient cities, concluding that this figure

---

[30] I have also discussed elsewhere some of the difficulties in calculating a 'minimum existence' level and in using it to mark poverty (Oakes 'Constructing Poverty Scales', pp. 367–71).

[31] C. R. Whittaker, 'The Poor in the City of Rome', in C. R. Whittaker, *Land, City and Trade in the Roman Empire* (Variorum; Aldershot: Ashgate, 1993), p. 4.

of 70% constitutes a reasonable estimate for the overall total who are at or below subsistence level, his categories PS6 and PS7.[32] This figure then guides his use of further percentages from Whittaker. Whittaker cites studies of several pre-industrial cities that fairly consistently show 4–8% of the population unable to earn a living and a further 20% permanently in crisis through low wages and other causes.[33] Friesen combines the two to give his estimate for PS7, people below subsistence, as 28%.[34] Whittaker cites 30–40% as a figure for small artisans, etc. who could sometimes temporarily fall below subsistence.[35] Friesen takes the 40% as his figure for PS6, people at subsistence level, preferring the upper end of Whittaker's 30–40% range in order to bring the total of PS6 and PS7 close to the Florence figure of 70%.[36] For PS4, 'moderate surplus resources', and PS5, 'stable near-subsistence', Friesen sees no basis for a particular point of division among the remaining 29% of the population that make up these categories. He very reasonably argues that the lower category would be considerably larger than the upper one and guesses at a division of 7% for PS4 and 22% for PS5.

It is easy to shoot at the first person who puts his or her head over the parapet and seeks to make progress in an important but difficult field. Friesen's work gathers together much of the best available evidence and uses it to estimate a shape for the non-elite social structure that is sufficiently specific to provide a framework for substantive discussion of the social location of the various members of Pauline churches mentioned in the New Testament. The extensive interaction there has been with his work shows the value of the progress he has made. Also, I have been rather startled to discover that the figures in our model can be mapped very closely onto his. In Table 2.2 above, the 67% in the lowest equivalent housing size is very close to his 68% for PS6 and PS7. The other figures then inevitably fit his total for PS4 and PS5, although it would be mischievously arbitrary to divide our upper non-elite range into 100–400 m^2 (22%) and 400–1,000 m^2 (7.5%) simply to fit with Friesen's PS5 and PS4!

Having said all this, the rapid increase in the availability of first-century socio-economic evidence indicates that the next steps forward in this kind of numerical modelling must surely come not from a comparative methodology, such as that of Whittaker and Friesen, but from

---

[32] Friesen, 'Poverty in Pauline Studies', pp. 344–5, esp. n. 69.
[33] Whittaker, 'The Poor in the City of Rome', p. 4.
[34] Friesen, 'Poverty in Pauline Studies', p. 344.
[35] Whittaker, 'The Poor in the City of Rome', p. 4.
[36] Friesen, 'Poverty in Pauline Studies', pp. 344–5.

analysis of evidence from the Roman empire itself. Our Pompeian space-distribution model is offered as a tentative step in this direction. Further progress looks likely in the future from analysis of further types of socio-economic evidence such as skeletal remains (marking aspects of health and lifestyle, although the patterns of evidence are complex) or food remains (one could imagine a social scale based on diet, as evidenced by latrine waste from various houses!).

The space-distribution model and the study of Pauline Christianity

As we have seen, our model broadly supports the figures for first-century social structure suggested by Steven Friesen. Against Gerd Theissen and the other 'New Consensus' scholars, who see Pauline Christians as covering a wide social range including the lower reaches of the elite, Friesen backs Justin Meggitt in placing the Pauline Christians only in non-elite categories and in generally representing those categories in terms of poverty.[37] Friesen's elaboration of social structure is intended to move forward from Meggitt's sharply dichotomized picture of society – all rich or poor – by articulating the differences within the non-elite 97%. Ironically, in doing so he opens up again the idea of social difference within the Pauline communities. This allows in the possibility of problems in those communities being due to social difference – the type of explanation offered by Theissen (although without the factor of specifically elite behaviour that is important in the work of Theissen and other scholars such as John Chow and Andrew Clarke).[38]

It is difficult, however, to move forward in exploring the social dynamics of the Pauline communities on the basis of Friesen's model of social structure. The essential limitation is that there is no real sense of vertical scale in his differentiation among the non-elite. He seeks to work in relation to poverty and, like Stegemann and Stegemann, his characterization of the non-elite is determined by that basis. His categories are 'below subsistence', 'at subsistence', 'near subsistence', and what we could call 'a moderate distance from subsistence'. Three of the categories, covering

---

[37] Friesen, 'Poverty in Pauline Studies', pp. 348–58.
[38] Gerd Theissen, *The Social Setting of Pauline Christianity: Essays on Corinth* (Edinburgh: T. & T. Clark, 1982); John K. Chow, *Patronage and Power: A Study of Social Networks in Corinth* (JSNTSup 75; Sheffield: Sheffield Academic Press, 1992); A. D. Clarke, *Secular and Christian Leadership in Corinth: A Socio-Historical and Exegetical Study of 1 Corinthians 1—6* (Leiden: Brill, 1993).

90% of the population, simply put people on one side or the other of a line, or on the line. The fourth category places people an undefined distance above the line. No analysis of social dynamics in a group can make much progress on the basis of this kind of scale.

Our space-distribution model does not yield specific figures for wealth or income (although, as argued above, there will be a correlation with income). However, it does offer a real vertical scale based on a significant economic variable. If, for instance, a house church consisted of five households and we placed them on our scale in accordance with the general distribution of space among the population, we would end up with something like two households in the 0–100 m^2 bracket, one in the 100–200 m^2 bracket, one somewhere between 200 and 400 m^2, and one larger than that, but probably between 400 and 600 m^2. Reflection on the likely social dynamics between five such households would offer a way into a range of issues in the Pauline house churches.

In reality, we ought to be a little more subtle than this. A house church would not generally consist of a random set of the urban population. In particular, the socio-economic level of the person hosting the house church is bound to have affected the social make-up of the group. A complication that we must also address is that Paul was not writing to Pompeii. For letters from Paul to house churches in other medium-sized urban settings this would not be such a pressing issue but, as we have already seen, Rome was a rather different place. We need to think about the extent to which, and the ways in which, the tremendously rich social evidence from Pompeii can be put to some use in thinking about Paul's letter to Rome. To these tasks we will now turn.

3

A model craftworker house church for reading Romans

An important scholarly tradition, from classic work such as that of Hans-Josef Klauck to recent studies such as that of Roger Gehring,[1] has placed the very early Christian groups into Roman houses. Jerome Murphy-O'Connor uses the Anaploga villa at Corinth to give this idea a specificity that has allowed it to have considerable impact on understanding Paul's writings (especially 1 Corinthians 11). He also uses it to argue that the maximum number which could have fitted into a house church meeting was about 40.[2] Carolyn Osiek and David Balch dispute that figure, using examples of large Pompeian houses in which considerably more could meet.[3] They also emphatically assert that houses of the traditional Roman form were the primary places of meeting.[4] Balch has since regretted this assertion, suggesting that we should also consider alternative possible settings in apartment blocks, such as the Insula Orientalis at Herculaneum.[5] In an article that appeared at the same time, David Horrell challenges Murphy-O'Connor's use of the Anaploga villa. Horrell suggests that a more typical environment for a Christian group meeting is to be found in places such as an upstairs hall in buildings east of the theatre at Corinth.[6] For the

---

[1] Hans-Josef Klauck, *Hausgemeinde und Hauskirche im frühen Christentum* (Stuttgarter Bibelstudien 103; Stuttgart: Verlag Katholisches Bibelwerk, 1981); Roger W. Gehring, *House Church and Mission* (Peabody, Mass.: Hendrickson, 2004), ET of Roger W. Gehring, *Hausgemeinde und Mission* (Bibelwissenschaftliche Monographien 9; Giessen: Brunnen Verlag, 2000).

[2] Jerome Murphy-O'Connor, *St. Paul's Corinth: Texts and Archaeology* (Good News Studies 6; Wilmington, Del.: Glazier, 1983), p. 156.

[3] Carolyn Osiek and David L. Balch, *Families in the New Testament World: Households and House Churches* (Louisville: Westminster John Knox, 1997), pp. 201–2.

[4] Osiek and Balch, *Families*, pp. 16–17.

[5] David L. Balch, 'Rich Pompeiian Houses, Shops for Rent, and the Huge Apartment Building in Herculaneum as Typical Spaces for Pauline House Churches', *JSNT* 27 (2004), p. 28.

[6] David G. Horrell, 'Domestic Space and Christian Meetings at Corinth: Imagining New Contexts and the Buildings East of the Theatre', *New Testament Studies* 50 (2004), pp. 349–69.

interpretation of Romans, Robert Jewett very sharply contrasts meetings in houses and meetings in apartment blocks, which he calls 'tenements'. The 'house church' has an elite patron and meets in his or her large house. The group is characterized by social hierarchy. The 'tenement church' meets in an apartment block and is patronless and egalitarian.[7] Jewett sees a house-church model of early Christian life as leading to an understanding of Paul's ethics in terms of what Gerd Theissen calls 'love-patriarchalism', reinforcing the social order while ameliorating it with mutual love.[8]

A key argument of the present book is that scholars have generally been looking at the wrong houses when looking for types of house in which a typical early Christian group would have met. The elite were a tiny percentage of society. They must have formed an even lower percentage of house-church members. The majority of house churches are unlikely to have included a member of the elite, in which case they will not generally have met in elite houses. Ironically, the main exceptions to this were probably household house churches among slaves, such as may well be indicated in Romans 16.10–11. Since most early Christians who met in houses probably did so in non-elite houses, this breaks down the main social contrast usually drawn between churches based in houses and those based in apartments.[9] If our house church is hosted by a craftworker, the social structure of the group that meets there is unlikely to be radically different from that of a church hosted by a similar craftworker in a space in an apartment block. There will be social hierarchy in both cases (beginning with the hierarchy in the host's household).[10]

To help in NT interpretation, we want to reflect on the nature of the groups that we would expect to meet in the kinds of spaces that were inhabited by the non-elite, but which were large enough for a reasonably sized group to meet. To represent such a group, meeting in a fair-sized craftworker's house such as that of Holconius, we will construct a model:

---

[7] Robert Jewett, *Romans: A Commentary* (Hermeneia; Minneapolis: Fortress, 2007), pp. 64–5, citing a range of scholarship from Floyd Filson, 'The Significance of Early House Churches', *JBL* 58 (1939), pp. 105–11, to Anton Weiser, 'Evangelisierung im Haus', *BZ* 34 (1990), pp. 64–77.

[8] Gerd Theissen, *The Social Setting of Pauline Christianity: Essays on Corinth* (Edinburgh: T. & T. Clark, 1982), pp. 11, 107. Jewett also cites Wayne A. Meeks, *The First Urban Christians: The Social World of the Apostle Paul* (New Haven: Yale University Press, 1983), p. 76.

[9] Moreover, Balch, 'Rich Pompeiian Houses', pp. 36–7, stresses the degree of continuity between elite houses and aspects of many apartment blocks.

[10] We will continue our discussion on comparing meetings in houses and apartments when we turn from Pompeii to Rome below.

a simplified representation of what we might expect a typical such group to be like.[11] In addition to a model based on this Pompeian house, we will construct a version of the model that is modified to take into account differences between Pompeii and the context in Rome that Paul might be envisaging as he dictates his letter.

Before we get going on these tasks, we need first to defend the idea that consideration of the types of gentile lives attested in Pompeii is relevant to the interpretation of Paul's letter to the Romans.

Specific social types in Pompeii and among the expected hearers of Romans

Our picture of the impoverished life of the stoneworkers may be drawn from Pompeii but, if this was the case in Pompeii, there will certainly have been many such situations in Rome, both as it really was and as Paul envisaged it (whether accurately or not). Paul expected there to be poor people in the house churches (see e.g. 1 Cor. 11.22). It is reasonable for us to think about how any of his letters would have sounded to first-century poor people. Our Pompeian stoneworkers offer concrete instances of the type 'near-destitute craftworker'. As long as we do not make our reading of Romans dependent on details of the stoneworking trade, it looks reasonable to ask how the text of Romans relates to this social type as instantiated in the Pompeian stoneworkers. The instantiation of the social type in the particular concrete case gives us the conceptual means – the imaginative means, even – to think in a specific way about how the letter would relate to issues facing a near-destitute craftworker. If we tried to carry out the same exercise with 'near-destitute craftworker' purely as an abstract concept, we would in any case probably end up unconsciously reifying the concept in an imaginary person, but would do so without the first-century contextual control that the evidence of a specific Pompeian case gives us.

The claim to be among the types of people whom Paul expects to be in house churches is also clearly justified for two of the other social types presented in Chapter 1: a low-status slave and a craftworker who has the capacity for hosting a house church. Our fourth social type, the sexually exploited slave Iris, is introduced because of the sharp issues it raises for

---

[11] On models, see Bruce J. Malina, *The New Testament World: Insights from Cultural Anthropology* (London: SCM Press, 1983), p. 17; John H. Elliott, *Social-Scientific Criticism of the New Testament* (London: SPCK, 1995), pp. 40–8.

the nature of Paul's communities and of his moral discourse. These issues have made such slaves a recent focus of scholarly discussion.[12]

Each of these four social types was present in all the Pauline towns and cities. We can be confident that the first three types, at least, were among the hearers that Paul was expecting for Romans. The Pompeian houses enable us to represent these types of hearers in ways that relate to specific first-century evidence. They thus offer the potential for clarifying our understanding of Paul's letter, both as originally heard and as he expected it to be heard.

There are two, or possibly three, provisos to be made. One is that we may need to allow for any systemic differences between a social type in Pompeii and its equivalent in Rome. Holconius, our Pompeian craftworker with a fair-sized house, would, in Rome, have much smaller, less conveniently organized accommodation. He would probably also have rather fewer possessions and less wall decoration. A second proviso is that we need to allow for our social types being Christians. We are interested in the type 'near-destitute Christian craftworker' rather than 'near-destitute craftworker' in general. The use of a reasonably realistic model craftworker house church actually raises tricky questions about the use of defining labels such as 'Christian': for certain types of people in the model it is quite hard to think about what membership, or even attendance at meetings, really involved. However, whatever labels we use, our hearers need to be people who would have heard the letter. This provides constraints on the social types and on our use of the Pompeian evidence for each case. To take an obvious issue: if we are imagining Christian versions of the stoneworkers and the cabinet-maker, we may want to suggest that the *lararia* in each house had gone out of use[13] (or maybe not, which would raise further issues). However, in general, there seems little reason to suppose that house-church membership excluded the social situations of the stoneworker, the bath-stoker or the cabinet-maker – we would not, for example, expect a Christian Holconius to have given up owning slaves – and Iris is included specifically because of the potential tension of her social type being part of a house church. A third issue, which could constitute a proviso, is more difficult to judge. Do the social types that we use as potential hearers of Romans need to be ones that relate in specific

---

[12] Jennifer A. Glancy, *Slavery in Early Christianity* (Oxford: Oxford University Press, 2002), ch. 2; Carolyn Osiek and Margaret Y. MacDonald, *A Woman's Place: House Churches in Earliest Christianity* (Minneapolis: Fortress, 2006), ch. 5.

[13] Cf. Balch, 'Rich Pompeiian Houses', p. 37.

ways to synagogues? This question plunges us into scholarly complications and we will deal with it separately.

How we can actually use individual social types to help in understanding the letter is clearly a major further issue. We will discuss it at the beginning of Chapter 5.

The expected hearers of Romans

One of the characteristics of the present book is that it uses historical evidence in a different way from most previous studies of Romans. Previous scholars have tended to use historical evidence, whether external to the text or within it, to construct a specific theory about the situation of Romans. They have then read the letter in relation to that theory about the situation. So, for instance, Andrew Das reads the letter in relation to tension between gentile 'god-fearers', whose previous attachment to synagogues had been ended by the Edict of Claudius (see below), and other gentiles.[14] Robert Jewett reads it in relation to Paul's intended mission to the 'barbarians' in Spain, which raised issues that intersected with the consequences of, again, that edict.[15] Instead of using historical evidence to build specific situational theories and consequent readings, this study uses historical evidence to put flesh on to a more general situational scenario: that Romans is a letter written for house churches in Rome in the middle of the first century. Unlike the more specific situational scenarios, this general scenario is something with which almost all scholars will agree.[16]

The comparison between these two approaches can be seen in the two main aspects of Wolfgang Wiefel's classic article, 'Die jüdische Gemeinschaft in antiken Rom und die Anfänge des römischen Christentums', translated into English as 'The Jewish Community in Ancient Rome and the Origins of Roman Christianity'. In a masterly piece of compact argument he presents overwhelming evidence of anti-Jewish feeling in early imperial Rome, then compares this with Paul's positive valuation

---

[14] A. Andrew Das, *Solving the Romans Debate* (Minneapolis: Fortress, 2007), pp. 201–2.

[15] Jewett, *Romans*, pp. 58–9, 87–91.

[16] An exception to the house-church (or tenement-church) consensus would be Mark Nanos, *The Mystery of Romans* (Minneapolis: Fortress, 1996), who would see the Christians in Rome as belonging to synagogues. This is a powerful alternative paradigm for conceptualizing the early Christian movement. However, his theory has difficulties both in its depiction of synagogue handling of gentile Christians and in exegesis of Romans: for instance, in his interpretation of 13.1–7 as relating to synagogue authorities, pp. 289–336. See Das's response to this point, *Solving the Romans Debate*, pp. 146–7.

of Israel in Romans, which culminates in the saying, 'all Israel will be saved' (11.26). He concludes,

> We have shown the existence of a strong anti-Jewish sentiment in Rome at the time of Nero and before. Positive statements regarding all of Israel appear for the first time in Paul's letter to the Romans and must be seen against this background.[17]

Leaving aside his slightly contentious implicit contrast between Romans and Paul's other letters, what Wiefel has done is to use historical evidence to set up a key aspect of the first-century cultural context in Rome, 'anti-Jewish sentiment', and then argue for reading Romans in relation to that cultural context. This is valuable work and we will seek to build on it in Chapter 6, when we read the material on Judaism in Romans in relation to the likely attitudes of a moderately educated gentile whose cultural reference points are Graeco-Roman and who shares his culture's general disdain for Jews: characteristics that are all likely to have been true of our Pompeian cabinet-maker, Holconius.

However, the aspect of Wiefel's article that has influenced scholars most, forming a key plank of many commentaries, is a four-page section halfway through. In this, he sketches a possible specific situation for the writing of Romans. Claudius probably issued an edict which expelled the Jews from Rome in 49 CE, after rioting that Wiefel sees as relating to Christianity. Among the expelled Jews were the earliest leaders of the city's house churches, such as Prisca and Aquila. By the time Paul writes, several years later, Prisca, Aquila and no doubt many other Jewish Christian leaders have returned. How might we expect the now-established gentile leadership of the house churches to react? It could well be in an unwelcoming way, to which Paul's rhetoric of mutual acceptance in Romans 14—15 would be well designed to respond.[18]

It is not reasonable to make a commentary on Romans dependent on such a theory. Unless it is backed by fairly clear evidence in the text, it is too specific to be other than rather speculative. Although it is fair to see Romans 14—15 as evidence of likely tensions within or between house churches, about issues that may well relate in some way to Judaism, it is not reasonable to infer that such tensions relate to the return of Jewish Christians who had been expelled by Claudius. Many other scenarios would

---

[17] Wolfgang Wiefel, 'The Jewish Community in Ancient Rome and the Origins of Roman Christianity', in K. P. Donfried (ed.), *The Romans Debate* (Peabody, Mass.: Hendrickson, 1991 edn), p. 100.

[18] Wiefel, 'The Jewish Community', pp. 92–6.

fit such evidence: for instance that of Andrew Das, noted above. More-over, Wiefel has fallen into a trap that easily catches people who are looking to relate local evidence to local phenomena. He writes that the sequence of events following Claudius' edict 'explains why Jewish Chris-tianity did not regain its dominant position [in Rome]'.[19] What he does not take into account is that gentiles are the predominant addressees of all Paul's letters, wherever they are sent to. Rome needs no special explan-ation. Probably, either Paul just always wrote his letters as if to gentiles, or the Christian groups around the northern Mediterranean tended to be predominantly gentile from early on, irrespective of whether it was Paul who founded them.

Wiefel does argue effectively for the audience of Romans being gentile. In maybe slightly overstated fashion, he writes in relation to Romans 9—11, 'For Jewish Christians, a justification of the Gentile mission would have been in order, but not a glorification of Israel's virtues.'[20] Although this is not an entirely convincing characterization of those chapters, it is true that their rhetoric does appear to be pitched at gentiles rather than Jews or even 'god-fearers'. The point about gentiles can be, and frequently has been, made more broadly.[21] Our biggest clue to the expected hearers lies in the nature of the hearers 'encoded' in the text. The most promin-ent form of such encoding in a letter which is to be read out (hence 'hearers' rather than 'readers') to a group or groups is the characteriza-tion of the addressees. Paul's greeting speaks of his 'apostleship for the obedience of faith among all the gentiles on behalf of his name, among whom are you too' (1.5–6). With a few exceptions,[22] commentators agree that this implies that the addressees are gentiles. This conclusion is sup-ported at the end of the opening section, where Paul describes his desire to come to them so that he might 'have some fruit among you too, as among the other gentiles. I am a debtor to Greeks and barbarians, wise and fool-ish, so I have the desire to announce the gospel to you too in Rome' (1.13–15). He also turns to his hearers in 11.13 and says, 'I am speaking to you gentiles'. In drawing his letter towards its close, he says that he wrote

---

[19] Wiefel, 'The Jewish Community', pp. 95–6.

[20] Wiefel, 'The Jewish Community', p. 96.

[21] For example, Stanley K. Stowers, *A Rereading of Romans: Justice, Jews, and Gentiles* (New Haven: Yale University Press, 1994), pp. 29–33; Das, *Solving the Romans Debate*, ch. 2; Runar M. Thorsteinsson, *Paul's Interlocutor in Romans 2: Function and Identity in the Context of Ancient Epistolography* (Coniectanea Biblica NT Series 40; Stockholm: Almqvist and Wiksell, 2003), ch. 2.

[22] Most notably, C. E. B. Cranfield, *A Critical and Exegetical Commentary on the Epistle to the Romans. Vol. I: Romans I—VIII* (ICC; Edinburgh: T. & T. Clark, 1975), p. 68.

the letter because of 'the grace given to me by God, to be the servant of Christ Jesus to the gentiles' (15.15–16).

This consistently gentile pattern is disrupted in 2.17, in which Paul addresses a Jewish interlocutor: 'If you call yourself a Jew . . .'. In chapter 16 he sends greetings to Prisca, Aquila and various other Jews. In 15.7, he asks his hearers to 'welcome one another', writing in a context where he backs this up with points relating to Jews and gentiles (15.8–12). More systemically, the letter contains extensive material relating to law and other Jewish matters.

The evidence of Romans 16, that the letter was written for both gentile and Jewish hearers, is not a problem for our approach. We are not dependent on gentiles being the only expected hearers. They just need to be a significant group of them. The same point can be made if Paul occasionally turns to a Jewish interlocutor. Many hearers could still be gentiles. In any case, the interlocutor could be taken to be the hypothetical sparring partner of diatribe.[23] The prominence of Jewish issues in the letter is potentially more of a problem, because it could suggest that the gentile hearers whom Paul was expecting were all ones with a previous attachment to synagogues, i.e. 'god-fearers'. However, Paul appears to have a broad range of gentiles in mind. He firmly places the letter and its addressees in the context of his mission to the gentiles as a whole. Paul's debt 'to Greeks and barbarians' takes us well beyond the synagogue. Moreover, in line with Wiefel's point noted above, the rhetoric of 11.13–24, calling gentiles not to look down on Jews, is undoubtedly addressed to gentiles who were not god-fearers, attracted to synagogues.

Most scholars would agree that many of Paul's expected hearers were gentiles. It also seems safe to argue that many were likely to be members of households engaged in craftwork or other work of that socio-economic level, such as shopkeeping. The argument for this is partly about Pauline Christianity in general and partly about the people in Romans 16. The hearers of 1 Thessalonians are instructed to work with their hands (1 Thess. 4.11). This follows the example of Paul (1 Thess. 2.9). Such a presentation of himself suggests the likelihood of similar converts elsewhere. More broadly, few of the Corinthians were powerful or well born (1 Cor. 1.26), which puts them down among the non-elite of craftworkers and similar people: our study is not about craftwork itself but about people of such socio-economic levels. In Romans itself, we have Prisca and Aquila (16.3)

---

[23] Neil Elliott, *The Rhetoric of Romans: Argumentative Constraint and Strategy and Paul's Dialogue with Judaism* (JSNTSup 45; Sheffield: Sheffield Academic Press, 1990), pp. 127–32.

who, according to Acts 18.3, are craftworkers. As Peter Lampe argues, the names of many of the rest of those in Romans 16 make them likely to be at low socio-economic levels, as slaves or freed slaves or their descendants.[24] In fact, even if one were to follow Runar Thorsteinsson's argument that the greetings in Romans 16 are for Christians who are in Rome but not in the house churches that Paul addresses,[25] the list of people would still be indicative of the general social level among the house churches at Rome. (Even if we go further, with T. W. Manson, in the now rarely held view that Romans 16 contains names relating to Ephesus, not Rome,[26] this is still evidence for the general argument about the social level of Pauline Christianity as a whole.)

Lloyd Gaston argues that the 'implied addressees of Paul's exhortation [in Romans] are those with relatively higher wealth and status'.[27] Gaston does think there are also poor people among the Roman Christians: those who need hospitality as well as those called to offer it (12.13). However, the exhortation is to those who can give. This is an important argument. The expected audience of a text could be wider than the group that the text primarily addresses. In fact, one of Paul's other letters is a good example of such a text: the letter to Philemon. Paul sets up a broad audience, then addresses almost all his remarks directly to Philemon. However, that

---

[24] Peter Lampe, *From Paul to Valentinus: Christians at Rome in the First Two Centuries*, ed. M. D. Johnson, tr. M. Steinhauser (Minneapolis: Fortress; London: T. & T. Clark, 2003), pp. 153–83.

[25] Thorsteinsson, *Paul's Interlocutor*, pp. 63–6. He follows T. Y. Mullins, 'Greetings as a New Testament Form', *JBL* 87 (1968), pp. 418–26, in arguing that second-person instructions to greet someone carry greetings to people who are not among the addressees of a letter. However, the presence of gentiles in the list of those to whom greetings are to be sent actually forces Thorsteinsson's theory into what looks an unsustainable position. One might, at a stretch, argue that a letter addressed to 'all those in Rome beloved by God, called to be holy ones' (1.7) is sent only to Christian gentiles, not Christian Jews. However, it seems almost impossible to suppose that the letter is not at least addressed to all the Christian gentiles in Rome, including those named in Romans 16. In any case, Mullins's lexical argument is not convincing. A second-person plural instruction to greet someone may, of course, be a request to greet someone who is not among the recipients. However, Mullins's argument that it is generally so rests on an analogy with second-person singular instructions (where this is clearly true) rather than analysis of second-person plural examples. In fact the unambiguous second-person plural examples from Paul's letters are instructions to 'greet one another', that is, to greet other people who are among the recipients of the letter. The list in Romans 16 ends with just such an instruction (16.16).

[26] T. W. Manson, 'St. Paul's Letter to the Romans – and Others', in M. Black (ed.), *Studies in the Gospels and Epistles* (Manchester: Manchester University Press, 1962), pp. 225–41.

[27] Lloyd Gaston, 'Faith in Romans 12 in the Light of the Common Life of the Roman Church', in Julian V. Hills (ed.), *Common Life in the Early Church: Essays Honoring Graydon F. Snyder* (Harrisburg, Penn.: Trinity Press International, 1998), p. 260.

letter actually suggests why an approach via the wider audience is valuable. To ask how the letter would sound to other members of the church in Philemon's house – and even how it would sound to slaves of Philemon other than the named Onesimus – greatly sharpens the issues in considering how the rhetoric of Paul's appeal to Philemon works. This would also be true for Romans, even if Paul spent all his time calling for almsgiving: it would be interesting to think about how such rhetoric would sound to the poor as well as to those better off. However, Paul is far from concentrating most of Romans on such issues. The presence of a few calls to share resources and to associate with the poor is no reason to categorize the primary addressees of the letter as well off. Most of the letter's rhetoric could address people of a range of socio-economic levels.

Stanley Stowers, on whom Gaston draws, sees the key social group among Paul's audience as being the 'upwardly mobile'. This is important for Stowers's understanding of Romans because he sees this group as particularly likely to have an interest in an ethic of 'self-mastery',[28] a central issue in his reading of the letter. In this, Stowers is using Wayne Meeks's work, which sees such upwardly mobile people, whose 'achieved status' was higher than their 'attributed status', as key active members of Paul's circle.[29] Stowers points out that many of those named in Romans 16 were probably slaves or freed slaves, quite likely including some from the imperial household (cf. Phil. 4.22), members of which were often notoriously upwardly mobile.[30] However, the existence of some well-known cases of upward mobility is not an argument for its general prevalence. In the first century, social mobility was of political importance, especially because a significant proportion of new members of the elite were descendants of freed slaves. However, the elite were such a small number that this only involved a tiny percentage of the slave population. Such mobility was extremely rare for slaves, even those owned by the emperor. The greatest mobility that most slaves could hope for was liberation to a probably impoverished old age. As Peter Garnsey and Richard Saller note, social mobility was controlled and effectively rationed by existing members of better-off groups. This patronal control of entry to higher groups was 'a crucial element in the stability of the Roman system of inequality'.[31] For

---

[28] Stowers, *A Rereading of Romans*, p. 75.
[29] Meeks, *The First Urban Christians*, p. 73.
[30] Stowers, *A Rereading of Romans*, pp. 78–9.
[31] Peter Garnsey and Richard Saller, *The Roman Empire: Economy, Society and Culture* (London: Duckworth, 1987), p. 125.

the great majority of first-century people, upward social mobility was extremely limited. The people in Romans 16 probably fell into this great majority.

Romans 16 gives evidence of a number of groups among the people receiving the letter. 'The assembly in the house' of Prisca and Aquila (16.5) is a craftworker-led house church. 'The brothers and sisters with' Asyncritos et al. (16.14) are presumably another house church, as are 'all the holy ones with' Philologos, Julia and the others (16.15). 'Those belonging to Aristobulus' (16.10) sounds like a predominantly slave house church, as does 'those who belong to Narcissus who are in the Lord' (16.11). If time and space permitted, it would be interesting to read Romans in relation to issues as they would affect a slave-household house church. However, the nature of the Pompeian evidence, and the prominence of craftworkers in the general scholarly view of Pauline Christianity, mean that a craftworker house church looks most likely to provide a fruitful model for an initial attempt to use the Pompeian archaeological evidence to help us understand the text of Romans. Our aim will be to use a model gentile craftworker house church to explore the social dynamics of part of Romans as it would relate to such a group. Romans 12 contains much material that makes it look a fruitful text to study in this way. We will discuss our approach further when we turn to this text in our next chapter.

To use the Pompeian evidence to construct a model suitable for reading Romans, we need to proceed in two steps. First, we will construct a Pompeian model craftworker house church. If a house church met in a house such as the Cabinet-Maker's House, with Holconius as its host, what might we expect its social make-up to be? As well as being an important first step towards producing a model for studying Romans, this Pompeian model should, in itself, be of interest for reflecting on the social dynamics of Pauline communities in other Graeco-Roman urban settings. The second step is to modify our Pompeian model to make it suitable for Rome. The social structure of a group hosted by a cabinet-maker in Pompeii would have many features in common with a group hosted by such a person in Rome, so some transfer of model is clearly possible. However, apartment life in high-rent Rome would also impose various constraints and changes in the make-up of such a group. Any Pompeian model needs to undergo significant modification to produce a model suitable for Rome. To take the most obvious point: a cabinet-maker who could afford a Pompeian house that was able to accommodate a church meeting of 40 could only afford a limited workshop and a few upstairs rooms in Rome. It would be surprising if he could host a meeting of more than, say, 30. The social range of the cabinet-maker's dependants and close contacts would probably be similar in Pompeii and Rome. However, the specific shape of that group would differ somewhat. We will seek to take such points into account in constructing our models.

Towards a Pompeian model house church

In a random group of 40 Pompeians, we would expect there to be about five householders (one in eight) and 35 people who were not household-ers. If our random 40 fitted our model of the total population (Table 2.2), the social breakdown in terms of family occupation of space would be as in Table 3.1 (where 'family' means householder, spouse and children).[32] This random group thus includes 10 slaves, 17 others with either no inde-pendent space or space in the smallest category, seven in families with space between this and the size of the Cabinet-Maker's House (310 m²), five other non-elite in families with that or greater space, and one member of an elite family. Consideration of the social dynamics of a group that some-how consisted of this random 40 would be worth while. It would begin

Table 3.1 Breakdown of random 40-person Pompeian group in terms of family occupation of urban space

Space occupied by family of the person (m²)	Number of people
More than 1,000	1
600–999	1
500–599	1
400–499	1[1]
300–399	2[1]
200–299	3
100–199	4
0–99	7
No space	20 (including 10 slaves)
Total	40
Number of householders	5

[1] The figures for 300–399 m² and 400–499 m² are actually 1.5 each, but the model requires whole numbers of people.

---

[32] Family members (spouses and children) are taken as occupying the same space as house-holders. The 50% of the population who occupy no space have been separated out from the 17% who occupy some space but less than 100 m².

Table 3.2 Breakdown of random 40-person Pompeian group excluding all families wealthier than the 300–399 m² group

Space occupied by family of the person (m²)	Number of people
300–399	2
200–299	3
100–199	5
0–99	8
No space	22 (including 11 slaves)
Total	40
Number of householders	4

Note: The figures are recalculated from Table 2.2 and then rounded off. For example, the figure for the 300–399 m² category is 4% of 40 × 100 ÷ 89 = 1.8, rounded to 2. The number of householders is (40 ÷ 8) × (78 ÷ 89) = 4.4, rounded to 4.

to indicate some of the issues that interest us. However, such a random set of people would never come together as a group. Apart from various social barriers that would discourage it, the set of people is from too many separate households. Any actual such group of 40 would be concentrated in fewer households. To construct our model house church we need to move beyond a purely random group.

Our best starting point is probably the house-church host. For a model craftworker house church we need a host who is a craftworker with accommodation large enough to host a house-church meeting. The cabinet-maker of House I.10.7 at Pompeii looks ideal. The size of group that could meet in a coherent space in his house – in the garden, portico and 'dining rooms' – is probably of the order of 40. This would seem a reasonable number for a house church.

It is reasonable to assume that house churches generally met in the largest house available. This would imply that any other householders in the church had houses smaller than Holconius the cabinet-maker. If we chose a random group of 40 Pompeians from whom the 22% of householders who were significantly wealthier than Holconius had been removed, we would get essentially the same group as in Table 3.1 (there would have been only one householder wealthier than Holconius in the original random group of 40 Pompeians). If we take the further step of assuming that none of their families would join the group either, we get a random group that is skewed by the removal of the wealthiest 11% of the population, those in families with houses of 400 m² or more (Table 3.2).

Again, the social breakdown of this group is interesting. It represents something like the social pattern we might expect in a house church if every person was an independent actor. However, both general historical conditions and New Testament evidence imply that, to a considerable extent, household members followed the actions of householders (e.g. Acts 16.15, 33; 1 Cor. 1.16). This most obviously applies to members of Holconius's own household. Although in large households it was known for slaves and other household members to participate in cults other than those in which the householder participated,[33] for smaller households such as that of the cabinet-maker, the household must usually have followed the religious practice of the householder, especially when the householder held a position of responsibility in the cult and the cult was conducted on his premises. Let us assume that all the cabinet-maker's household attend house-church meetings. Given the size of his house and the extent of the craftwork carried on there, we could expect him to have a household of about ten. He would probably have a wife, some children (say, three), a few craftworking slaves (say, three), a domestic slave, and maybe also an extra dependent relative.

Even if this was itself a household church – just these ten people – we would already see many of the social relationships and disparities that would make the potential impact of Paul's teaching on the group very interesting: gender differences; owner and slaves; dependency and authority; household hierarchy. We also see that not all members of a 'craftworker house church' would actually be craftworkers. To be pedantic, we could talk of a 'predominantly craftworker house church' or a 'craftworker-hosted house church'. However, we will stick to the more straightforward expression, even though our craftworker house church would tend to include various non-craftworkers.

We need 30 more people to make up the house church. Let us try modelling one extreme option, that no one other than householders has independence of decision, so the house church is entirely made up of complete households.

All the households are smaller than that of the cabinet-maker. Because the households are small, the number of householders is higher than the Pompeian average. If we estimate average household sizes as eight, six and four for houses in the 200–299 m², 100–199 m² and 0–99 m² ranges, respectively (based on the layouts of the various sizes of house and on workable figures for Pompeii as a whole), this gives us between five and

---

[33] 'Cult' here means a religious ritual practice. 'Participation' could mean any of a range of things from mere attendance in the vicinity of a sacrifice to acting as the sacrificing priest.

Table 3.3 A hypothetical Pompeian model house church consisting entirely of complete households from houses 310 m² and smaller

	Householders	Other family members	Other household members
From house of 310 m²	1	4	5
From house of 200–299 m²	1	3	4
From houses of 100–199 m²	2	6	3
From houses of 0–99 m²	3	8	0

six householders in a group of 30.[34] Let us round this up to six.[35] Following our usual space distribution, one of these households would be in the 200–299 m² category, two in the 100–199 m², and three in the 0–99 m² range. If we also assume an average family size (householder, spouse and children) of four, this produces a model like Table 3.3.

This is about the simplest conceivable craftworker house church of 40 with a reasonable diversity of households. Fewer households would be involved if the house church consisted of Holconius, a few of his socially equal friends, and their households. This may sometimes have happened. However, since the house church would still be socially diverse (because it included the full range of members of each household), it would seem unreasonable to restrict the householders in it to Holconius's social level. Given the range of contacts that Holconius would have, it seems more typical that some poorer householders would be included. Moreover, Paul's letters themselves suggest that Christian households of varying socio-economic levels met together (see esp. 1 Cor. 11.17–34). It seems more reasonable to take a craftworker house church as having a range of household incomes, as in the present model.

This simplest form still involves up to three categories of people (householder, family, other household) from each of seven households. Moreover, these categories themselves break down in crucial ways relating to gender, age and whether a person is a slave (given the nature of craftworking households we might guess that, say, nine of the 12 'other

---

[34] In our model, 70% of 1,250, i.e. 875, Pompeian householders have houses smaller than 300 m². At the estimated sizes, they and their households comprise 4,750 people $((175 \times 8) + (275 \times 6) + (425 \times 4))$. Therefore, the number of householders in the group of 30 is $875 \div 4,750 \times 30 = 5.5$.

[35] The round-number estimates of household sizes look, if anything, slightly on the large side for the bottom two categories, so it seems better to produce a model with six slightly small households than one with five slightly large households. In Table 3.3, this results in one person fewer in both the 0–99 m² and 100–199 m² categories.

household members' were slaves). We can certainly see at least 20 distin-guishable social types (e.g. female slave from house 200–299 m^2) in our simplest conceivable house church of 40. We can therefore multiply the points made earlier, on the basis of social diversity within the cabinet-maker's household, about the potential social dynamics of Paul's teaching. In par-ticular, as there are now several households in the model, issues are raised about how Paul's instructions work across household boundaries. This issue is further sharpened by the considerable socio-economic differences between the households.

In New Testament texts, as well as indications of entire households professing allegiance to Christ, there is clear evidence of church members whose household head was not a Christian (e.g. 1 Cor. 7.13; 1 Pet. 3.1). A reasonable model ought roughly to lie somewhere between our skewed random group and our hypothetical complete-household house church. There must also have been the possibility of the occasional house-church member who was from a family wealthier than the house-church host.

A Pompeian model craftworker house church

If we begin from our complete-household house church of Table 3.3, we need to change it in three ways to produce a reasonable model. First, we need to reduce the number of householders from seven to a number closer to the four or five in our random groups of 40 Pompeians. We will reduce it to six, taking out one householder and his household. Second, we are now assuming that allegiance to the householder's religion is not total, although still very important. Let us take about 75% of household members as being with the householder (except for the totally loyal denizens of I.10.7). This means reducing the 'other family members' and 'other household members' by about a quarter. Third, we need to bring the new people into the group of 40: those from households where the householder is not part of the house church, and those who are home-less. Our model now looks something like Table 3.4.

The most significant difference between this model and the complete-household house church is the advent of the 10 people from households whose householder is not part of the church. Such people, whether slave or free, raise further complications for the social dynamics of the house churches and for the issues raised by Paul's teaching. Issues of authority and of scope of action would seem particularly complex. If the four from families with a non-Christian householder are distributed randomly

Table 3.4 Social breakdown of the Pompeian model craftworker house church

	Householders	*Other family*	*Other household*
From the house of 310 m²	1	4	5
From the house of 200–299 m²	1	2	3
From the house of 100–199 m²	1	3	1
From house, of 0–99 m²	3	6	—

From families with householder not in church: 4
Slaves or dependants from the other households: 4
Homeless: 2

Table 3.5 Comparison between random distributions, complete-household house church, and Pompeian model craftworker house church

Space occupied by family of the person (m²)	*Random group of 40*	*Random group skewed to exclude families wealthier than cabinet-maker*	*Hypothetical complete-household house church*	*Pompeian model craftworker house church*
more than 400	4	—	—	1
300–399	2	2	5	5
200–299	3	3	4	4
100–199	4	5	8	5
0–99	7	8	11	10
No space	20 (10 slaves)	22 (11 slaves)	12 (9 slaves)	15 (9 slaves)
Total	**40**	**40**	**40**	**40**
Number of householders	5	4	7	6

across the social spectrum, there is also the possibility that one or two are from families wealthier than the house-church host.[36]

If we re-express our model craftworker house church and the complete-household house church in the same form as the breakdown of our random and skewed random groups in Tables 3.1 and 3.2, we can see how they compare (Table 3.5). The most significant observation from Table 3.5

---

[36] Allocating four people randomly using our space-distribution model puts one in the 0–99 m² bracket, one in 100–199 m², one in 200–399 m² (probably the lower half) and one above 400 m².

is that the social profile of each of these four groups is fairly similar. Although we began with the social distribution represented in our random group of Pompeians, this is not changed beyond recognition by the kinds of assumption used to move from this to our other three groups. The pattern remains one which spreads out at the lower socio-economic end, and which includes a fairly steady minority of slaves. The most important inference from the pattern is that any plausible group of this kind will be thoroughly socially stratified, even though most such groups contain no members of the elite. There is no escape from social stratification by moving a group down the socio-economic scale. All likely house churches will have been socially stratified, whether they met in the House of the Menander or a workshop in an apartment building.

Comparing our model house church with the other groups in Table 3.5, we notice two slight oddities. One is the high number in the 300–399 m^2 range. The presence of the whole of the cabinet-maker's family disrupts the expected social profile of the church, giving it a socio-economic 'bulge' at the top. This is presumably an innate characteristic of house churches. We used the size of the Cabinet-Maker's House to estimate both how large his household was and how large a meeting the house could accommodate, a figure that we then took as the size of the house church. Since his household, in a way, fills the house, it is rather inevitable that it will tend to form a disproportionate part of the church membership. In our model, this goes with a relative shortage of members on the next socio-economic rung down, leaving the cabinet-maker's family somewhat distanced, socially, from the bulk of the membership.

The second oddity is the sharp drop in the 100–199 m^2 figure compared to the complete-household house church. This stems, of course, from the fact that we removed an entire household from that range in order to reduce the number of householders in the house church to a more reasonable figure. We could equally have taken out the household from the 0–99 m^2 range, with even odder-looking results. This is an inevitable problem of building a model involving small whole numbers of householders. We could avoid the problem Solomonically, by chopping some householders in half. In fact, we could produce a model house church full of decimal numbers of people: 9.7 slaves and so on. It would be all right to have a model like that. It could be envisaged as the notional average profile of a number of house churches. However, such precision would be illusory. Our whole method from start to finish has been full of approximations. The point of the numbers in our model is to give us a general feeling for the likely shape of a typical house church that could have met

Table 3.6 Social description of the Pompeian model craftworker house church

Forty people in total, comprising:

1 A craftworker whose house has a plan size of *c.* 300 m², his wife, children, a few (male) craftworking slaves, a (female) domestic slave, a dependent relative.
2 Several other householders (mainly, but not necessarily all, male) with smaller houses, some (but not all) of their spouses, children, slaves and other dependants.
   Their houses are within a range from about 20 m² to just under 300 m².
3 A few members of families whose householder is not part of the house church.
4 A couple of slaves whose owners are not part of the house church.
5 A couple of free or freed dependants of people who are not part of the house church.
6 A couple of homeless people.

in a medium-sized, non-elite Pompeian craftworker's house, and which fits the socio-economic profile evidenced by a survey of Pompeian housing. The mathematical work has all been aimed at helping us get an idea of the shape that corresponds to the concrete evidence in a reasonable way. Without the numbers, scholars have tended not to give proper thought to the likely social shape of house churches.

Having seen this shape, we now need to pull back from overdependence on the specific figures in our model. That model can probably be best described as a list of types of people in the house church, together with some indications of the relative sizes of the groups (Table 3.6). From the earlier mathematics we can see that the key uncertainty in the model is the point of balance in numbers between group 2 and groups 3–5. The relative sizes of group 2 and the others depend on where we put first-century household behaviour on the spectrum from complete independence of individuals' action to complete uniformity of household action. The relatively small size of groups 3–5 in our model reflects the impression that household members usually, although not always, acted together in matters such as religious allegiance. The number of members of group 6, the homeless, is sadly a matter of guesswork.

The model does not distinguish between free-born people and freed slaves. We can expect that a number of the householders will have been freed slaves, especially those in the smaller houses. The distinction between free-born and freed was, however, a very significant one and provides a further form of social diversity that may need to be considered in reflecting on the potential impact of Paul's text.

Another dimension that the model does not describe is that of likely relationships between some of the people in the house church. Although we have avoided trying to construct the model by mapping the potential contacts of people in Holconius's household,[37] undoubtedly such relationships would exist between house-church members, either because the relationship was a factor in drawing someone into the house church or because being fellow house-church members led to the development of a relationship. To take a fairly prosaic example, a carpenter might come into contact with the group and the gospel through carrying out work for Holconius at periods that were too busy for the workers in his own household to cope with. Conversely, someone with needlework skills who joined the house church might be given work in connection with the furniture-making. Other likely relationships between house-church members would include being relatives, neighbours, friends, trade associates, suppliers, customers or, in an informal sense, clients.

The diverse and unpredictable nature of the possible relationships prevents us from formally building them into our model. However, they do need to be borne in mind when using the model, especially where the relationship involves dependency and authority. For example, in assessing some of Paul's instructions that imply the creation of relationships with equal standing between the participants, we should think about these not only in relation to household relationships of gender or servitude (which are directly part of the model) but also in relation to (informal) patronage and other such relationships of dependence that would be common where, as in our model, there are significant differences of socio-economic standing between members of the group.

---

[37] We could try to create our Pompeian model craftworker house church by taking the cabinet-maker and his household, then reflecting on who they would know and, hence, which kinds of people might be particularly likely to be members of a house church based in his house. This would have considerable merit as a descriptive exercise. As Klauck, *Hausgemeinde*, p. 19, rightly notes, the family of the host would tend to act as a 'germ cell' (*Keimzelle*) from which the church would grow. However, two important limitations mean that we will not follow this route. First (and there is a hint of theology here, as well as historical assertion), the formation of the early Christian groups seems likely to have been a little more anarchic than this. Many people other than friends or close associates of existing members seem to have joined the movement. For instance, the narratives in the Acts of the Apostles are full of such incidents (e.g. Acts 8.12; 10.47–48; 16.14). Second, the exercise of working outwards from the 10 members of a household is too uncontrollable to produce a reasonable model of a group of 40. Each member of the household leads rapidly to so many possible contacts that the model could take any of a large number of wildly differing shapes.

A further type of information is implicitly encoded in our model. As has been happening all along, the Pompeians in the model are sorted according to house-plan size. In the model these are given just as bare figures. The evidence discussed in Chapter 1 and in many other studies of Pompeii, makes these figures a gateway into a large supply of specific social and cultural evidence about the life of the particular kinds of first-century people in the model.

Every Pauline context is somewhat different. However, the extensive detailed evidence from Pompeii offers a route to thinking about the nature of early house churches in a way that ought to be helpful across the range of Graeco-Roman urban settings. Some points will need to be varied according to the setting, but a model craftworker house church based on Pompeian evidence should offer a framework that can form a basis for consideration of a range of issues in Pauline texts that relate to house-church life.

A model craftworker house church for reading Romans

Paul had probably never visited Rome by the time he wrote his letter. He is very definite that he has not done so as a Christian missionary (Rom. 1.10–15; 15.19–24). Since this is the case, we need to be careful in considering the extent to which archaeological and historical knowledge of Rome is relevant to the interpretation of Paul's letter.

This is quite a different question from that of the interpretative relevance of archaeological and historical knowledge about first-century life in general. Paul is a first-century writer, writing with first-century assumptions. All the evidence – archaeological, textual or comparative – that can be brought to bear on this fact is important in seeking to understand Paul's writings. However, he could be writing to Rome with an assumption that social conditions there were very much the same as in Corinth, where he was sitting. More generally, he might picture house-church life as following a similar basic pattern wherever it was, with the real variations being caused by external events such as persecution.

If this is the case, our Pompeian model craftworker house church could, without alteration, be a good basis for interpreting Romans as Paul expected the letter to be heard. The use of the model is more problematic if we are interested in how the letter was actually heard in Rome. That requires us to think more seriously about Rome itself. However, if Paul had a generalized picture of house churches and took a broad-brush approach to instructing them (particularly in a wide-ranging passage such as Romans 12), then the Pompeian model should be useful for understanding the text.

On the other hand, despite probably never having visited Rome, Paul, like everybody in the Mediterranean world, will have had an image of Rome. He also knew people, such as Prisca and Aquila, who had lived in Rome before he met them. Furthermore, the specificity of Romans 14—15, in particular, suggests that he did hear news from the Roman house churches.

His image of Rome must have conceived it as crowded, bustling and full of immigrants from around the world. Almost certainly, he will have envisaged tall apartment blocks into which most people were crammed. If he had heard from Christians in Rome, he would probably have known something about the sorts of locations in which they met, and the kinds of sizes of house churches that had been formed. Our model craftworker house church would more likely be useful for interpretation of Romans if we could modify it to take account of these factors.

What we cannot do is to carry out again the whole analytical process of this and the previous chapter using data from Rome. The method would simply not work. Once most people live away from the ground floor, it is impossible to produce even an approximate social structure on the basis of distribution of ground-floor space. For instance, if we worked from the *forma urbis*, the astonishingly detailed (but now fragmentary) plan of the city created in the third century CE,[38] we would conclude that Rome was primarily a city of shopkeepers, who must have spent their time selling goods to each other. Instead, we ought to begin from our Pompeian model, then do the following: consider probable commonalities between the social situations of craftworkers in Pompeii and Rome; explore and take account of factors that will have produced differences in their social situations; increase our level of caution about specific numbers in our model.

Our focus is not on the city of Rome as a whole. Peter Lampe uses a range of arguments to locate the early Christians predominantly in low-lying, peripheral areas of the city.[39] Although some of his approaches are open to improvement (for instance, his argument relating Christian burial sites to areas of residence ought to be conducted in the context of a broader study of the relationships between Graeco-Roman burial sites and places of residence: otherwise, the evidence is very hard to evaluate),

---

[38] See, for example, A. Wallace-Hadrill, '*Domus* and *Insulae* in Rome: Families and Housefuls', in David Balch and Carolyn Osiek (eds), *Early Christian Families in Context: An Interdisciplinary Dialogue* (Grand Rapids: Eerdmans, 2003), p. 6.

[39] Lampe, *From Paul to Valentinus*, ch. 3.

his cumulative case is fairly convincing. He then investigates the social characteristics of these low-lying peripheral areas and, again, although some questions could be raised (especially over his description of the term *insula* in the fourth-century *regionaria* as meaning a 'rental dwelling': see Wallace-Hadrill for discussion of the term),[40] he paints a convincing picture of these as densely populated quarters full of apartment blocks and craftworkers, especially immigrants.[41] This is especially the case for the Transtiberim area of the city.[42]

As has been mentioned above, Robert Jewett argues the case for most of the Christian groups at Rome being tenement churches, operating without patronage. He sees the social pattern in these groups as egalitarian, especially in the two listed in Romans 16.14−15, for each of which five leading figures are named.[43] Jewett is undoubtedly correct that most of the groups met in apartment blocks rather than houses. Apartment blocks were too prevalent at Rome for this to be otherwise. Roger Gehring's argument that their accommodation provides insufficient space or catering facilities for such meetings underestimates the range of types of space in such blocks and the feasibility of bringing food in.[44] In any case he accepts that meetings could take place in workshops,[45] which seem generally to be among the most likely spaces for a Christian group to meet in an apartment block. Whether 'tenement church' is the best term for the groups depends on the connotations of the term. I am a little wary of using the term 'tenement' because, for me, it connotes a fairly uniformly shabby block of consistently poor housing. First-century apartment blocks were typically more diverse than this, comprising, from the ground floor upwards, shops or workshops and their living spaces, then fairly opulent apartments, then several floors of increasingly poor homes. In any case, this study seeks to dissolve some of Jewett's contrast between a house-church model and a tenement-church model by arguing that the elite-funded house-church model never was appropriate for most study of Pauline texts − that we need instead something more like a craftworker-led model for a house church if it is to be fairly typical of Pauline communities.

---

[40] Lampe, *From Paul to Valentinus*, p. 53; Wallace-Hadrill, '*Domus* and *Insulae*', pp. 7–10.

[41] Lampe, *From Paul to Valentinus*, ch. 4.

[42] Lampe uses the modern Italian name, Trastevere.

[43] Jewett, *Romans*, p. 65.

[44] Gehring, *House Church and Mission*, pp. 149–50. He seems correct, though, in arguing, against Jewett, that temporary removal of partitions to create large spaces would generally not be possible.

[45] Gehring, *House Church and Mission*, pp. 135, 140, 150.

In fact, once we focus on non-elite housing, the dividing line between 'house' and 'apartment' becomes difficult to draw. Like most blocks of Roman housing, the Insula of the Menander is a solid block. The houses, apartments and workshops all abut each other. It is very difficult to tell whether or not some of the two-storey buildings are pairs of apartments with a shared entrance. Even the House of the Menander has at least two upstairs apartments above parts of it. We should not do away with the distinction entirely: spacious atrium-and-peristyle houses are different from apartment blocks in Ostia. However, for the non-elite, the social difference between accommodation that we might call a house and what we might call an apartment was often not great. I am also conscious of the long scholarly tradition of the *Hausgemeinde* (and as Klauck's term, 'house community', highlights, the 'church' element of house church is at least as open to challenge as the 'house' part). The essence of 'house church', to me, is the meeting of Christians in someone's own home (which may also be a workshop), rather than in a building specially constructed for worship.[46] For these reasons we will continue to call the early Christian groups 'house churches' even when they meet in apartment blocks.

Jewett's suggestion of an egalitarian social structure is a useful starting point for considering the extent to which we can adapt our Pompeian model for use in Rome. Our Pompeian study suggests that any hope of finding a section of society that is non-hierarchical is, sadly, illusory. Jewett's point about egalitarianism might be correct about leadership of the groups, but it seems unsafe for him to describe this as the 'social pattern'.[47] However far down the social spectrum we go, we keep finding social hierarchies. Even among the slaves of a single household we would find a hierarchy.

Jewett may be thinking of a group that, in general society, would have been socially differentiated, but has become egalitarian under the influence of Christian teaching. Our method has been to draw an appropriate group from society in general and report on the social situations of its members. Our model therefore inherently expresses society's hierarchies. This seems to me the most useful kind of model to employ as a starting-

---

[46] This point in fact opens up a converse issue, that of the increasing adaptation of domestic space over the following few centuries to be dedicated to church use (a classic study is L. M. White, *Building God's House in the Roman World: Architectural Adaptation among Pagans, Jews and Christians* (Baltimore: Johns Hopkins University Press, 1990)). Such adaptations actually form the core of what some scholars mean by 'house church', as can be seen in Klauck's shift from talking of *Hausgemeinde* in the earliest period to *Hauskirche*. For me, the further such adaptation goes, the further we move from the key elements of 'house church'.

[47] Jewett, *Romans*, p. 65.

point for interpreting Paul's text. The text might turn out to appear to be intended to give such a group an egalitarian social pattern (although it is hard to imagine how it could in a full sense, without Holconius ceasing to be a householder and the slaves ceasing to be slaves), but it seems unlikely that an egalitarian social pattern is a realistic or useful starting point for reading the text. In any case, the rhetoric of Romans 12, to which we will turn shortly, seems unlikely to be directed at a group that is already egalitarian.

The major social patterns of the situation of the craftworkers in our Pompeian model seem likely to be maintained if we are switching to a craft-worker model suitable for Rome. The basic structure of a household would remain the same: householder, family, slaves (if any), other depen-dants (if any). However, the average size of households would probably decrease. Householders other than the house-church host would still tend to have smaller accommodation than him or her. There would still be a tendency for household members to follow householders but, as before, this would not always be the case, so the house church would still be like-ly to include some people whose householder was not a Christian. Many of the likely relationships between people in the group would be the same in Rome: friend, neighbour, relative, customer, supplier, casual employee, (informal) client.

The most dramatic change would be in the size and nature of the space that a cabinet-maker such as Holconius could expect to rent if he were transplanted to Rome. Jerome Murphy-O'Connor places Prisca and Aquila in Rome in a ground-floor workshop with mezzanine living accommodation and estimates that they would be able to host a house-church of between 10 and 20.[48] This looks rather too small for a craft-worker house-church host such as Holconius. If we take rents in Rome to be about double those in Pompeii,[49] we might reasonably assume Holconius to rent about half as much space in Rome as in Pompeii. In Pompeii, he had 310 m² of ground-floor space, 75 m² of which was gar-den, probably less expensive than housing. On the other hand, he also had about 90 m² of upstairs rooms. Let us allow him about 160 m² in Rome.

---

[48] Jerome Murphy-O'Connor, 'Prisca and Aquila: Traveling Tentmakers and Church Builders', *Bible Review* 8.6 (1992), p. 49.

[49] As noted in the previous chapter, by gathering figures from various sources, Stegemann and Stegemann estimate the minimum existence for a family of four to be 250–300 denarii per annum in the country, 600–700 denarii in a town, and 900–1,000 denarii in Rome (Ekkehard W. Stegemann and Wolfgang Stegemann, *The Jesus Movement: A Social History of its First Century*, tr. O. C. Dean Jr (Minneapolis: Fortress, 1999), p. 84, table 8).

In Pompeii, he used about 100 m² for work and storage. He would need something approaching that amount in Rome too, although the higher rentals would probably make the size of his business a little smaller. The key point is that the demands of his craftwork would mean that most of the reduction in space in moving from Pompeii to Rome would be felt in the living accommodation. What might he rent in Rome?

The best-preserved first-century apartment block in Rome is the Insula Aracoeli. It was laid out in what is a typical fashion, except that it had only one frontage because it was built onto the rock face at the foot of the Capitoline Hill. The ground floor is a row of shops/workshops, each generally of about 30 m². Each of these was connected by a wooden staircase to a first-floor (US: second-floor) room of the same size. The second floor was a series of large connected rooms that could have formed an apartment of about 400 m². The third and fourth floors were both laid out as a large number of rooms, mainly of 10–15 m² but with one of 35 m². These rooms could presumably be rented out singly or in various combinations to constitute apartments.[50]

If Holconius was renting space in an apartment block like this one (although not in such an expensive central location), he would probably have needed to rent two of the workshop units. This would have given him two workshops of 30 m² each and, above them, two first-floor rooms of similar size. To make up his notional 160 m², he could then also have rented an apartment on the third or fourth floor consisting of a 15 m² front room – with the luxury of windows – and a couple more 10 m² ones – without windows. He, his family and his domestic slave would probably live in the apartment, with the craftworking slaves and the odd dependent relative living over the workshops.

The Insula Aracoeli is rather inconvenient for Holconius. One workshop-plus-room-above unit is too little for him, but two is rather too much, leaving him only able to afford very cramped family accommodation. However, configurations of apartment blocks did vary somewhat, so he would presumably have been able to find something more like a 45 m² workshop with a similar-sized mezzanine room for storage and for the slaves to sleep. This would allow him a more manageable 70 m² living apartment somewhere higher in the block or in another block nearby. A 45 m² workshop would give a fair amount of space for a house-church meeting. It would be a lot less than was available in Holconius's house in Pompeii. It would also be a far less pleasant space: spartan; dark if the doors were

---

[50] Wallace-Hadrill, '*Domus* and *Insulae*', pp. 14–15 and figs 2–3.

closed, open to the street if they were open; in a very noisy environment; heavily encumbered with materials, tools and work in progress (although in this particular case, some might have been able to be sat on!); lacking in the cooking facilities and latrine that were available in the house in Pompeii. However, the amount of space would presumably allow, say, 30 people to gather.

If Holconius and his household have been trimmed, let us say, to eight by the higher cost of living in Rome (one child fewer, one slave fewer), but still form the core of the house church, this means 22 other people. The general shape of the descriptive form of our Pompeian house-church model (Table 3.6) is probably still going to be roughly correct, except for the house sizes. The main determinant of the balance between 'several' householders and 'a few/a couple' of people of various types from households with non-Christian householders was the degree to which household members followed the practices of their householders. This would presumably be similar in Rome and Pompeii. The size of the group needs scaling down. 'Several' householders was about five in Pompeii (plus Holconius). We might be looking at three (plus Holconius) in Rome.

However, the category 'householder' itself becomes problematic at the lower end of the social spectrum of apartment dwellers. In Pompeii, even our near-destitute stoneworkers occupied a significant space with a closable street entrance. In Rome, they would be unlikely to be able to afford to rent a workshop at all. They might well be reduced to renting just a part-share in a room to live in, high in an apartment block. In Rome, there will also have been significant numbers of migrant workers, living away from their families. The proportion of homeless people will have been higher too, particularly among immigrant groups, from which the churches often drew members. As well as the ethnic dimension of a group drawing in many immigrants, we need to be aware of the economic dimension of immigrant status, making poverty and endemic insecurity more likely.

Looking at the social description of our Pompeian model (Table 3.6), there is no reason to exclude any of the categories of people from our model for a craftworker house church at Rome. We should add a seventh category to cover people such as the stoneworkers and migrant workers, who have a roof over their heads but are living in rented shared rooms rather than in a conventional household. Given that such people were probably common in areas such as Transtiberim, we should put 'a few' into our model house church (more than 'a couple', fewer than 'several'). Although the proportion of homeless should be raised, the absolute number may not rise because the overall size of the house church is smaller.

Table 3.7 Social description of the model craftworker house church in Rome

Thirty people in total, comprising:

1 A craftworker who rents a fairly large workshop (*c.* 45 m²) and some separate living accommodation, his wife, children, a couple of (male) craftworking slaves, a (female) domestic slave, a dependent relative.
2 A few other householders (mainly, but not necessarily all, male) who rent less space than the householder above, some (but not all) of their spouses, children, slaves and other dependants. The rented spaces would be either workshops with mezzanine living areas or apartments on upper floors of apartment blocks.
3 A couple of members of families whose householder is not part of the house church.
4 A couple of slaves whose owners are not part of the house church.
5 A couple of free or freed dependants of people who are not part of the house church.
6 A couple of homeless people.
7 A few people who are renting space in shared rooms (e.g. migrant workers separated from their families).

The model (Table 3.7) is a hypothetical group designed to be representative of the likely social composition of craftworker house churches in Rome. It is important to bear in mind that, even if this model was, by some fluke, a perfect representation of the average composition of these house churches, we would still expect any specific individual house church to vary from this, with some social types being overrepresented and others underrepresented or missing altogether.

The reader may feel that our final model is disappointingly unmathematical, given the amount of mathematics that preceded it. It might be felt that the same result could have been achieved without the mathematics and without involving Pompeii at all. In response, I would take you back to the models of ancient society presented by Alföldy and Lenski, with their lack of articulation of the shape of non-elite society. It would be very difficult to construct a model non-elite group from these starting points. In contrast, Pompeii offers us masses of detail about non-elite society, both in its general shape and in the social and cultural details of what various kinds of non-elite life involved. Our mathematical analysis was an attempt to put this evidence into some sort of useable order. This process showed many of the complexities of non-elite lives and of the relationships between them. That background gives a better basis for modelling house-church life and for analysing the issues which relate to this in Pauline texts. Even in our final, Rome-based model, there is implicit mathematics in the broad relationships between the sizes of the sub-groups. There is also considerable implicit reference to the Pompeian material evidence that indicates aspects of what being a first-century craftworker could involve. It was inevitable that detailed figures would fall away in our final model. This is Rome, not Pompeii, so detailed estimates of figures would be too tenuously based to be worth while. Also, and maybe more significantly, our model is intended to help us read the letter to the Romans. Such a task does not need numbers. What it needs is a sense of the shape of the social diversity within a representative group.

4

Romans 12 for a model craftworker house church

We have used Pompeian evidence, together with consideration of differences between Pompeii and poor areas of Rome, to give us some sense of
what it means to talk about a group of about 30 non-elite people who
might gather for Christian meetings somewhere such as a workshop in
an apartment block in Transtiberim. The key impression is of social
diversity and social hierarchy, even when the wealthiest member is only
a craftworker with a modest household. We have expressed this social
pattern in our model craftworker house church (Table 3.7). We have
also argued that such groups are likely to have been among the types of
hearers that Paul expected when he wrote Romans.

We will now turn to a passage that deals with issues of social dynamics, Romans 12, and consider how the points raised by the text would relate
to our model house church. This could be thought of as an exercise in
considering the likely early reception of the letter. However, since the model
is designed to represent hearers expected by Paul, the exercise could also
be seen as a way of raising possibilities for what he intended in terms of
practical application of what he was writing. A third way of looking at
the exercise is as a study of the nature of the text itself. By seeking to
put it into an appropriate socio-cultural context (by considering the text's
potential impact on the model group), the exercise could be seen as
providing some socio-linguistic illumination of the text.[1]

The reading of Romans 12 will be offered in the form of a translation
and running commentary. Some brief notes on translational issues are given
after many of the translations.

---

[1] As, for instance, in systemic functional linguistics. For the use of this in NT studies see Todd
Klutz, *The Exorcism Stories in Luke–Acts: A Sociostylistic Reading* (SNTSMS 129; Cambridge:
Cambridge University Press, 2004).

Romans 12.1–2: A communal living sacrifice

12.1 So I urge you, brothers and sisters, because of* God's mercies, offer your bodies as a living, holy sacrifice, pleasing to God – your form of worship that makes sense.

2 And don't** go along with the pattern of this age, but be transformed by the renewing of your*** mind. This will mean you are able to discern what God's will is – what is good and pleasing and perfect.

* *Lit. 'through'.*

** *Some willingness to use typical abbreviations in spoken English, such as 'don't', seems more likely to catch the sense of the letter as a text to be read out than does the consistently formal register generally used in Bible translations.*

*** *Following P[46], etc. in omitting ὑμῶν, but then adding 'your' in translation, for sense.*

Paul turns from explaining God's salvation (in Romans 1—11) to calling the hearers to action in view of God's mercy. It is not immediately clear what these actions mean in practice but, as we shall see, there is plenty in chapter 12 that would involve both sacrifice and non-conformity for members of a craftworker house church.

The communal bodily sacrifice is their 'rational worship' (12.1). If some of the male members of the house church were previously (or still) members of a trade (or other) association, they would be used to communal meals beginning with a token sacrifice to a patron deity.[2] All of the house-church members will have experienced both the token sacrifices of domestic cults and the large-scale sacrifices paid for on behalf of the city by wealthy patrons sponsoring festivals and games. Some in the house church will individually, or as a family, have offered what to them were quite substantial sacrifices to particular goddesses or gods on special occasions such as childbirth. The religion of a house church is to involve a total, ongoing communal sacrifice by everyone. This new religious

---

[2]   Associations (*collegia*) were a range of types of voluntary group. Some were linked to a trade but they functioned more like clubs than what we would think of today as trade associations. Philip A. Harland, *Associations, Synagogues and Congregations: Claiming a Place in Ancient Mediterranean Society* (Minneapolis: Fortress, 2003), pp. 57–74, gives an excellent account of the evidence of religious activities by associations. Although he is right in stressing the seriousness of the religious activity (in reaction to previous scholarship), it still seems likely that in most association meetings, the proportion of time devoted to sacrificial activity per se was relatively limited.

practice is of a different order from the token sacrifices of association meals or the domestic cult. Unlike the civic cults, the house-church 'sacrifice' is provided by everyone. Unlike the sacrifices on special occasions, Paul calls for a living, and hence continuing, action. In contrast to individual sacrifice, the 'sacrifice' here is a unified act ('sacrifice' is singular) performed collectively ('your bodies', plural). It is an act in which all types of people in the house church can take part because the sacrifice is not of the body of an ox, affordable only by the wealthy, but of their own bodies. Even for the slaves, whose bodies belonged to other people, their body was still the physical realm over which they could exercise the most control. They might own no goods at all, but they could still take some actions.

Romans 12.3: A new scale of value

12.3 For, through the gift that I have been given, I say to each one among you that you shouldn't think more highly of yourself than you ought. Instead you should assess soberly, as God has distributed to each an amount* of faith.

* *Although Cranfield's reading,[3] followed by Jewett in his translation, 'measuring rod',[4] is supported both by lexical frequency and theological considerations, the above translation, which broadly follows that of Dunn,[5] seems better to fit the sentence and Pauline usage.*

Paul cites his gift (and calling) then urges 'each one among you' not to overestimate his or her worth but to assess people using the measure of the amount of faith given to them by God (12.3). Unrealistic boasting and inflated opinions of oneself were condemned and mocked by ancient writers.[6] However, Paul is not calling for realistic assessment of oneself on the usual scales of status and intellect. He does away with these scales of achievement and inherited qualities by putting in a scale based on unmerited gift. This has profound implications for the craftworkers, which will be reinforced in the coming verses.

---

[3] C. E. B. Cranfield, *A Critical and Exegetical Commentary on the Epistle to the Romans. Vol. II: Romans IX—XVI* (ICC; Edinburgh: T. & T. Clark, 1975), p. 615.
[4] Robert Jewett, *Romans: A Commentary* (Hermeneia; Minneapolis: Fortress, 2007), pp. 741–2.
[5] James D. G. Dunn, *Romans 9—16* (Dallas: Word, 1988), pp. 721–2.
[6] See Jewett, *Romans*, p. 295, n. 10.

The first effect is to undermine the honour system.[7] Graeco-Roman elite males competed vigorously for honour. In particular, civic offices were held for the sake of the honour that the offices gave. Honorific inscriptions are among the most common epigraphic finds from the period. Some inscriptions show that a limited number of elite women seem also to have sought honour, especially by means of benefaction.[8] Competition for honour extended to the non-elite. In craft associations, the titles of officeholders often replicated those of the city.[9] It seems clear that such offices were also sought for the sake of the honour they gave. In the Insula of the Menander we have already encountered the graffiti exchange between Severus and Successus, fitting a 'challenge and riposte' pattern, in which concerns of honour and dishonour are central. Paul's call to change the way in which one assesses oneself and others undercuts the urge to compete for honour. No one can seek office in the house church for the sake of the honour it might give. There is no basis for seeing oneself as superior when the only measure is faith, a gift from God.

As well as undermining competition for honour, this change of attitude undermines the status system.[10] The 30 people in the model house church stood in a status order that would be broadly agreed by them and by society as a whole. There were subtleties and scope for limited differences of opinion, but there was a fairly clear scale running down from the wealthiest free-born male householder (unless someone else in the house church was particularly well born) to the lowest-level slave. Free-born was above freed, which was above slave. Male was above female. Adult was above child. Wealthy was above poor. Wealth could cut across some other factors. If the church included a relatively well-off widow householder,

---

[7] Cf. Neil Elliott, *Liberating Paul: The Justice of God and the Politics of the Apostle* (Sheffield: Sheffield Academic Press, 1995), p. 201; Philip F. Esler, *Conflict and Identity in Romans: The Social Setting of Paul's Letter* (Minneapolis: Fortress; London: SPCK, 2003), p. 313. For Halvor Moxnes, 'Honour and Righteousness in Romans', *JSNT* 32 (1988), p. 75, in the soteriology of Romans, 'Paul breaks with the competition inherent in an honour society': 'Behaviour among Christians should reflect God's free granting of honour'. For Moxnes this unifies the letter, with ch. 12 relating closely to chs 3–4.

[8] A classic example is Eumachia of Pompeii. Paul Zanker, *Pompeii: Public and Private Life*, tr. D. L. Schneider (Cambridge, Mass.: Harvard University Press, 1998), pp. 93–101, describes her as using the construction of her large building in the forum 'for direct self-promotion' (quote on p. 97).

[9] G. H. Stevenson and A. W. Lintott, 'clubs, Roman', in *Oxford Classical Dictionary*, ed. S. Hornblower and A. Spawforth (Oxford: Oxford University Press, 3rd edn, 1996), pp. 352–3.

[10] On status, see Peter Garnsey and Richard Saller, *The Roman Empire: Economy, Society and Culture* (London: Duckworth, 1987), pp. 118–22, 199.

she would probably have had higher status than poorer male house-holders. Her status would also be affected by the number of children she had raised.[11] Paul's call does away with the relevance of all this in assessing one's position. All is faith, a gift.

Romans 12.4–5: Symmetrical relationships in Christ across household boundaries

12.4 For just as in one body we have many parts, and not all the parts have the same function,

5 just so, we who are many are one body in Christ and, individually, we are parts of each other,

Paul sets up the issue of diversity of function in the one body in Christ (12.4–5). His use of 'we', encompassing himself and the hearers, at first suggests that he is thinking of the whole Church, spread around the Mediterranean. However, this soon appears less likely because the gifts and consequent ministries in vv. 6–8 look like those of a single congregation, not an overall movement (for example, there are no apostles). Similarly, his assertion that, in the body, we are 'members of one another' sounds like an exhortation about the connectedness of all Christians: him and them; the Roman house churches and those as far away as Jerusalem; the diverse house churches in Rome.[12] However, the close relevance to house-church life of what he says immediately before and afterwards suggests that he intends 'members of one another' (12.5) also to be taken as about relationships within each house church. In that case, 'members of one another' becomes a radical assault on the hierarchical assumptions that flowed from the status system. Paul is also effectively challenging the boundaries of the household.

Craftworking families knew the importance of interdependence within the household. In the first century, very few free-born people worked

---

[11] This is seen, for instance, in the removing of a woman's need for a guardian if she had three children (or four, in the case of a freedwoman!) (Gaius, *Institutes* 1.145, 194).

[12] Where scholars contextualize Romans 12, they generally follow this route of relating it to interaction between diverse house churches, especially between 'Jewish' and 'gentile' ones: e.g. Ben Witherington III with Darlene Hyatt, *Paul's Letter to the Romans: A Socio-Rhetorical Commentary* (Grand Rapids: Eerdmans, 2004), pp. 281, 292, 294. The strength of this approach is its link between ch. 12 and the later chapters. However, this is also a weakness because it lessens our sensitivity to the issues in ch. 12 that relate more naturally to life within house churches than to interaction between the groups.

regularly for large craftworking enterprises. Where large-scale production took place (as, for example, in some pottery manufacture) it tended to depend on slave labour. Most free-born craftworkers worked in family units. If the amount of work exceeded what a group of close relatives could handle, the family tended to acquire one or more slaves. The household typically handled every process, from preparation of materials to final sale.[13] This is particularly clear at Pompeii in the case of bakeries in which flour mills, ovens and serving counters can be seen together.[14] Craftworkers would readily apply to the household Paul's metaphor of a body, all of whose parts had specific functions (as long as he allowed for some multi-tasking). However, the 'parts/members of one another' metaphor would be more contentious. Although a craftworking family would appreciate the truth of the interdependence of the household members, that interdependence operated within a strong hierarchy of privileges and duties. There was social distance as well as interconnectedness. To make the householder and a slave interdependent, in a close, symmetrical, reciprocal relationship, challenged the most fundamental conceptual structures of the household.

Paul goes further. This intimate interconnectedness goes beyond the household. Craftworker households were separate units of production. There could be elements of co-operation with other households, especially for access to expensive resources such as kilns, or, socially, in associations. However, the households were essentially in competition with each other. While a craftworking family would acknowledge an interconnectedness within the household, they would only do so to a very limited extent beyond that. Paul proclaims the close interconnectedness of every member of the house church, across any household boundaries. Just as a challenge to household hierarchy undermines the essential nature of the household, so does a challenge to the integrity of the household's boundaries.

The symmetry of the relationship of interdependence in the one body in Christ, across any household boundaries, also undermines a fundamental relationship between households in the Graeco-Roman world, that of patronage. If the householder of Pompeii I.10.7 had an ongoing relationship with the stoneworkers in I.10.6 it was probably one of patronage. This would be even more likely in Rome, because the probable inability

---

[13] Roger Ling, 'Working Practice', in Roger Ling (ed.), *Making Classical Art: Process and Practice* (Stroud: Tempus, 2000), p. 100, describes a house-cum-workshop from Aphrodisias in which the production side is evidenced by unfinished sculptures, tools, etc., and the sales side is indicated by the location and design of the space, with two broad doorways onto a public piazza.

[14] For example, House VII.2.22.

of a tenant of a 40 m² workshop in Pompeii to afford any viable workshop in Rome would make the stoneworkers more dependent on those
with enough money to rent a workshop. Ancient writers tend to focus
their stories about patronage on the elite and their political supporters.
However, in social-scientific terms, patronage is a broader phenomenon
in which the poorer are dependent on the wealthier for access to goods
and services, and where the richer provide such access in return for
benefits such as unpaid work or, in particular, the giving of honour.[15] The
householder of I.10.7 controlled eight times as much space as the
stoneworkers of I.10.6. This was a huge social gulf and any relationship
across it was bound to be strongly asymmetric. The giving of honour to
patrons depended on, and reproduced, such asymmetry. The asymmetric
exchange on which the stoneworkers may have depended for their liveli-
hood, and which was one element in the patronal householder's main-
tenance of his position in society, was under threat if the symmetrical
relationships as 'parts of one another', which Paul was announcing as the
situation in Christ, came about.

All these issues of honour, status and patronage are, in principle,
brought into question by what Paul says in vv. 3–5 about thinking and
about the one body in Christ. However, just as it was not immediately
clear, in vv. 1–2, what the practical content of bodily sacrifice and non-
conformity was to be, so it is not clear in vv. 3–5 how far-reaching Paul's
apparently radical assertions are meant to be. We need to read on to get
more sense of the implications.

Having said that, we ought to note that vv. 3–5 do provide indications
of the likely implications of vv. 1–2. Bodily sacrifice and non-conformity
seem to be about changed communal behaviour – behaviour different from
what would be normal for a group of first-century people.

Romans 12.6–8: The diverse gifts that make a house church work

12.6 having gifts that, in line with the grace given to us, are diverse. A
gift could be prophecy* in accordance with faith,

7 or service with the service**, or someone who teaches*** with the
teaching,

---

[15] For a definition and description of key characteristics of patronage, see S. N. Eisenstadt and
L. Roniger, *Patrons, Clients and Friends: Interpersonal Relations and the Structure of Trust in
Society* (Cambridge: Cambridge University Press, 1984), pp. 48–9.

8 or someone who exhorts with the exhortation, someone who shares with generosity, someone who leads with eagerness, someone who shows mercy with cheerfulness.

* Lit. 'whether prophecy'. Exegetes have tended to interpret the list that follows primarily as instruction in how various ministries are to be performed. In the first instance it seems more a celebration of both the diversity and the quality of the gifts that God gives to the Christian community through the people in it. At a secondary level this would, indeed, also encourage the people performing the various ministries to do so in the way specified (not that it is always clear what that way means).

** Paul literally repeats the word 'service', διακονία.

*** Lit. 'the one who teaches'.

Verse 6 takes us back to God's allocating action, already mentioned in v. 3. Here we get the first practical challenge to household hierarchy. Normally, the householder allocates the tasks, either directly or through an intermediary such as his wife or grown-up son (the households in our model house church are too small for formal intermediary figures such as stewards). In a house church one might have expected roles to be allocated by the householder of highest status, who would also tend to be the church's host. Paul takes away that prerogative. It is not apparent how the church was to discern which gifts each member had. However, Paul clearly intends it to be a 'charismatic' process under the control of God, not a person.

We do not know how radically the ministries were distributed. If, for example, a slave woman was gifted with leadership and led the church, the upset to conventional authority patterns would have been extraordinary. On the other hand, if she prophesied, this would be far more in line with the norms of a society in which prophesying slave women were a well-known phenomenon.[16] Two of the gifts have possible financial implications. These are 'sharing' and 'showing mercy'. Does that imply that such ministries would only be given by God to wealthier members of the house church? Only two or three members of the model church have full control of significant amounts of money: the householders of the larger (although still rather small) apartments. If some gifts are only for the wealthy, where does that leave the 'charismatic' nature of the distribution of gifts? Could we also say that 'teachers' are likely to be literate, which

---

[16] As instanced in Acts 16.16.

limits the pool, or that 'leaders' are likely to be those with leadership experience, that is, especially householders? We cannot really tell. The principle that the prerogative of allocating roles in the church belongs to God, not the member of highest status, seems clear. However, it is not clear how radical the allocation of roles was in practice.

'Sharing' and 'showing mercy' take us to a new kind of issue. Even the wealthiest of the craftworkers in the model house church are not very well off, and some in the house church are almost, or actually, destitute. 'Sharing' resources constitutes a financial sacrifice, presumably particularly by the wealthier households. Since they would generally have had very little surplus to spare, one effect would be to lower their wealth from what it would otherwise have been. This in turn affects the status of the household and householder in society. It is also a practical sign of the breaching of the household's boundary. The resources of the household were normally for the people in the household, especially the householder. They were not to leak across the boundary into other households. The financial sacrifices move to a further level if the sharing is to be beyond the house church. This is not clear here[17] but it is explicit further on.

'Showing mercy' could also be primarily an economic issue.[18] In a craftworker house church there would be issues of 'showing mercy' related to discipline, especially of slaves. However, given the limited number of slaves that small craftworkers would own, more common occasions for 'showing mercy' among craftworkers could be financial. Indebtedness must often have arisen, between craftworkers or between them and their suppliers and customers. 'Showing mercy' could mean cancelling debts or deferring payment. Given the acute poverty of some members, it could also refer to donating money or food to them. 'Showing mercy' might also refer to almsgiving to people outside the Christian community.[19] Several possible ways of interpreting 'showing mercy' involve economic sacrifice by some in the house church.

---

[17] Jewett seems correct in asserting that the language probably indicates that this is sharing within the group, rather than beyond (*Romans*, pp. 751–2). He is probably also reasonable in seeing this as taking place particularly in common meals.

[18] Dunn supports this by appeal to the common association, in various Jewish texts, of 'cheerfulness' with giving (*Romans 9—16*, p. 732).

[19] Jewett stresses this, fearing redundant repetition of the idea of 'sharing' if 'showing mercy' also relates to mutual support in the group (*Romans*, pp. 753–4). This concern seems outweighed by the consideration that this list of gifts as a whole seems focused on life within the group.

Romans 12.9–10a: Family love beyond family boundaries

12.9 Love is without pretence*: people hating what is evil,** clinging to what is good,

10a loving each other with brotherly*** love,

There is no verb in the Greek phrase. Most commonly in such cases, the verb to be supplied is ἐστίν ('is'). This sentence and the others in vv. 9–13 are effectively instructions: 'Love without pretence. Hate what is evil', etc. The Greek form cannot be reproduced in English. However, it appears that the effect of the Greek is to express the instructions as though they are a general description of a loving Christian community. To give this effect, I have supplied indicative verbs rather than imperatives. As the reader can see, this still produces a passage that any reasonably sensitive audience would see as instructional. However, any awkwardness that direct instructions on these topics might have caused is diffused by the indirect form of presentation.

**Lit. just 'hating what is evil', without 'people'. However, the Greek for 'hating' is plural, so it is misleading to translate as 'Love is without pretence, hating what is evil',[20] because it implies that 'love', a singular term, does the hating.*

***If an elegant gender-neutral term were available it might be good to use it. φιλαδελφία is a term that could cover love of sisters as well as love of brothers. The Egyptian ruler Ptolemy II Philadelphus gained his epithet through marrying his sister (who carried the same epithet for the converse reason).[21] However, it is also conceivable that the term 'brotherly love' evoked not only family affection but also the behaviour of certain male groups. See the discussion below.*

The implied call for love that is 'unhypocritical' or 'without play-acting', as one might rather literally translate 12.9a, reinforces the points above. Love that is unhypocritical is presumably marked by practical action on behalf of those loved, instead of mere platitudes. It is presumably also a force against maintaining hierarchies of status and competition for honour in the Christian community. Love without play-acting would have been rather tricky to manage in most pre-modern societies (and is difficult enough now!). Even among the non-elite, life was structured by formal relationships in which the participants were expected to act

---

[20] Cf. Jewett, *Romans*, p. 755.

[21] Dunn is incorrect in implying that Ptolemaic usage was an example of *Philadelphus* used in a broader sense than family love (*Romans 9—16*, p. 741). His other instance, from 2 Macc. 15.14, is more cogent.

and react primarily in accordance with their societal role, rather than with individual spontaneity. Where we might expect relationships to be characterized by affection, particularly between spouses and between parents and children, behaviour was often rather formally ritualized. 'Love without play-acting', although not a direct attack on the ritualized relationships of the first century, does, in principle, engender a new way of interacting that would produce a range of major changes for all of the types of people in our model house church.

This is sharpened further by the call to love each other with brotherly love (12.10).[22] This challenges family boundaries. The household was the basic social and economic unit. It is more difficult to generalize about what kind of unit the family was.[23] Levels of affection varied. Levels of allegiance also varied (as is most clearly seen in the practice of exposure of some babies). At its minimum, the family was the unit to which the honour of the *paterfamilias*, the head of the family, was most closely tied. However, there clearly were also generally degrees of affection and allegiance in relationships between spouses, parents and children, and siblings. These were combined with the obligations of *pietas*, which involved respect for parents and ancestors. In any case, the ties among the relatives in a house-hold (or beyond the household to siblings) differed from the relationships with other household members such as slaves. In advocating brotherly love, Paul undermines the boundaries of kin relationships, just as he has earlier undermined the boundaries of the household. As many scholars have noted, Paul creates a 'fictive kin' relationship among the Christians.[24] One particularly difficult area for house churches to work this out, in practical terms, was presumably in how owners should relate to slaves. Different, but equally acute, difficulties would be raised by the incorpor-ation of those, such as homeless people, with whom no one in the house church would normally have had any connection, let alone one that could be described in family terms. The practical implications of such new con-nections could presumably be far-reaching and potentially problematic for

---

[22] Jewett argues that 'each other' would normally be too obvious for Paul to include but is added here to address divisions between house churches (*Romans*, p. 761). In fact, the Greek term, ἀλλήλους, is common in Pauline vocabulary and need carry no implication of divisions existing (compare, for instance, 1 Thess. 4.9).

[23] We are using 'family' in the sense of 'kin' rather than the rather different sense of the Latin term *familia*. For the study of Roman families see, for example, Keith R. Bradley, *Discovering the Roman Family* (Oxford: Oxford University Press, 1991); Suzanne Dixon, *The Roman Family* (Baltimore: Johns Hopkins University Press, 1992).

[24] For example, Bruce J. Malina and John J. Pilch, *Social-Science Commentary on the Letters of Paul* (Minneapolis: Fortress, 2006), pp. 362–3.

literal families who were being encouraged to expand their effective kin network in this way.

Turning this point around, homeless and other 'detached' people would no doubt be delighted at incorporation into something that functioned as if it was a kin group. This would be particularly striking for migrant workers, who would often be acutely aware of the detachment from family that was involved in them coming to Rome to look for work. In fact, for migrant workers and, more generally, for immigrant groups, it is common for fictive or marginally real kin networks to be an important social and economic resource. I think of stories of successive groups of Jews arriving in the Strangeways area of Manchester, fleeing from pogroms in Russia. They talk of extended hospitality given because people were very distant cousins or because they were effectively regarded as cousins through having come from the same region.[25] However, this example indicates a key feature of such groups: their underlying ethnic basis. Although it would be reasonable to expect that some house churches in Rome may have developed among particular ethnic groups, this seems unlikely to have been an overall pattern. It is clear that if the house churches in Rome were founded by Jews, they very rapidly stopped being exclusively ethnically Jewish. Such early multi-ethnicity probably set a continuing pattern.

For half a dozen members of our model house church, a fictive kin relationship presents a particularly difficult issue. These are members of families or households whose head is not part of the church. It is one thing for Christian householders to extend the effective boundary of their family to encompass other people in the house church. It is a different matter for a non-Christian householder to discover that some of their family, slaves or other dependants have been incorporated into such a group. The non-Christian householder would probably see this as the action of the householder who was the house-church host. The non-Christian householder could well see this as an attempt by the Christian householder to steal some of the allegiance of household members. This could easily become a source of trouble.

More generally, the implications of the essentially egalitarian 'brotherly love' must have been difficult to work out across various boundaries, such as those of gender and servitude. More subtly, φιλαδελφία is not a common word (except in references to the towns of that name) so it is difficult to be sure of its connotations when used in an extended sense

---

[25] As in the novel by Maisie Mosco, *Almonds and Raisins* (London: New English Library, 1979).

as Paul does here, in relating it to Christian groups rather than to actual families. The term 'brother' is used of members of associations.[26] It could be that Paul's usage of φιλαδελφία would evoke ideas of loyalty within an association. If the term did evoke such a usually all-male, convivial setting, this could do subtle things to the sense of identity of women and others who would not usually see themselves in that situation. Conversely, the nature of φιλαδελφία would be changed by the inclusion of such groups. This kind of point is actually raised by each of the more egalitarian elements of this chapter. They sound like ideals rooted in Greek elite male groups, among whom certain ideas of friendship arose.[27] For Paul to ascribe such ideas and practices to the types of people in our model house church is potentially complex and far-reaching.

Romans 12.10b: Mutual honouring in a hierarchical world

12.10b outdoing each other in giving honour,

Paul's implicit call to 'outdo each other in giving honour' (12.10) presumably refers to giving honour to each other. To us, this may seem relatively insignificant. Honouring each other tends not to be a major issue for us: maybe a matter of taking care to hold the door open for each other. Actually, this is quite a good practical example of part of the difference between now and the first century. If, at church, I hold a door open for someone, it is not revolutionary, whoever it may be. In a first-century house church, if a slave held a door open for their master, no one would notice. If a master held a door open for a slave, this would be very radical. However, the matter goes much further than this. As we have already seen, honour was a crucial issue for first-century life. The giving and receiving of honour – and competition for it – was a central driver for many kinds of action. A slave did not, in principle, have any honour. For women, children and freed slaves, honour was an ambiguous category. Honour focused mainly on freeborn male heads of households. In our model house church, this means just a few people out of a total of 30. Paul's call implies giving each person honour individually, rather than all honour just being rolled up into the householder's honour. It implies the slave-owners giving honour to their slaves. In first-century terms this is outrageous. It is very difficult

---

[26] Richard S. Ascough, *Paul's Macedonian Associations* (WUNT 2.161; Tübingen: Mohr Siebeck, 2003), pp. 76–7; Harland, *Associations*, pp. 31–3.

[27] See Alan C. Mitchell, 'The Social Function of Friendship in Acts 2:44–47 and 4:32–37', *JBL* 3.2 (1992), pp. 255–72.

to see how it could have been put into effect. Even if we were to entertain the (implausible) assumption that none of these house churches included slaves, we would still be left with honour being given in all sorts of abnormal directions.

All this is in the context of the fatherhood of God. The honour of all the church members is essentially focused in God, through Christ. As Romans 8 has made clear, all Christians are God's children. As such they have a derivative share in God's honour. 'All Christians' includes slaves, so they share in this honour in the same way, and to the same extent, as free-born Christians. The basis of honour in the house churches has no connection with human status. In Christ, the honour distinctions of ethnicity, servitude and gender are defunct.

The potential social implications of all Christians being children of God are extremely wide. In view of that, honour is probably a relatively manageable issue for Paul to pick up on. The same can be said of the mutual love and allocation of house-church ministries that are main strands in the chapter so far. Even though it is hard to imagine how our model house church would work these out in practice, it is far easier than if Paul had called for action on the really hard-edged issues: free your slaves! redistribute your wealth! The Jerusalem church in Acts followed such a radical road, although Luke does not then trace such radicalism on into the subsequent churches. The utopianism of NT eschatology is surely this radical. The New Jerusalem must be a free, equal society. The celebratory procession in the air in 1 Thessalonians 4 must also be of free, equal people. But Romans 12, although radical to an extent, is not fully so. It does call for not conforming to this age. Its call for a renewed mind is to lead to new practices. However, it does not call for radical changes to social structures that would be unambiguously visible to outsiders. Outsiders might see that the stoneworkers appeared better fed than one would have expected, given their likely income. Outsiders – especially those with access to Christian-led households – might see more respect shown towards slaves. However, the householders would still be householders, with much the same status in society as before. The slaves would still be slaves. The house-church meetings, including their meals, might operate in ways that would scandalize observers who happened to see them. The meetings might be such as to appear to outsiders to be transgressive in the way that Saturnalia celebrations were ritually transgressive – when slaves gave the temporary illusion of being free.[28] However, in contrast

---

[28] John Scheid, 'Saturnus, Saturnalia', in *Oxford Classical Dictionary*, pp. 1360–1.

to the annual Saturnalia, house-church meetings were sufficiently regular that they constituted a significant part of life. A slave who was treated as if a free person, for one or more periods every week, was actually living a different life from that of a normal slave. If this was coupled with being treated with some respect during the rest of the week, this was a markedly different life, albeit without the really radical step: freedom.

Romans 12.11: Hard work

12.11 not slacking in eagerness, fizzing with the Spirit, acting as slaves to the Lord,

Paul's earlier rhetoric has tended to imply raising the slaves in the house church to various aspects of the status of free people. Verse 11 probably tends in the opposite direction, addressing the free people rather as though they were slaves. Its exhortation to hard work, enthusiasm and service sounds the kind of message that a speaker might say to a group of slaves. The rhetoric of Romans 12 is fascinatingly different from that of the 'household codes' of Colossians, Ephesians and 1 Peter. In the household codes, the rhetoric of service is separated out from the rhetoric of love and kindness. The wives, children and slaves are to serve and respect: the husbands, parents and masters are to be loving and kind. In Romans 12, both types of rhetoric are directed at everyone. All, including slaves, are to be loving. All, including the householders, are to be slaves to the Lord and not to be lazy (one of the common literary characterizations of slaves). Of course, the rhetoric is not quite the same because the instruction is 'serve the Lord' rather than 'serve your owner as if serving the Lord' (cf. Eph. 6.7), although, in our model house church, there are about half a dozen slaves whose owners are also members, so they might hear some encouragement to good service as slaves. More systemically, the rhetoric is considerably different because it is directed at everyone. Having lifted them all up to seats at a convivial gathering, Paul pushes them all firmly down into the world of hard work and service. All are of high status in God's eyes. All need to serve.

Of course, for our craftworker house church, this is not as radical an assertion as it would be for a group that included members of the elite. Our cabinet-maker is the wealthiest person in our model. He rents more space than anyone else and has well over ten times the resources of the poorest church members. However, he works with his hands. Although he has a couple of craftworking slaves and some family members to help him, he himself wields a chisel. He is probably far from being wealthy enough to let others work while he enjoys leisure. Everyone in the house church works hard. At the other end of the model's economic spectrum, the homeless also work. They would not be recipients of the Roman citizen grain dole.[29] They would be too marginal to city life for that and, in any case, are likely to be immigrants, not citizens at all. The homeless have to scrape whatever living they can, either through economically marginal work such as collecting firewood, or through begging or theft. All these are work in the sense of requiring time and effort.

This is rhetoric of hard work for people who are used to it. The effect of Paul's call is to divert some of the limited supply of effort into the Christian work of the house church. Since first-century life means that everyone is already stretched, the effect of increased Christian work is a decrease in the other work needed for survival. Time given to meetings is time not available for craftwork. Cooking food for the homeless in the church, and maybe beyond, means less time for other domestic work. Half an hour moving the part-finished furniture around to allow the meeting to happen is not only half an hour lost from work today but also half an hour lost in setting the room up again for work tomorrow. To become 'lazy' in all this would not be a matter of inaction but of returning the focus of all your action to the business of survival that the six non-Christian craftworkers in the row of workshops are devoting all their attention to, thus getting ahead of you.

There are, however, resources for service. The reference to the spirit is, given the extensive use of the term earlier in the letter, probably a reference to the Spirit of God. Power for the 'boiling' ('fizzing') comes from the Spirit put within the Christian, rather than being a matter of pure human effort.

Romans 12.12: Hope, endurance and prayer

12.12 rejoicing in hope, enduring through suffering, devoting themselves to prayer

Verse 12 offers the further resources of hope and prayer, but also draws attention to suffering. Hope, suffering and prayer actually form a closely linked group in the extensive rhetoric of chapter 8.[30] The key drive in that

---

[29] Garnsey and Saller, *The Roman Empire*, p. 83.
[30] Jewett helpfully compares the opening of the verse to the argument of 5.1–5 (*Romans*, p. 763).

chapter, towards endurance under suffering, is fuelled by hope and sustained by prayer. Romans 8.25–26 captures the co-ordination: 'but if we hope for what we don't see, we wait for it with endurance. In the same way also the Spirit helps us in our weakness, for we don't know how to pray as we ought, but the Spirit itself intercedes with wordless groans.'

The suffering in Romans 12.12 may or may not be for the sake of Christ. I have argued elsewhere, on Philippians, that long-term suffering for one's faith tends to have a strong economic component.[31] In the relatively impoverished context of a craftworker house church in Rome, economic issues are likely to be important in relation to suffering, whether or not the suffering is because of their faith. For instance, one form of suffering that could strike anyone in the house church is illness. Looking at the model house church, we might expect about a dozen of the 30 to have been in families that could pay for occasional, reasonably competent medical help. However, the general standard of medical practice was such that this may not have made a dramatic difference to the chances of dying from the illness.[32] Physicians available in a poor area such as Transtiberim are likely to have been particularly scarce and poorly trained. A possible bonus for our specific model house church is that Holconius probably did part-time surgery alongside his cabinet-making. Whether this was actually to people's advantage is another question.

As well as the frequent danger of death, especially for children, the elderly, and women during and shortly after childbirth, illness had immediate and possibly long-term economic effects. Time for work was lost and disabilities might result. This would be a particular threat for slaves, who would fear being thrown out of the household because of becoming too unproductive to be worth feeding.[33] All the above points apply also to the possible consequences of injuries, whether sustained by accident, by attack (whether because of their faith or the general dangers of the dark streets and apartment blocks), or by violent punishment. This last possibility was, of course, particularly likely to happen to slaves.

For the craftworking households in the house church there were also various possible directly economic forms of suffering: boycotts by customers

---

[31] Peter Oakes, *Philippians: From People to Letter* (SNTSMS 110; Cambridge: Cambridge University Press, 2001), pp. 96–9.

[32] For a few of the classic primary sources on this see Jo-Ann Shelton, *As the Romans Did: A Sourcebook in Roman Social History* (New York: Oxford University Press, 2nd edn, 1998), pp. 87–9.

[33] On slavery, see Keith R. Bradley, *Slavery and Society at Rome* (Cambridge: Cambridge University Press, 1994).

or suppliers – or charging of excessive prices – damage to stock or premises, denial of access to shared resources such as warehousing. There could also simply be poverty due to adverse market conditions. For house-church members from households headed by a non-Christian, there were possibilities of serious suffering if relations with the household head broke down. Children might be disinherited, wives might be divorced, freed slaves might lose vital patronage, actual slaves might be violently punished, fined out of their *peculium* (the money they were customarily allowed to hold, even though it technically belonged to their owner), or sold into a worse situation. All in all, for various groups in our model house church, suffering would frequently have a major economic component.

Endurance is a slightly curious concept. For most first-century people, in most forms of suffering, they had little choice of action. They became ill. They either recovered or died. Surviving the illness was not generally a matter of effort. The same could be said of poverty or experiencing violence. If the suffering was because of their faith, endurance presumably meant sticking with Christ and with the house church despite whatever pressures were being brought to bear. Sometimes the burden of this must have fallen on Christian members other than those directly attacked. If one member lost their source of food, presumably others would tend to help. This could easily reach the point where some of the Christian households were under economic strain. Then, the endurance that would be needed would be to keep on giving support to fellow-Christians rather than backing out of the house church or holding its poorer members at arm's length. This last scenario would also apply if the suffering was not a result of being a Christian. Viewing the house church as a group, the group's endurance under suffering would lie particularly in being willing to absorb the range of shocks caused by the suffering that various of the members would undergo. There would always be a temptation for the group to split at that point, setting adrift those who were suffering.

Romans 12.13: Giving and hospitality

12.13 sharing in the needs of the holy ones, pursuing hospitality.

The sharing that Paul writes of here could be within the house church. He calls all the Christians in Rome 'holy ones' (1.7). In that case, the instruction would express the necessary economic consequences of mutual love, as we have been discussing above. Hospitality could also be a key issue within the house church. Taking one of the scenarios discussed above: the child or wife of a non-Christian might get thrown out of the family home by a non-Christian householder. In such a case, hospitality would mean the giving of shelter – quite possibly long-term. Such hospitality was likely to be an acute economic burden on any household of the sizes we are envisaging in the model house church.

Paul may well, however, be thinking further afield. In chapter 15, he uses the term 'holy ones' to refer to the Christians in Jerusalem (15.25, 26, 31), in the context of the bringing there of the collection of money from the gentile churches of Asia Minor and Greece. His phraseology in 15.26, 'the holy ones who are in Jerusalem', implies that he could also use the term of Christians in general, as one would expect from 1.7. In 12.13 it is particularly noticeable that he switches to this term from the language of mutuality he has used earlier and will soon return to. Instead of 'sharing in the needs of each other', as one might expect from 'love each other' (12.10) and 'be of one mind with each other' (12.16), we read 'sharing in the needs of the holy ones'. This is a substantial fresh challenge to the craftworker house church. Not only must they sustain the economically marginal mix of people within the group, they are also called to provide money for house churches elsewhere.[34] In places where Paul talks about how to gather money for the Jerusalem collection, he asks for members of churches to put aside regularly amounts that they can afford (1 Cor. 16.2; 2 Cor. 8.13–15). However, the economic pressures of craftworking existence among the apartment blocks of Transtiberim would tend to make any donation very difficult.[35]

Similarly, hospitality could refer to the well-known issue of giving hospitality to travelling missionaries and other visiting Christians. This could be something that was rather harder in Rome than in the more spacious setting of smaller towns. Paul stayed with Prisca and Aquila at Corinth (Acts 18.3). If, in Corinth, they had a house like that of the cabinet-maker in Pompeii, we can easily imagine them finding room for him. However, if Holconius moves to Rome, he not only loses half his space but has to give over a higher proportion of his space to craftwork. Finding space for Paul in the limited accommodation could be difficult. More broadly, the

---

[34] Jewett suggests a specific application of both the sharing and the hospitality to the needs of Jewish Christian leaders returning to Rome after the lapsing of Claudius' edict of expulsion (*Romans*, pp. 764–5). The difficulty of making such a specific application is particularly evident where Jewett's argument about this specific call for hospitality repeatedly appeals to studies that show hospitality as a very general phenomenon in early Christianity.

[35] Peter Stuhlmacher, *Paul's Letter to the Romans: A Commentary*, tr. S. J. Hafemann (Edinburgh: T. & T. Clark, 1994), p. 196, sees this, together with 12.8, as evidence of regular collections for the poor, distributed by specially commissioned members of the church. That may be overreading the degree of organization implied by the instructions.

issues about the cost of providing for people also apply for guests from beyond Rome. In fact, the costs would probably be greater because of expectations about the type of hospitality that would be provided for particularly honoured guests.

Both the giving and the hospitality raise issues about which types of people Paul is addressing. The only ones who could offer hospitality would be the families whose householders belonged to the church. In terms of adults, this means Paul addressing only about eight people. In fact, given the very constrained space of the householders poorer than Holconius, one suspects that the instruction effectively addresses only him. However, in a broader sense, more people in the house church could be involved in hospitality. Even though the guest might be bound to stay in Holconius's apartment (maybe relegating his children to the workshop mezzanine space), others in the group could contribute work or food.

'Sharing in the needs of the holy ones' could probably, to some extent, be done by everyone, even if some contributions were very small. However, there would be differing constraints on various types of people. The householders would have clearest access to money. However, their money was what sustained the household and its craftworking enterprise. Any giving away of household money would clash with the householder's responsibility to those dependent on him (or, possibly, her). It would also make him poorer. This would threaten to destabilize his status, causing difficulties for his position in networks of people on whom he was dependent (such as a patron), or who were dependent on him. Family members of Christian or non-Christian householders would not, legally, have independent possession of money, even if they were adults.[36] However, by custom, they could control some money. The amounts would tend to be much more limited than the householder's own money. However, family members might actually feel more freedom to dispose of money that they did have: it would not feel like part of the main household fund. Slaves were in a similar but worse position. Their *peculium*, gained mainly from tips, would often have been very limited. They would also be quite likely to be urgently saving their *peculium* to buy their freedom.[37] Freed slaves would have money of their own and liberty to give it away. However, the sums involved, at the craftworker level of society, would generally be small and would generally be very difficult to spare. Migrant workers would also have money and the freedom to use it. Their constraint would be similar

---

[36] Garnsey and Saller, *The Roman Empire*, p. 137.
[37] A. F. Rodger, 'peculium', in *Oxford Classical Dictionary*, p. 1130.

to that of householders because migrants would tend to be gathering money to support relatives in the place that they came from. The homeless would be constrained by their absolute poverty. A complicating factor that could affect any of those with legal control over money was debt. The net economic worth of some in the house church could easily be negative.

Romans 12.14: Bless, rather than curse, your persecutors

12.14 And bless those who persecute* you**! Bless and don't curse.

* The Greek word also means 'pursue', forming a verbal link with v. 13.

** As in 12.1, it could be right to follow P⁴⁶, etc. in omitting ὑμῶν (although the evidence is much weaker than with 12.1). However, as in 12.1, we ought to add 'you' in the translation, for sense.[38]

For most of us, cursing is a matter of rudeness: effectively a form of insult. In the first-century world it was seen as a concretely effectual form of interaction. One of the most common types of textual find from antiquity is *defixiones*, curse tablets. In a recent episode of the British popular archaeological TV programme *Time Team*, two of these small lead items were found in the remains of a Romano-British temple near St Albans.[39] Cursing your persecutor would be viewed as a way to take actual revenge (see below) or to get rid of the persecutor and the persecution. One major temptation among members of the early Christian movement, convinced that they had access to the God of the universe, must surely have been to seek to use his power to curse their enemies. In fact, we do know examples of people using Christian terminology in such a way. A fourth-century example runs as follows:

> Holy God, Gabriel, Michael, do what is sufficient for me, Mesa. Lord God, strike Philadelphe and her children. Lord, Lord, Lord, God, God, God, strike along with her Ou[. . .]sou. Christ have mercy upon me and hear me, Lord.[40]

---

[38] Jewett omits 'you' and reads this as a 'generic formulation "bless the persecutors"', with an application to the Roman authorities who had conducted the deportation under Claudius (*Romans*, pp. 755, 766). As in the previous verse, it looks unreasonably speculative for Jewett to attach this rather generic instruction to such a particular scenario.

[39] *Time Team*, first broadcast Channel 4, 4 January 2009.

[40] Papyrus in Greek, Institut français d'archéologie orientale, Cairo; recorded in Marvin W. Meyer and Richard Smith, *Ancient Christian Magic: Coptic Texts of Ritual Power* (Princeton: Princeton University Press, 1999), p. 51, no. 29, tr. Marvin W. Meyer (capitalization altered). See also pp. 183–6, Robert K. Ritner's introduction to the section on curses. With thanks to Todd Klutz for this reference.

Such cursing extended throughout society. Anyone in our model house church could have engaged in it.

Paul urges that, instead, Christians should bless their persecutors. Again, we should probably think of that in quite concrete terms.[41] If Christians prayed for good to come on their enemies they probably expected this to be effective. For Christians to do this was probably felt to be something of a sacrifice. This is especially so if we follow scholars, such as Bruce Malina, who argue that this was a limited-good society.[42] In that case, if good things were transferred to your enemy as a result of your prayers, other people (such as you) would be losing out.

The call to bless one's persecutors would be particularly problematic for those who had suffered heavily or repeatedly at their hands. If the persecution was because of their Christian faith, such a situation might involve a family who had suffered economic ruin as a result of how someone on whom they depended economically had reacted to their conversion. If the term 'persecutor' is more general, one would think particularly of the suffering, sexual or more generally physical or mental, that owners frequently caused their slaves. In some such situations, an unconditional call to bless the persecutor could be deeply problematic in a number of ways.

Romans 12.15–16: Family sympathy beyond family boundaries; involvement with the poor

12.15 Rejoice with people who are rejoicing. Weep with people who are weeping.

16 Be in agreement with one another.* Don't be carried away to grandiose ideas but to lowly people.**

'Do not be wise in your own eyes'.***

* Lit. 'Thinking the same thing as one another'.

** Lit. 'not thinking high things but getting carried away to the humble'. In fact, the Greek term translated 'humble' could be masculine or neuter. Witherington offers the viable alternative 'carried away to lowly tasks'.[43]

*** Proverbs 3.7.

---

[41] Malina and Pilch, *Social Science Commentary on the Letters of Paul*, p. 278.

[42] Bruce J. Malina, *The New Testament World: Insights from Cultural Anthropology* (London: SCM Press, 1983), ch. 4.

[43] Witherington, *Paul's Letter to the Romans*, p. 296. He describes this text as anti-hierarchical.

Verse 15 calls on the hearers to be alongside people in all the highs and lows of life (some churches have maybe taken this too far by only ever having contact with most people at weddings and funerals!) – or, reading it slightly differently, to be alongside people who are doing well and alongside people who are doing badly. All types of people in the house church will have had some experience of an expectation to laugh or cry at appropriate occasions. Celebration and mourning were expected of all members of a household. More widely, Rome was repeatedly convulsed by excesses of one or the other, in which the entire population were encouraged to join. Imperial birthdays or triumphs engendered huge festivals. Major funerals brought large-scale mourning. At family level too, funerals in particular were to involve everyone. One intended effect of the common practice of manumitting some slaves in a will was to produce a particularly committed group of mourners.[44]

Paul's thoughts undoubtedly go beyond formal events. As indicated above, we may need to read him as thinking of categories of people who habitually weep because of their long-term circumstances. Social norms must have dictated who could fully laugh with whom, and who could weep together. There are certainly stories of slaves weeping at their owners' misfortunes, such as going into exile.[45] Generally, these stories operate in one direction only. The slave feels the pain of the master. The master rarely feels the pain of the slave. If he does, it would be very unlikely that he would be seen to weep over it. Paul calls for all to laugh with any who laugh, and all to weep with any who weep. Laughter and tears are a matter not of duty but of fellow-feeling. They are to cross any social barriers that would prevent this. This means the more powerful weeping with the less powerful. It also means a willingness to laugh or weep with people outside your own household, people with whom society would not have viewed you as being sufficiently closely connected for such a display of emotion.

'Be in agreement with one another' (12.16). This phrase particularly has the sound of the norms of elite male friendship.[46] The unity of thought that Paul urges here is also a prominent feature of the rhetoric of unity in Philippians (2.1–4). In terms of our model craftworker house church, the thought is astonishing. Again, the power lies in the symmetry of the

---

[44] Dionysius of Halicarnassus, *Roman Antiquities*, 4.24.4–8, complains about this practice.

[45] Ovid, *Tristia* 1.3.20; Pliny, *Letters* 3.14.3. With thanks to Roy Gibson and Alison Sharrock for these references.

[46] See Mitchell, 'Social Function of Friendship', pp. 255–72.

instruction. Paul is not calling the house church members to be in agreement with the host, the member of highest status, but with each other. Holconius is to think the same thought as the unemployed, homeless dockworker, who is destitute and entirely uneducated. This wonderfully confounds common sense. Just as the gifts in the house church are distributed to all by God, the wisdom in the house church is distributed to every one of them. These people, who from an educational point of view are a completely ragtag bunch, are to have the kind of unity of mind that was normally thought to flow from the long, considered discussions of the symposium or the philosophical school. Holconius absolutely was not to think he could push on ahead of the house church, paternalistically thinking their thoughts for them because he had been to school for longer than the rest of them and had memorized many fine maxims from the classic writers (although he had not gone on to the gymnasium or to a rhetorical or philosophical school – his was a non-elite education).[47] The house church was to be a community of thought.

Paul then produces a strange-looking contrasting pair that is very difficult to render in good English: literally, 'not thinking high things but getting carried away to the humble' (12.16). Ταπεινός, 'humble', is not here a moral category but a social one. Paul is probably not urging Christians to associate particularly with people who have the virtue of not thinking too highly of themselves (although it would make the contrast in the verse very neat). In this period, ταπεινός was much more commonly used to denote the poor. It tended more towards being pejorative than complimentary.[48] For a Jewish writer such as Paul, the writings of the prophets probably did give this kind of poverty a positive connotation: the humble poor were often seen by the prophets as looking to God for help. However, it is probably the poverty of such people, rather than any praiseworthy attitude of their minds, that Paul is thinking of here. The attitudes that Paul is focusing on are those of his hearers. In some sense, they are not to look up but to move down, towards the poor. This movement represents the attitude that his hearers are called to have, and which may also be evoked by the quotation from Proverbs about not being wise in one's own eyes.

---

[47] S. F. Bonner, *Education in Ancient Rome: From the Elder Cato to the Younger Pliny* (London: Methuen, 1977).

[48] For an extended study of the term, see Klaus Wengst, *Humility: Solidarity of the Humiliated. The Transformation of an Attitude and its Social Relevance in Graeco-Roman, Old Testament-Jewish and Early Christian Tradition*, tr. J. Bowden (London: SCM Press, 1988).

Paul is calling his hearers to look to (so as to associate with) the poor rather than to 'higher things'. Thinking of our model house church, we need to consider whether the poor in question are those within the house church or those outside. Undoubtedly, if wealthier people in the house church were not associating fully with the poorer members, this text would encourage them to do so. However, the argument above about 'the holy ones' (v. 13) probably applies here too. If Paul had been thinking about the poor just within the house church we might have expected the language of mutuality that he uses elsewhere.

This interpretative issue could go either way. It could be that the middle of v. 16 borrows the mutuality language from the beginning of the verse, making the middle part a practical explanation of the first part. In that case, the whole verse would be directed primarily at the upper socio-economic end of the house church and could be paraphrased something like: 'Be in agreement with one another, which involves you (the more educated house-church members) not getting too "highfalutin" in your ideas but getting drawn into the ideas of the poorer church members. Don't be wise in your own eyes!'

On the other hand, on balance, it is probably more attractive to see v. 16 as addressing the whole house church, with the second clause being about how the whole group should position itself in society: 'Don't spend your time in grandiose thinking but commit yourselves to the poor'. The house church is not to become a comfortable debating society but a group constantly involved with the poor beyond the house church. If something like this reading is correct, it would probably make the house-church members very nervous. As first-century craftworkers, their resources were always marginal. As a community that includes some people who need economic support, they are financially stretched. Now, in the space of a couple of verses, Paul has added, first, the expectation of supporting Christians elsewhere in the empire, and then the expectation of engaging constantly with the poor in their part of the city. Where is the money to come from?

Romans 12 does not explain how house-church finances might work. There are clear signs in some texts, such as 1 Timothy, that some desire to regulate church financial help arose quite early in the Christian movement. Here, there is no such argument. Romans calls churches to be groups that, in social terms, primarily look 'down' to action in engagement with the poor, rather than 'up' to intellectual debate (as, in its own manner, 1 Timothy does too: see 1 Tim. 1.3–7, and cf. 1 Tim. 5). We tend to think of intellectual activity as socially neutral – that anyone can engage in it.

In the first-century world, a contrast between intellectual activity and practical action was a contrast between wealthy leisure and the working life of the poor. The contrast in the central clause of 12.16, between high thoughts and association with the poor, is not, in a first-century context, a strange contrast at all.

Romans 12.17–21: Against Christian retributive violence

12.17 Do not pay back anyone evil for evil, but aim to do good before everyone.

18 If it is possible, as far as it rests with you, be at peace with everyone.

19 Dear friends, don't avenge yourselves. Instead, leave room for the real wrath,* because it is written, 'Vengeance is mine, I will repay',** says the Lord.

20 But rather, 'If your enemy is hungry, feed him; if he is thirsty, give him a drink, because, by doing this, you will heap burning coals on his head'.***

21 Don't be overcome by evil, but overcome evil with good.

* Lit. 'But give space for wrath'. Translators need somehow to indicate that the wrath is not that of the Christian who is not avenging himself or herself. Some translations (e.g. NRSV) do this by specifying it as God's wrath. 'Real', in the translation above, is intended to perform the same function. It is meant in the sense of 'substantial', with Paul implicitly contrasting the weight of God's anger with any puny action that Christians might be tempted to take on their own account.

** Deuteronomy 32.35.

*** Proverbs 25.21–22.

In vv. 12 and 14 it is not clear whether the 'suffering' and 'persecution' refer to such things happening on account of the Christians' faith and practice. The chances of this being the case are greatly enhanced by Paul's apparent assumption in vv. 17–21 that they are being attacked. The fact that he gives more space to this than to any preceding issue in the chapter shows that he is extremely concerned about the possibility of Christians taking violent action in revenge for attacks.

In fact, Christians are not necessarily being attacked specifically because they are Christians. Individual house churches, or connected sets of house churches, were substantial groups of people, including quite a number of young men, both slave and free. Rome was full of such groups.

Everything, from Roman history to modern study of group behaviour, demonstrates that one of the main things which groups do is to defend their interests. In Rome, gang warfare repeatedly broke out between *collegia* ('associations') or similar groups such as rival ethnic groups or supporters of particular politicians.[49] As soon as house churches functioned as groups, there would have grown up a degree of solidarity that would have made some group members want to defend others who were attacked – for any reason, whether religious intolerance or robbery. Even without the existence of the group, if, for instance, Holconius's daughter was mugged by a known criminal in the neighbourhood, Holconius would, if he was able, almost certainly go round with his slaves and relatives and beat the man savagely, taking any belongings that they found, in revenge for the robbery. It would be very difficult for Holconius to stop doing this just because he became a Christian. In fact, one might rather expect the practice to spread. If an isolated widow joined the house church and, at some later point, was attacked in the street, one would expect the house church as a whole to feel responsible for taking revenge on her behalf. A small Christian mob might go round to find her attacker. Apart from obvious precautions such as avoiding going out alone at night, this was how defence worked in the streets of Transtiberim. Even the most neutral-looking defensive strategies, such as Holconius's daughter going shopping accompanied by one of the male slaves, only worked because of the implied threat of violence from the slave if she was attacked.

Even if the house-church members somehow lived without engaging in this normal process of defensive violence, they could face trouble from other groups. A house church gets founded in a particular apartment block. It attracts members and grows to a size of about 30. It is not a temple that people are visiting for public or semi-public rituals. It is a group of people meeting together to eat, support each other and engage in religious activities. The obvious question arises: on whose 'turf' has this group been created? For instance, a local 'crossroads' (*compitalis*) association, who meet to eat and drink together, socialize, and engage in religious activities in connection with the *lares* of the crossroads,[50] might take offence

---

[49] Mary Beard, John North and Simon Price, *Religions of Rome. Volume I: A History* (Cambridge: Cambridge University Press, 1998), pp. 184, 230. Harland, *Associations*, pp. 164–6, shows how this related to the politics of the first century BCE in Rome and argues that it should not be seen as true of associations across the empire. His argument is fairly reasonable although his picture, being mainly based on association inscriptions, is likely to over-correct scholarship in the direction of seeing almost all associations as very benign.

[50] Beard, North and Price, *Religions of Rome*, p. 139.

at the creation of another religious group in their area. If it was Jews or some other ethnic group, the crossroads association might (or might not) understand. Such people were known to gather in ethnic groups. But the Christians seemed to be drawing in anybody. The crossroads association might seek to 'encourage' the house church to shut down or go elsewhere. This would not be 'religious' persecution as such. It would be the kind of negative group interaction that was rife in Rome. If violence did break out, and there was some networking between house churches in the city, a church that was attacked might seek help from other churches and the scale of trouble could escalate. On top of these possibilities, there probably would have been some actual 'religious' persecution and Christians being tempted to revenge.

It is very difficult for most of us to imagine how radical a change of behaviour was called for by teaching such as this by Paul, or in Jesus' injunction to 'turn the other cheek'. Relatively few of us will have depended on violent retribution as our standard means of defence, prior to exposure to Jesus' teaching. We will have been used to the idea of picking up the phone to call the police instead. In ancient Rome, nothing short of a major riot or the murder of a member of the elite was likely to attract the attention of the urban cohorts or the *vigiles*, the local force whose main remit was to deal with fires.[51] You were on your own – or, rather, you were part of whatever group you belonged to that might defend you. The streets of Rome were, roughly speaking, those of the two HBO TV series *Rome*. Many readers will baulk at the depictions of sex and violence in that series but its sense of the social dynamics of Roman street life is very powerful and has a reasonable degree of historical probability. The second series, in particular, has a street-level major subplot of a feud between two particularly violent associations struggling over issues of control of illicit income and over issues of honour and insult (this is all a counterpoint to the struggles between Octavian and Mark Antony).

For us, renunciation of violent revenge costs little (at personal, if not necessarily at national level). For the members of a craftworker house church in first-century Rome, it could cost their lives. We may baulk at Paul's appeal to God's vengeance and to the teaching of Proverbs that makes doing good to your enemies into a sort of punishment of them. We would rather have a world in which defence was not needed: in which no one, even God, needed to carry out vengeance on our behalf. But neither Paul nor his hearers is in that world. In dealing with this desperately important practical

---

[51] Nicholas Purcell, 'vigiles', in *Oxford Classical Dictionary*, p. 1598.

issue, Paul takes vengeance out of the hands of the Christians, placing it firmly in the hands of God. God will, so they do not need to. In fact, if they do, it will get in the way of God's fuller vengeance. Paul's instructions should create communities where faith – faith in God's judgement – gives them the confidence to opt out of the cycle of violence.

At the end of Romans 12

If we were to carry on into Romans 13, the above reading gives us a rather natural transition into Paul writing about the attitude of the house church to the authorities.[52] Beyond that, we come to material on debt and love that takes us back to some of the themes we considered earlier. In these, and the further issues in chapters 13—15, reflection on the potential practical consequences of the text for a socially diverse house church in the apartment blocks of Transtiberim is clearly an important exercise to carry out as part of the overall enterprise of seeking to understand these chapters.

---

[52] Cf. N. T. Wright, *Paul: Fresh Perspectives* (London: SPCK, 2005), p. 78.

5

Primus, Sabina, Iris: justice, survival, tension

A campaign speech, a sermon, and Romans

If a text is written for a diverse audience, an important analytical step is to consider how the text would sound to people from each part of the audience.

When a Republican presidential candidate speaks to a televised meeting of party supporters in the run-up to a US presidential election, the speech is written for an audience with several components. First, there are the supporters in the hall. Most of them are looking for reinforcement of key Republican values, to spur them on in their efforts to get the local vote out in favour of their candidate. There will also be known subgroups among the supporters. For instance, there could be a significant number of Hispanic Republicans in the town, who could be watching out for particular issues in the speech. The press and TV reporters are also in the hall. They are looking for newsworthy stories, points relevant to New York or wherever they are based and, if they are really lucky, gaffes that can be shown again and again. Beyond the hall are the TV audience and those who read the papers. In particular, there are the swing voters. The candidate knows that his or her election depends on detaching people at the right of the Democratic support base and persuading them to vote Republican this time, especially those in certain key states. Any good analyst of US political speeches will consider each of those angles.

A campaign speech is an extreme case of a text responsive to diversity, because the candidate is trying to gain everyone's vote. To move closer to the mark, consider sermons. All of us who attend places of worship will have had the experience of sitting through a particular kind of useless sermon. We sat there and thought, 'Does this person not realize the range of types of people in the congregation? Doesn't the preacher realize that he or she has been going on for half an hour about issues that are irrelevant to two-thirds of the congregation?', or 'Doesn't he or she realize that in raising such-and-such an issue, then dismissing it in three sentences, they were touching on something particularly sensitive for certain groups in the congregation, so the subject should have either been left alone or dealt with far more carefully?', or 'Doesn't the preacher realize that constructing his or her main point on the basis of an allusion to the rules of cricket is going to leave it rather opaque to many in the congregation?'

A good preacher, on the other hand, is aware of their congregation, in all its diversity. A sermon is not a campaign speech. It is not constructed by stitching together points, each designed to be popular with a particular group in the audience. However, a good preacher thinks through the range of people in the congregation and considers what will be relevant and intelligible to various groups, and which issues will need particularly sensitive handling because of the situations of various people. If we are analysing a good sermon, and we know something about the make-up of the congregation, it will be valuable to consider how the sermon might look from the viewpoint of various of the groups who would be listening to it.

Whether Romans is, in this sense, like a good sermon is something that needs to be investigated. It might be that considering Romans in relation to various first-century social types reveals a letter that is irrelevant to most of them, offering relevant and intelligible material only to a fraction of the house-church members. It might, for instance, as Stowers suggests, be sharply aimed at the upwardly mobile who have an interest in self-mastery.[1] In that case, we would expect there to be only an accidental scatter of material that happened to be relevant to other groups. On the other hand, we might discover substantial amounts of material, located at significant points in the text, that appeared to respond to a range of possible agendas and a range of types of people.

Traditionally, scholars have read the letter, decided what agenda it is setting, then explored that agenda, drawing in first-century social and cultural material where it illuminates that agenda. This is clearly highly valuable. However, its key limitation is that the scholarly twenty-first century viewpoint is used to decide what agenda it is that the letter is setting. The method of this and the following chapter will be to use the Pompeian socio-cultural material to suggest some agendas that particular types of people in the Roman house churches might bring to the text when they heard it. We will consider the extent to which the text relates to each agenda and to related aspects of the social situation of each type. This is

---

[1] Stanley K. Stowers, *A Rereading of Romans: Justice, Jews and Gentiles* (New Haven: Yale University Press, 1994), p. 75.

of particular value since the chosen social types are likely to have been among the expected hearers of the letter. An exception is Iris, whose possible presence among the expected hearers is itself a question of interest.

To move from social types to specific agendas is clearly a radical simplification that could in fact lose the first-century concreteness of the social types we drew from the archaeological evidence at Pompeii. Primus the slave could become simply a cipher for an agenda of justice. In that case we would be back to me, as a twenty-first-century scholar, simply bringing a twenty-first-century justice agenda to a first-century text. I hope I have not done that, but the reader will have to judge. In fact, my research process involved reading the whole text in relation to each social type (and several others besides our four). This resulted in a complex set of overlapping issues and potential agendas. Primus, Sabina and Iris, in particular, overlap considerably in their situations and likely interests. To present some of the key issues in an intelligible way, this has all been reduced to linking one or two agendas to each social type in the following analysis.

Many readers will realize that, methodologically, I am indebted to a strand of feminist scholarship that draws heavily on first-century evidence to elucidate relationships between the text and aspects of the lives of first-century women. The concern about gender brings the issue of social differentiation into sharp focus. A key stage in the development of my own interest in social diversity was the reading of Lilian Portefaix's *Sisters Rejoice: Paul's Letter to the Philippians and Luke–Acts as Received by First-Century Philippian Women*.[2]

However, the strength of this feminist approach is also a limitation. If we are properly to analyse texts in relation to social diversity among their expected hearers, we need to consider the full range of that diversity: male as well as female, richer, poorer, slave, free. We also need to consider each type of person not in isolation, but within the kinds of first-century social structures in which they are located. To clarify these structures, even a study focused specifically on women needs to spend plenty of time studying first-century men. The concern to consider the full range of social diversity and its potential impact on texts led to my attempt to model first-century Philippian society and the Christian community there.[3] It also led to me inflicting role-playing on fellow-students in the NT graduate seminar at

---

[2] Lilian Portefaix, *Sisters Rejoice: Paul's Letter to the Philippians and Luke–Acts as Received by First-Century Philippian Women* (Coniectanea Biblica, NT Series 20; Uppsala/Stockholm: Almqvist and Wiksell International, 1988).
[3] Peter Oakes, *Philippians: From People to Letter* (SNTSMS 110; Cambridge: Cambridge University Press, 2001), chs 1–2.

Oxford and in various other settings,[4] then to publication of an experimental study, 'Jason and Penelope Hear Philippians 1:1–11'.[5] My hope is that, by considering a text in relation to a range of the social types among its expected hearers, we stand a chance of hearing some of the nuances of the text as it was written for its diverse audience. This is clearly a complex and difficult task. The present study can only perform a few simple experiments in this direction and see whether they yield any interesting and potentially useful results.

Four hearers and Paul's ideas of salvation

If study of the lives of kinds of people who heard Paul's letters can only help us to understand social issues raised in those letters, this is a fairly limited gain. Consideration of the lives of non-elite first-century people should help us better understand a wide range of aspects of his letters. It should help us better understand, for instance, his ideas about salvation as well as his ideas about how people in house churches should relate together. Having given our previous chapter over to consideration of the text in relation to the social dynamics of house-church life, we will now leave those issues out of consideration and will focus on other aspects of Paul's gospel, especially the ideas of salvation.

We have imagined four people, representing aspects of social conditions in four Pompeian houses. Primus is a slave from House 4, right at the bottom of the social heap. Sabina is a stoneworker from House 6, more or less destitute. Iris is a slave barmaid from House 2–3, forced to work as a prostitute. Holconius is a cabinet-maker-cum-surgeon, the householder of House 7. I have tried to imagine listening to the soteriology of Romans from each of these viewpoints. The great limitations of my, or any of my readers, doing this are obvious. However, the attempt, however stumbling, to listen from a range of first-century non-elite viewpoints must be important.

It has certainly changed how the letter sounds to me. I found that the readings relating to each of the four social types sounded different. In each

---

[4] For a creative set of role-playing studies on Romans, see Reta Haltemann Finger, *Paul and the Roman House Churches: A Simulation* (Scottdale, Penn.: Herald Press, 1993). These fascinating studies require a degree of commitment and organization beyond most churches of my acquaintance. However, they do have the virtue of including recipes.

[5] Peter Oakes, 'Jason and Penelope Hear Philippians 1:1–11', in C. Fletcher-Louis and C. Rowland (eds), *Understanding, Study and Reading: Essays in Honour of John Ashton* (JSNTSup 153; Sheffield: Sheffield Academic Press, 1998), pp. 199–212.

case, much to my surprise, Paul's letter seemed repeatedly to address issues that we could expect to have been of major concern for that type of hearer. To Primus, conscious of his disadvantaged social position and of the unfair advantages of those above him, Romans brought an insistent message of a God who would bring justice, punishing people such as Primus's owner and raising the status of someone like Primus to an unimagined level. To Sabina, desperately struggling from day to day, Paul brought a message praising endurance and promising survival – now, to an extent, and certainly after death. To Iris, torn by the tension of a prostitute's existence, a tension exacerbated by awareness of Christian teaching, Romans presented a rather complex soteriology of the body. This included extensive acknowledgement of the tension of life, some possible, though perhaps problematic, instruction on ways forward, and a promise of final resolution of tension. Holconius's cultural reference points were gentile. He was also embedded in Graeco-Roman society with connections in all social directions: a patron above him, family and clients below him, trade associates and customers beside him. Apart from the socially challenging kind of teaching we have discussed in the previous chapter, an aspect of Romans that seems likely to have particularly struck someone like him is the pervasive Jewishness of Paul's gospel. Paul is forthright and unapologetic about that Jewishness. At the same time, he defines and describes gentile Christian life in ways that stand in a complex relationship to Jewish culture. Holconius is also a house-church host. As such, he would be interested in the nature of the group that was filling his workshop regularly. He hears Paul presenting a strongly defined group soteriology. The odd bunch of people in the workshop are presented as having an astonishing identity.

In Chapter 3, we noted that one essential proviso for our four model hearers was that they were Christians. This could lead us into the almost impossible task of trying to distinguish between what the hearers knew already and what they were hearing for the first time: between what was common Christian knowledge and what came fresh from Paul in Romans. I wish to avoid this task, not just because of its impracticality, but also for methodological reasons. Unless a text is clearly intended as a reworking of, or response to, earlier traditions, the task of interpreting the text will at least include elucidation of the text as it stands. In terms of our approach here, that involves trying to hear the text from the point of view of each model hearer as though the specific soteriological ideas in it are new to him or her (although we can allow that they had some prior idea of some basic points, such as that salvation came to people through

Christ). In reality, many of the Roman Christians had presumably heard some Pauline ideas through his former companions mentioned in Romans 16. However, for the purpose of this exercise we will read the letter as though Paul's ideas about salvation came fresh to the hearers in it.

As I said, all this deals with non-elite diversity at only a very basic level. The reality would have been far more complex. I cannot as yet see a way into much more complexity without making readings of the letter dependent on too much detailed speculation. For the current exercise, we will simply take each character in turn and read the letter in relation to issues that seem likely to have been particularly prominent for each of them.

Primus and the God of justice

For many ordinary people around the world today, a key concern is with the perceived injustice of their situation. They are held down, poor, oppressed, while others, who are more wicked than they are, enjoy wealth and freedom. Krister Stendahl criticized scholars for their obsession with the 'introspective conscience of the West', riddled with concern about personal guilt.[6] This point can be made again, in a slightly different way. Western churches and scholars are indeed often concerned about personal guilt and forgiveness. For many poor Christians, although there is bound to be concern about personal guilt, surely the main paradigm for concerned thought is, 'I am faithful, but I do not receive justice'?

Primus epitomizes such concerns. He sees himself as being stuck at the absolute bottom of the heap, despite being faithful to Christ and behaving well, while others in the household – especially his owner – are faithless and wicked. Primus's concern is with the injustice of this situation. No doubt he would have moments of feeling personal guilt, and would hope for forgiveness, but his key interest is in God putting right his situation – and such situations more broadly. Two aspects of Paul's gospel relate strongly to Primus's concerns: the gospel's promise of justice and the gospel's announcement of transformed status.

Justice

One of the most common mistakes of NT scholars is to take God's justice as a given, not needing comment, and to move quickly on to God's forgiveness, which is seen as remarkable and academically interesting. For

---

[6] Krister Stendahl, 'The Apostle Paul and the Introspective Conscience of the West', in Krister Stendahl, *Paul Among Jews and Gentiles* (Philadelphia: Fortress, 1976), pp. 78–96.

most people in the world, the need for justice is probably a bigger perceived issue than the need for forgiveness. For a gentile slave such as Primus, it is likely that the most striking news of the Christian gospel was that a God existed who would bring justice for Primus, punishing his oppressors and improving his position. Although Primus is at an extreme of the spectrum of social positions among Paul's hearers, this message of justice would be core good news for most of them (whether they heard the message of God's justice first from a Christian missionary or from a Jewish teacher in a synagogue). Romans powerfully reinforces the message of God's justice.

The gospel puts the situation right for believers by revealing the righteousness of God (1.16–17). Justice must be a central element of God's righteousness. Most interpreters contrast the revelation of God's wrath (1.18) with the revelation of God's righteousness. However, the grammar of the passage is against this. 'For the wrath of God is revealed': the 'for' tends to link this to the previous verses. More significantly, for Primus and other oppressed people, it is excellent news that God's anger is revealed 'against all the ungodliness and injustice of people'. As Paul's litany of condemnation continues, Primus would probably hear it as especially relating to his owner, and people like that. In 1.23, Paul attacks the worship of images of mortal humans. For a bath-stoker in Pompeii I.10.4, the most frequently seen examples were on the shelf set up as a shrine just along from the door to the bath complex. They may represent ancestors.[7] When Paul describes people given over to 'impurity' and various sexual practices, the most prominent examples for Primus would be his owner and friends when holding certain parties. Verse 27 might also remind Primus of his owner taking advantage of various slave boys.

At the end of what a slave might see as a very reasonable description of the evils of society, Paul concludes with the accusation that people not only do what they know to be evil, but approve of others who do so (1.32). Primus knew that his owner and his owner's friends wholly approved of each other's immoral behaviour, as did most people who Primus saw in society around him. Paul then attacks 'every man who judges' (2.1). To the slave of a member of the elite, this would again seem a criticism of his owner and those on the same social level. The most prominent posts

---

[7] Amadeo Maiuri, *La Casa del Menandro e il suo tesoro di argenteria* (Rome: La Libreria dello Stato, 1933), pp. 100–6; John R. Clarke, *The Houses of Roman Italy, 100 BC–AD 250: Ritual, Space and Decoration* (Berkeley: University of California Press, 1991), pp. 192–3. However, Roger Ling, *The Insula of the Menander at Pompeii. I: The Structures* (Oxford: Clarendon Press, 1997), p. 61, argues that the significance of the busts is unknown.

in their political careers were as magistrates of various kinds. A slave would know that these elite men were clearly guilty of many crimes. For them to act as judges was an outrage against God's justice. A low-level slave might also hear a criticism of senior household members such as stewards, who would judge and punish slaves while probably doing evident wrong themselves.

For God judges truly (2.2). There is no escape from his judgement (2.3). The hard-hearted, unrepentant judges mock the kindness of God and face 'wrath on the day of wrath and of the revealing of the just judgement of God who will give to each according to their deeds', giving honour to those who endure in doing good (such as Primus) and bringing wrath and anger on the disobedient and unjust (most other people, in Primus's view) (2.3–8). This applied to Jew and gentile alike because – a statement that would bring joy to a slave's heart – God shows no favouritism (2.9–11). This judgement of God, carried out through Jesus, was an essential part of Paul's gospel. It would all happen 'on the day when God will judge the secret things of people, in accordance with my gospel, through Christ Jesus' (2.16).

Paul moves on from this topic to talk about Jews (2.17—3.20). In doing so, he gives a noble role to the Jewish Law in the process of God's justice coming to fruition. As the Law speaks to those under the Law, it somehow makes the whole world 'accountable to God' (3.19). This does mean that there are limits on what the Law can do: since its function is about making sin known, it is not itself capable of bringing justification (3.20). As Paul says later, the Law cannot be the basis of inheritance because its function is to bring wrath (4.14–15). However, the bringing of wrath is a positive function. It is part of God's judging the world, which Paul sees as essential (3.6). Although he spends most of the letter depicting another side of the gospel, God's judgement recurs several times. In 9.22 it relates to Pharaoh and others. In 12.17–21 it is a motive for Christians not taking revenge themselves. In 14.10–12 it is a motive for not judging other Christians.

This may all seem disturbing. That is probably because of the perspective of the comfortably off in the West. Most Christians in the West are not driven by longing for God to judge the world in favour of the righteous oppressed. Faced with the news of God's justice and judgement, we are more likely to fear it. This is often particularly because we feel that it would threaten people who we like but who are not active Christians, or because we can only imagine the idea of judgement as something based on marginal, arbitrary criteria, such as subscribing to particular lists of doctrinal ideas, or behaving in line with a number of moral norms (while other moral issues may be ignored). For Paul, God's judgement is 'through Christ Jesus' (2.16). This excludes it being based on doctrinal or moral arbitrariness. Moreover, Paul can also sometimes sound rather universalist. He ends the whole argument of chapters 1—11, 'for God has imprisoned everyone in disobedience so that he might have mercy on everyone' (11.32). However, God's justice, which involves God's judgement, was essential to Paul's message. Luke probably has this right in his depiction of Paul's proclamation in Acts. Jews knew of God's justice and judgement. In Acts 13, Paul proclaimed to the synagogue at Pisidian Antioch the forgiveness in Jesus (Acts 13.38, although with a warning). But to the gentile governor Felix, Paul talked of 'righteousness and self-control and the coming judgement' (24.25), and the punchline of his sermon on the Areopagus was that God was calling all people to repentance, 'as he had set a day on which he would judge the world in righteousness, by a man whom he had marked out, having given a guarantee to all by raising him from the dead' (17.31). A slave perspective on what Paul writes in Romans about justice, judgement and wrath probably brings us closer to the shape of Paul's proclamation than do the typical Western church and scholarly presentations of Paul, which tend to 'airbrush' the theme of judgement out of Paul's gospel.

New status

For a slave such as Primus, God's justice needed to have two sides. It needed to bring down those who oppressed Primus. It also needed to raise him up. While the early part of Romans promised judgement through Christ, much of the rest of the letter promised a new, better life. For a bathhouse stoker, there was an astonishing rise in status on offer.

The most modest of the improvements in the status of a slave was remarkable enough. Paul's idea of salvation effectively gave everyone equal status. He emphatically put everyone under sin (3.19). Then everyone needed to undergo redemption (3.24), as though they were slaves needing to be freed. All then owed their existence to mere gift (3.24). Moreover, unlike in the harsh lottery that had left Primus born into slavery, all those in Christ received the same gift. No wonder there was no longer any scope for boasting![8] How could masters any longer boast over slaves? Or free-born people boast over slaves? All stood in Christ in the same way. The same point can be inferred from chapter 6. All were crucified with Christ (6.6) – a death for a slave – and all were raised with Christ, as new people, born

---

[8] Hearing ποῦ . . . ἡ καύχησις; rather like ποῦ σοφός; etc. in 1 Cor. 1.20, and giving the boasting a general referent of claims of superiority of any kind.

on the same basis into the same status. The rhetoric about enslavement and freedom in 6.15–23 further reinforces this slightly. However, it could be that Paul is here just using slavery as a metaphor for moral subjection and freedom, so it would probably not be heard as giving a strong message about status. On the other hand, the passage does make everyone equally morally responsible. This would be a sharp change for a slave, who would previously have had little moral sense ascribed to him, but would have been viewed rather like a donkey, to be controlled by carrot and stick.

Being declared a 'holy one' (1.6–7) would further boost Primus's status: not only is he now on a level with the free population but he is among the special people who are particularly linked to a deity. The opportunities for a slave to be linked to a cult so strongly as to acquire some of the cult's sacredness would be very limited. A slave might be bought by a cult and become a temple functionary, but this was not something that a slave could bring about. A fairly wealthy slave could sometimes join certain associations (an inscription at Philippi lists slaves among the *cultores* of the god Silvanus).[9] However, belonging to a religious association did not normally make the members sacred. In any case, this required amounts of money that a low-level slave, such as Primus, would not have. Free-born people could become priests of various cults. However, this was mainly the preserve of the elite.

As I have argued elsewhere, people can be designated as holy not only by use of holiness terminology but also by describing them either as being separated from general society or as being closely linked to a deity.[10] Paul repeatedly describes his hearers by using separation language such as 'chosen', 'elect', 'predestined' (Romans 8.28–33; 11.7; 16.13). He also stresses their links to God. They are 'beloved by God' (1.7; 5.5; 8.35, 39; 9.25). Above all, they are children of God, brothers and sisters of Christ (8.14–17, 29). Paul's ascription of holiness to slaves such as Primus makes them part of a select group within society: religiously special and, on that account, worthy of particular respect.

There can be no higher status for a human than to be a child of God (8.14–16). For Primus, to be told that he was a son of God was staggering. This put his status above the whole of society. In fact, the only person

---

[9] Peter Pilhofer, *Philippi II: Katalog der Inschriften von Philippi* (WUNT 119; Tübingen: Mohr Siebeck, 2000), nos 163–6.

[10] Peter Oakes, 'Made Holy by the Holy Spirit: Holiness and Ecclesiology in Romans', in Kent E. Brower and Andy Johnson (eds), *Holiness and Ecclesiology in the New Testament* (Grand Rapids: Eerdmans, 2007), pp. 167–8.

on a par with Christians, as a son of a deity, was the emperor. The Caesars had been making this claim on their coinage since the days of Octavian's struggle with Mark Antony, prior to Octavian becoming the emperor Augustus. Of course, Primus would even see himself as above the emperor, because Primus no longer saw the emperors' fathers as deities. Another similarity with the emperor was that the Christian's sonship came about by adoption (8.15). In the ancient world this put the adopted person into the lineage of the adoptive family, something very hard for us to conceive of. However, it can be seen clearly both in the chain of paternity claimed by the emperors and, effectively, in the genealogies of Jesus in Matthew 1 and Luke 3, which both run via his adoptive father, Joseph. For a slave, any adoption was a sharp increase in status. It could only come with freedom. It gave him or her a family and a lineage, neither of which slaves had, but which were the fundamental basis for status in the ancient world.

Two elements of Romans 8 further enhanced the status of a slave such as Primus. First, he was made an heir (8.17). Many urban slaves gained freedom. Only a few were fortunate enough to gain inheritances. It did happen sometimes. Some slaves inherited their owner's estate, becoming wealthy. Some freedmen of this kind were prominent in Roman society. Paul's other announcement was that the Christians were central to the future of the whole cosmos (8.18–21). Primus was at nearly the most peripheral position possible in society. Paul moves him to the centre. The whole universe is made to be dependent on what will happen to people like Primus.

So Paul proclaims a marvellous new status for slaves who are listening to the letter. Of course, the slaves would then have questions about what their new status, which Paul was declaring as a present reality, would mean in practice in the life of house churches and households. That, of course, takes us back to our previous chapter, where we saw that the practices that Paul called for were potentially very radical, although with a certain social ambiguity.

Sabina and the gospel of survival

Although getting justice is a key concern for many ordinary people around the world, there is a yet more fundamental concern: the need for survival. This produces two key questions for the gospel. How will God help me (and my family and others like me) to survive from day to day? Will God enable us to survive after death – which threatens us daily and has already taken away so many others?

These questions faced Sabina more sharply than Primus. He was 'at the bottom of the heap', even of urban slaves. He was furious about, and frustrated by, the world order that kept him down. However, as a slave with a physically demanding job in a wealthy household, he would probably be adequately fed, clothed and sheltered. His owner had a financial interest in his health. All this might change if and when Primus became permanently unfit for his work but, for now, survival was not a major issue for him.

Sabina was in a much more tenuous position. As freed slaves, she and her husband had formal links to their former owner as patron. However, they were not the kind of clients who were of political value, so they would probably receive little economic help from their patron. This was especially so because they would probably either have paid their patron a significant sum of money for their freedom or have been freed when they reached an age at which their economic value became marginal.

The kind of low-value stoneworking they seem to have done would not have earned much. Moreover, the situation of such craftworkers in Rome would probably have been even more marginal than in Pompeii. In Pompeii they were tenants of the smallest kind of workshop. In Rome, they could probably not afford even that. Such craftworkers would have to live in whatever cramped accommodation they could find, and probably look for work as jobbing stoneworkers, going round to work at people's houses or getting periodic surplus work from workshops. In either case, the problems of day-to-day economic survival would be acute.

Help for endurance

As we saw in the previous chapter, Paul's instructions to the house churches in Romans 12 would, if followed, bring some practical help to poor people like Sabina. The repeated emphasis on love in general and on 'brotherly love' (12.9, 10; 13.8–10; implicit in other verses) must have had some practical edge. More specifically, help might come to Sabina in response to Paul's points about 'sharing', 'showing mercy' (12.8), 'sharing in the needs of the holy ones' (12.13) and 'associating with the lowly' (12.16).

In addition to these calls for practical help, Paul offers some theological support. Endurance is a surprisingly persistent minor motif in Romans. Paul's first description of the requirement for salvation is not merely 'doing good' but 'endurance in doing good' (2.7). Suffering leads to hope by producing 'endurance' and 'character' (5.3–4). This hope is guaranteed by God's love being poured into our hearts through the Holy Spirit (5.5). The endpoint of a major section of chapter 8 is that, because we have hope (the word comes five times in two verses!), 'we wait with endurance' (8.25). 'Enduring' when suffering is part of a list of behaviour encouraged in chapter 12 (12.12), although this injunction is not particularly high-lighted. Finally, and very enigmatically, endurance is a key element in the winding up of Paul's argument about the strong and the weak. After call-ing for 'the strong' not to please themselves but for each to please their neighbour (15.1–2), he cites the example of Christ, who did not please himself. Paul backs this up with a quote about the insults of those who insulted God falling on the psalmist (15.3; Ps. 69.9). Paul then continues,

> For as many things as were written beforehand were written for our teach-ing, so that through endurance and through the encouragement of the scriptures we might have hope. May the God of endurance and of encour-agement grant you to be one in mind with each other in accordance with Christ Jesus[. . .]   (Rom. 15.4–5)

Given the main topics of chapters 14—15, it is a considerable surprise that endurance is emphatically made an issue here. It certainly tends not to be an issue in scholars' reconstructions of what is happening in these chapters. Paul also ends this whole section, and with it the main body of the letter, by stressing hope. The 'root of Jesse' is the one in whom the gentiles hope (15.12). Paul calls on the God of hope to enable the letter's hearers to 'overflow with hope by the power of the Holy Spirit' (15.13). This link between the Holy Spirit and hope reminds us of their link, in the context of suffering and endurance, in 5.2–5.

The letter certainly includes enough about endurance and hope for someone such as Sabina, whose life is a struggle, to hear Romans as an encouragement to endurance and, conversely, an acknowledgement of the fact that many faced a life of struggle. Alongside this would stand Paul's validation of present suffering, especially in chapter 8. Glory is conditional on suffering with Christ (8.17). Current sufferings will be outweighed by future glory (8.18). Creation is a place of frustration and groaning, which extends to Christians too (8.20–23). Then come the points about hope and endurance (8.24–25). Present existence is a time of eager waiting with endurance (8.25).

This material can worry Western Christians. If glory is dependent on suffering with Christ, what of those of us who suffer little? Also, isn't there also a danger that broad validation of suffering and an emphasis on endurance can lead to passivity in the fact of pernicious conditions, such as sexual abuse, that we ought to seek to change? The first of these questions should probably be allowed to hang in the air, as a nagging reminder that Christians should always be asking whether their discipleship is sufficiently radical. Paul would have been unlikely to have sided with later Christians who actively sought martyrdom. However – to make another unwarranted chronological leap – he would probably be staggered by the complacency of many current churches. The second question is very serious. As we saw in the previous chapter, Paul's exhortations, while having a sharp, socially radical edge, fall short of calling for structural social change. Slaves may be treated differently but they remain slaves. In present-day society, both the victims of abuse and others who find out about it – as, to an extent, we all do – often can and should take action to seek to change the situation. This extends to other forms of suffering such as poverty, although here the responsibility for action is almost all on the side of those with the wealth and power to bring about change.

Having said all this, it is still important, for suffering people such as Sabina, that the gospel validates their suffering and encourages them in their day-by-day endurance. Hope can itself have a transforming effect on day-to-day experience.

Paul goes on in Romans 8 to offer more for Sabina's daily life than validation and hope. He promises protection and internal help. The helper is the Holy Spirit, who, in Romans 8, seems particularly linked to the experience of suffering. The Spirit is the means by which Christians cry out (κράζομεν) 'Abba, father!' (8.15). This is not an unemotional declaration but a powerful affirmation and plea. The Spirit testifies to our identity as children of God (8.16). It is as those having the firstfruits of the Spirit that Christians groan, as creation groans (8.22–23). The Spirit helps us in our weakness, interceding with God in wordless groans (8.26). The exact nature of early Christian experience of the Spirit is one of the deepest questions in the study of early Christianity. However, Paul clearly saw the Spirit as a very active, palpable force in the believer's life. Paul promises to people like Sabina (and to others) an internal but practical help for daily living.

Romans 8.31–39 offer reassurance of protection for Paul's hearers. In Christ they will survive and even be victors (8.37) in any challenge that life or death can bring them. Paul picks up many of the issues that would be worries for Sabina. 'Who shall separate us from the love of Christ? Shall suffering, or distress, or persecution, or hunger, or nakedness, or danger, or the sword?' (8.35). Hunger and nakedness are primary effects of poverty. Danger is also most common for the poor (as current knife-crime statistics in the UK make particularly clear). Paul offers reassurance in the face of all these. In a sense, the Christian is protected. Sabina would surely have drawn some comfort as she faced these difficulties.

However, the fact that death is listed as one of the things unable to separate us from the love of Christ means that the Christian's protection is not so tangible as to prevent death. It is then just as well that Paul places substantial stress in Romans on life after death.

Eternal life

Life after death is one of the most emphatic themes in Romans 1—8. It is astonishingly underplayed by scholars. The same verse that introduces the motif of endurance also brings the first reference to the afterlife. 'Eternal life' is promised to those who 'by endurance in a good work seek glory and honour and immortality' (2.7). The same point is effectively made again in v. 10. God will give 'glory and honour and peace to everyone who does good'. The day of judgement, in v. 16, was for Primus the time when wrongs are put right. If Sabina was more interested in issues of survival, then that day would be seen as the day when endurance is rewarded and eternal life is granted.

In 4.17, Paul says that Abraham trusted in 'God who gives life to the dead'. Paul sees God's response to this as a pattern for God's response to Christians 'who believe in the one who raised Jesus our Lord from the dead' (4.22–24). This is primarily teaching about belief in what happened to Christ. However, if a central element of Christianity is belief in God as the one who raises the dead, this is bound to make Christians expect resurrection for themselves. In 5.2, the boast is in 'hope of the glory of God'. In 5.10, the past event of reconciliation with God guarantees the future event of salvation. Both the glory and the salvation would probably be heard by Sabina as expressions about eternal life.

Romans 5.12–21 and chapter 6 tend to be handled separately but they are in fact held quite closely together by the theme of death and life. This is seen most obviously in their parallel endings:

> so that, just as sin reigned in death, so also grace will reign through righteousness for eternal life through Jesus Christ our Lord. (5.21)

> For the wage of sin is death, but the gift of God is eternal life in Christ Jesus our lord. (6.23)

More broadly, across both chapters, sin is aligned with death, while Christ, righteousness and grace are aligned with life. Romans 5.12–21 sets up the gift of eternal life in Christ, in a world full of death. Romans 6 handles the objection that such grace undermines morals, but the chapter also restates this promise of eternal life.

Sabina knew about the reign of death and the presence of sin in the world (5.13–14). Through Christ, the gracious gift of justification had come to her (5.15–16). This gift of righteousness meant reigning in (eternal) life through Christ (5.17). This was a justification that meant life (5.18). She was one of the many established as righteous (5.19). Grace had overcome sin, so now it reigned, through righteousness, to provide eternal life in Jesus Christ, Sabina's Lord (5.20–21).

In chapter 6, Sabina's baptism was a burial with Christ that meant sharing his new life (6.4), sharing the pattern of his resurrection (6.5), confident that she would live together with him (6.8). This meant that her current life was life directed to God, in Christ (6.11), therefore a moral life. She was someone returned from the dead, so her body should serve righteousness (6.13). Sin produced death: obedience produced righteousness (6.16) – righteousness is aligned with the opposite of death. As a slave to God, she would receive holiness, the outcome of which would be eternal life (6.22). God's gift is eternal life in Christ (6.23). Despite the clear message of chapter 6 that new life in Christ was a life to be lived now, obediently, this chapter is still shot through with the promise of eternal life. That is the fundamental datum, set up in chapter 5, which is then a basis for moral exhortation in chapter 6.

Romans 7 runs off in another direction. However, it does return to the question of life: 'Who will rescue me from this body of death? Thanks be to God through Jesus Christ our Lord!' (7.24–25). Death and life continue into chapter 8. The new feature here is that life is linked with the Spirit: 'the law of the Spirit of life in Christ Jesus will free you from the law of sin and death' (8.2). In 8.10, the spirit (or Spirit) is life through righteousness (life and righteousness are again aligned). The Spirit is specifically that of 'the one who raised Jesus from the dead'. If this Spirit 'lives in you', 'the one who raises Jesus from the dead will also give life to your mortal bodies through the Spirit that lives in you' (8.11). Although this clearly has some reference to present life, it also implies life after death. As in chapter 6, this has moral consequences (8.12). Putting to death 'the deeds of the body' brings life (8.13). Eternal life may be implicit in being children of God (8.14–16) and, especially, in being 'co-heirs with Christ'. It is certainly implied by the promise of glorification with him (8.17). Even more direct is the announcement of 'the coming glory to be revealed in us', compared to which 'the sufferings of the present time will be as nothing' (8.18). This is then taken up as a point of comparison for the whole of creation, which will escape from frustration and decay when it comes to share 'the freedom of the glory of the children of God' (8.19–21). These have 'the first fruits of the Spirit': presumably the full harvest is to be enjoyed in the afterlife. They eagerly await 'the redemption' of their bodies (8.23). They will ultimately become like Christ (8.29). Having been predestined, called and justified, they will be glorified (8.30). Death cannot separate them from the love of Christ (8.35–39). In Romans, Paul hammers home – to an extent that scholars have rarely absorbed – the message that struggling Christians, such as Sabina, can be confident of eternal life.

Iris and the redemption of the body

Iris, the bar owner's servant girl, was in a role that typically involved slavery and sexual exploitation. This would inherently be a life of tension because she lacked final control over her body. Her situation was probably rather better than that of a prostitute in a full-time brothel. Sleeping with the customers was very unlikely to be Iris's main task. However, for her owner it was probably a particularly profitable aspect of the bar's business, so she was likely to be constrained to flirt frequently with customers, with a view to them paying to take her upstairs. Her own financial well-being would also have probably depended heavily on this.

As Jennifer Glancy has argued, the experience of tension inherent in the life of a sexually exploited slave would seem likely to be exacerbated if he or she joined a Christian group that heard Paul's teaching. His rhetoric directed against sexual immorality in general and, in particular, against men going to prostitutes, depicts the activity as incompatible with Christian life (esp. 1 Corinthians 5—6). Glancy concludes that, given the endemic sexual exploitation of slaves, it is difficult to see how slaves could exist in the kind of Christian group projected by Paul's rhetoric.[11] This is, of course, a paradoxical result because he knows of slaves in the house churches and addresses them, even in 1 Corinthians itself (1 Cor. 7.21–22; cf. 12.13).[12]

The contribution that our study hopes to make in this area is to consider how a less obvious text, Romans, relates to the existence of sexually exploited slaves. If such slaves were indeed part of house churches, how would Paul's letter sound? Romans includes little direct discussion of sexual issues. There is extensive material on sin and righteousness.

---

[11] Jennifer A. Glancy, *Slavery in Early Christianity* (Oxford: Oxford University Press, 2002), pp. 49–50, 58, 63–70.

[12] Cf. J. Albert Harrill, *The Manumission of Slaves in Early Christianity* (Hermeneutische Untersuchungen zur Theologie 32; Tübingen: Mohr Siebeck, 1995), p. 194.

However, I cannot see a way into understanding what the (undoubtedly varying) moral attitudes of slaves were to the actions that they were wholly or partly constrained to perform.[13] It therefore seems difficult to make much progress in relating Paul's rhetoric on sin and righteousness to this context. However, Romans also has significant rhetoric about the body. For a slave such as Iris, there would seem to be many elements of that rhetoric that related strongly to her situation.

Slavery is not a thing of the past. Moreover, it still tends to be strongly connected to sexual exploitation. Sexual exploitation often requires the kind of absolute control that only slavery, or some other totalizing force such as drug addiction, brings. Slavery in terms of debt bondage or fear of violence is common in the European sex trade. Churches tend only rarely to reach the victims. However, there are some church-related projects that do work in seeking to free people who are trapped in this way. Of course, a major difference from the Roman period is that slavery, and similar forms of coercion, are illegal, so the visibility inherent in an enslaved sex worker forming a link with a church organization now tends to involve the person being on the way to freedom. In the first century, slavery was a central social institution. The exploitation would continue, however visible it became.

In a different sense, Iris represents a much wider group of people. The experience of some tension in aspects of embodied Christian life must be almost universal. For many who are not slaves, there are other constraints that make bodily life a state of tension – a tension that may be heightened by the experiences the person has as a Christian.

The body: dead or alive?

Paul writes about bodily matters in Romans 6—8. In 6.3, Iris hears her baptism interpreted as a death and rebirth. This idea is developed through 6.1–11. For a slave who is constrained to do things that she dislikes and disapproves of, especially since her exposure to Christian teaching, a soteriology of death and rebirth is a hopeful one. It promises to deal with her condition in such a radical way that the constraints her owner places on her cannot affect it. Death is a powerful symbol for slaves. It is the one thing that they can almost always achieve irrespective of their owners' wishes.

However, the very radicalness of this idea of salvation raises a great problem for slaves. How can the 'old person' be dead? How can the 'sinful body'

---

[13] Cf. Glancy, *Slavery*, p. 64, on the difficulty of deciding what Paul himself would have thought about the issue.

have been done away with? How can they 'no longer be enslaved to sin'? A Christian slave is still physically enslaved to the owner. In Iris's case this means continuing to be compelled to action that Christian teaching saw as sinful.

There are various types of solution that people tend to adopt when faced with this kind of 'cognitive dissonance'.[14] Given what Paul has written up to this point in Romans, a hearer might adopt a sense of having a 'secret identity'. This is probably already inherent in Paul's description of the addressees as 'holy people', and the other epithets in 1.6–7. This gives the hearers an identity radically at odds with the way they are likely to have been perceived by those around them. Such a secret identity is reinforced by Paul's internalizing of the symbols of Jewish identity, when he writes of 'the one who is a Jew in the hidden place' and of 'circumcision of the heart' (2.29). Iris would probably feel that her Christian rebirth gave her a new identity, as a person of worth and integrity, that was essentially hidden from her owner.

However, the dissonance is still there. What Paul writes in 6.1–11 does not dissolve it by putting the new life solely in the future. Although he has some future-tense verbs for the blessings of the new life (6.5, 8), there are other points at which the new life is meant to be a present reality (6.4, 6, 11). In particular, his argument is directed towards the new life having current moral effects (6.1–2, 6–7, 10–11). Clearly, Iris could attempt to compartmentalize her life into areas over which she did or did not have control. However, this must be particularly difficult when the central problem is sexual exploitation.

Issues of physicality take a slightly different form in 6.12–23. Whereas 6.6 talks of 'the sinful body' (τὸ σῶμα τῆς ἁμαρτίας) which is 'done away with' or 'made of no effect' (καταργηθῇ), in 6.12–23 the body is almost neutral (6.12) and 'your members', the parts of your body, are completely neutral, able to be used either for sin or for righteousness (6.13, 19). When Paul writes, 'Therefore let sin not reign in your mortal body, so as to obey its [the mortal body's] desires' (or maybe 'lusts', ἐπιθυμίαι) (6.12), the Christian is presented with a choice as to what reigns in the body. The malign power, sin, is aligned with the body's 'desires' or 'lusts'. As we have seen, the idea of choice is itself a problem for a slave. However, one tendency in this verse that a slave such as Iris might adopt is towards asceticism. A tendency to denial of desires must, I imagine, be a relatively

---

[14] The term is that of Leon Festinger, *A Theory of Cognitive Dissonance* (Stanford: Stanford University Press, 1962).

common response to enslaved sexual exploitation. It could presumably strengthen a sense of personal autonomy. Just as death is an option for a slave, it is also in their power not to take advantage of ameliorations of their life that their owner offers them. Iris might, for example, refrain from getting drunk, despite the easy availability of wine in the bar and the numbing affect it would have on some of her worst moments.

It is worth us jumping forward at this point to 13.14, to see Paul again writing in an ascetic key, this time with a significant change of vocabulary: 'But put on the lord Jesus Christ, and take no forethought for the flesh (σάρξ) to carry out its desires'. As well as the use of 'flesh' here instead of 'body', two contextual points are also important. The instruction concludes a list of 'the deeds of the darkness' (13.12). This list of night-time deeds reads like a summary of what Graeco-Roman writers would see as typically going on in a bar such as Iris's: 'revelry and drunkenness, sexual immorality and indecency, fighting and jealousy' (13.13).[15] The second contextual point raises a *caveat* over how ascetic Paul is being. In 13.9, as in 7.7, Paul uses ἐπιθυμέω for the verb in the tenth commandment, 'do not covet'. In 7.7, he uses ἐπιθυμία as the equivalent noun. It would, however, seem unreasonable to restrict the translation of ἐπιθυμία in 6.12 and 13.14 to 'coveting'. Paul must surely be thinking of bodily desires in some wider sense than that. On the other hand, although the New International Version is undoubtedly over-translating when rendering ἐπιθυμίαι in 6.12 as 'evil desires', it is unlikely that Paul is being so ascetic as to include all 'desires' in his use of the word. Having said all this, there is considerable potential for Paul's hearers to interpret his words as a call towards a degree of asceticism, and this might be heard particularly by people such as Iris, for whom Christian life brought a certain level of cognitive dissonance.

For most of us, 'not doing evil' is rather easier than 'doing good'. Doing good tends to require us to think, to break out of the pattern of what we were going to do and do something new: a positive deed that would otherwise not have been done. For a slave such as Iris, the opposite could tend to be true. Her owner constrained her to do what she saw as wrong. But even slaves can do good deeds. Paul's hearers are urged not to 'offer your members to sin as instruments of unrighteousness' but to 'offer yourselves to God . . . and your members to God as instruments of righteousness' (6.13). Iris may have had little control over the extent to which her members were used for unrighteousness. In any case, as I mentioned at the beginning of this section, we do not know what a slave's moral attitude to constrained

---

[15] For references on the reputation of first-century bars see Chapter 1, n. 68 above.

actions would have been. Iris, and even other house-church members, might have written them off as not being her responsibility. As for doing good, the nature of a barmaid's work (even allowing for radical differences between then and now) could well produce many opportunities for righteous actions. Ironically, the heavy tipping that Iris might have received for some of the less righteous aspects of her work might have enabled her, even as a slave, to offer financial support to people who were destitute.

In Romans 7.1–13, Paul talks about a past relationship to the Jewish Law, the changed situation in Christ, and the role of the Law in provoking sin. This would not seem likely to have much impact on a gentile slave. However, part-way through v. 14, Paul switches to language about slavery. Having contrasted his 'fleshly' existence with the Law's spiritual nature, he unpacks this fleshly existence as being 'sold under sin'. As both Albert Harrill and John Byron argue (with very different results), Paul then continues to the end of the chapter with language relating to slavery.[16] The first-person voice in the passage is constrained to do what he does not want to, and prevented from doing what he wants. The speaker is dominated by his master, sin, which lives in him (7.20). A law 'in his members' 'imprisons' him in 'the law of sin' (7.23). He says that 'in my mind I am a slave to the law of God but, in my flesh, I am a slave to the law of sin' (7.25). He pleads for rescue 'from this body of death' (7.24) and finds that rescue in Christ (7.25).

Whatever one's view of what Romans 7 is about (Christian life? non-Christian life? Israel? Paul before conversion? Everyone?),[17] a slave would seem likely to view Paul as expressing his (or someone else's) experience in terms of theirs. More specifically, Paul was painting a picture of their present experience, as Christian slaves whose actions were constrained by non-Christian owners. Iris is sold into sinful control (7.14). She does what she hates (7.15). Although she is not from a Jewish background she has, through Christianity, come to know and approve of God's commands (7.22), yet she is forced to break them. Whatever the subtleties of Romans 7, for sexually exploited Christian slaves this is an expression of the acute tension of their present existence.

The beginning of Romans 8 then announces to them that, in Christ, they have been set free from 'the law of sin and death' (8.2). They face no

---

[16] J. Albert Harrill, *Slaves in the New Testament: Literary, Social and Moral Dimensions* (Philadelphia: Fortress, 2006), pp. 17–33; John Byron, *Slavery Metaphors in Early Judaism and Pauline Christianity* (WUNT 2.162; Tübingen: Mohr Siebeck, 2003), pp. 223–7.

[17] For a summary of some of the main views, see Robert Jewett, *Romans: A Commentary* (Hermeneia; Minneapolis: Fortress, 2007), pp. 441–5.

condemnation (8.1). For them it is obvious that the Law is fatally weak-ened, as a potential source of salvation, by the realities of the flesh (8.3). The arrival of God's son provides the means for sin to be condemned in the flesh without that condemnation dragging them down with it (8.3). Now, they can be regarded as fulfilling God's commandment because they live in accordance with their secret, spiritual identity rather than with their enchained, fleshly one (8.4). They know well that fleshly existence cannot please God. They rely on their spiritual existence (8.5–9).

This all sounds rather dualistic. Hearers whose disastrous experience of life drives them to evaluate the body rather negatively will inevitably hear Paul's 'body' and 'flesh' language as fairly inextricably linked. They are bound to identify the 'spiritual' life as one that is somehow detached from the traumas of the body. Such people seem likely to read the flesh–spirit duality of 8.1–8 as being similar to the flesh–mind duality of 7.25. If people hear 7.13–25 as being their present experience, the realm of the mind easily becomes the sphere in which the Spirit operates, a sphere contrasted with the uncontrollable sphere of the flesh. The same factors that seem likely to produce a dualistic hearing of 8.1–8 would also seem likely to promote the chances of reading Paul's instruction in 6.12 as a call to asceticism. Romans 8.9–13 would partially reinforce the dualistic impression, although it also blurs the lines. The assertion 'you are not in flesh' (8.9) resists a simple identification between 'flesh' and bodily life, however traumatic. The next verse adds the assertion 'your body is dead on account of sin' (8.10). This, of course, resists any literal application. In a third complication, Paul promises that 'the one who raised Christ from the dead will give life also to your mortal bodies through his Spirit that dwells in you' (8.11). Since Paul is clear that the Spirit lives in Christians now, he presumably sees life being given to their mor-tal bodies now. A dualistic approach to life can probably cope with the idea of walking around in what is, in terms of what matters, a dead body. It can cope with the idea that 'the real you' is somehow not in the flesh. However, life being put back into the body causes problems for the system. For Iris, walking around in what she views as a dead body could be a workable survival strategy. However, if she had been hearing Paul as promoting such a strategy, he is now somewhat withdrawing the possibility. The Spirit is somehow breathing life into this bodily situation that was rendered dead by sin. This is a call to a more complex life than a simple dualistic defensiveness. Somehow, the embodied life can be a sphere of the Spirit's action, even during the suffering that Paul is about to describe.

Romans 8.14–17 promises sonship, adoption, becoming a child of God. We have already commented on this in our other slave reading, by Primus. However, the language might have a particular resonance for someone such as Iris. Probably the owner of a small bar could not afford to buy an attractive female slave. It would be more likely that the owner had acquired Iris as an infant, 'exposed' by her parents by leaving her in a public place, to either be picked up and raised as a slave or die. Parental language must have been particularly evocative for such slaves.

At the end of this passage, Paul elevates the value of suffering. Glorification with Christ depends on suffering with him (8.17). Paul then relativizes the seriousness of current suffering by comparing it with the scope of the glory to come (8.18). For someone such as Iris, who may suffer considerably, each of these rhetorical moves may offer encouragement. There may be occasions when a promise of future glory to those who are suffering is problematic because of its palliative effect on wrongs that should be set right, rather than made more bearable. However, for most generations of slaves, unable to alter their basic situation, a strong future hope is a crucial resource.

Paul then once again validates the struggles of life in the tensions of the present (cf. Iris's hearing of 7.13–25). He puts the Christian's groaning in the context of creation's own travails (8.22–3). In fact the whole universe is like a groaning slave waiting for freedom (8.21). Paul also makes the Christian's groaning a work of the Spirit (8.23, 26). Iris's struggles are struggles that God is involved with, through the Spirit.

Finally, the body itself will be redeemed (8.23). Paul's tenses get confusing. Having announced adoption as having happened (8.14–16), he now places it in the future, and makes it identical to bodily redemption. This places one kind of limit on dualism. For Paul, salvation is never ultimately just a matter of the mind. The body too is redeemed. Conversely, it places a limit on the extent to which the Spirit gives life to mortal bodies now (8.11). Much of the freeing of the body is yet to come. A sexually exploited slave such as Iris recognizes this well. An 'over-realized' eschatology, which views the current life as a full enjoyment of God's blessings, would cut little ice with her, as with many in similar situations since then.

6

Holconius and the Jewish salvation
of a holy people

The relationship of parts of Romans to the social situation of Holconius the cabinet-maker has already received a fair amount of attention in our study. In Chapter 4, many aspects of our reading of Romans 12 had a particular relationship to him because he was the highest-status male in our model house church. Texts that represented any variation from the social status quo would tend to have had the deepest potential impact on him. In this chapter, we will consider two further aspects of Holconius's social situation: as gentile and as house-church host.

Despite the common acknowledgement that the primary addressees of Romans are gentiles, scholars have not really followed through the logic of it being a letter for a gentile audience. At Holconius's economic level, some of the possible cultural reference points of gentile life can be seen in features such as wall decoration. In his case, we have Greek mythology, represented in the Fall of Icarus and the Judgement of Paris in room 9, together with the more enigmatic cultural imagery of the banquet scene in room 8. I do not want to press the details of particular kinds of mythology: David Balch has recently done helpful work in this area.[1] I am more interested in a very general cultural point. Holconius's cultural reference points were not Jewish ones. By the time of Romans, when probably the great majority of Christians in Rome were gentile, there must have been many among Paul's expected hearers who came from a background with no Jewish cultural reference points, except for some basic biblical knowledge gained through Christian teaching. We can go further. General Roman evidence suggests that such people would probably not only lack Jewish cultural reference points but have a certain level of cultural disdain towards Jews, as people with strange ways who were not part of the cultural mainstream.

---

[1] David L. Balch, *Roman Domestic Art and Early House Churches* (WUNT 228; Tübingen: Mohr Siebeck, 2008), chs 2–7.

Scholars have tended to avoid reading Romans in relation to such an audience. The reasons are fairly obvious: Romans is full of material about Judaism, so one would expect it to have been written for people with a strong interest in the subject. However, it is interesting to ask how Romans looks if we turn this last point on its head. How would Romans sound to someone with little interest in, or knowledge of, Judaism? How would it sound to someone who accepted the message about Jesus but was rather embarrassed by the links to Judaism that this implied? How would it sound to a fairly typical gentile such as the Pompeian Holconius? After all, the typical gentile, with no prior connections to synagogues, is pre-sumably who Paul ultimately has in mind when he speaks of his calling to bring the gospel to the gentiles.

The shortage of scholarly work taking this kind of approach is particu-larly striking, given that most Christians, over the centuries, have fallen into this category: knowing and caring little about Judaism and tending to be somewhat anti-Jewish. In fact, historically, most interpreters have clearly fallen into this category themselves, and have shown it by essen-tially ignoring the Jewish character of Romans, 'rewriting' the letter as a handbook of (gentile) Christian theology. If, as we will consider below, the letter can be seen as introducing Christianity as a Jewish phenom-enon to gentiles who are uninterested in, and disdainful of, Judaism, this will have interesting practical resonances.

The second aspect of Holconius's social situation to be considered below is as house-church host. As a house-church host, Holconius would be one of a number of people who would tend to feel particular respons-ibility for the existence and well-being of the group. We ought to con-sider what the nature of this group, created by the salvation that Paul describes, would sound like to the types of people likely to host or lead the group. We need to consider what Paul's soteriology implies about the identity of the group.

Again, it is rather surprising that Pauline scholars have not given much thought to how his letters would sound to people who had a particular sense of responsibility in relation to house churches. This is a category of people who we know to have been among the expected audience of all Paul's letters. We would expect him to have given particular thought to people such as house-church leaders when he was composing his letters. Although we tend to think more of the Pastoral Epistles as texts for church leaders, such people must also have been in view in letters addressed to entire groups of church members.

Exploration of aspects of Paul's ideas of salvation in Romans that pertain to group identity touches on issues relevant today as well as then. What does it mean for Christian salvation to create a group, rather than simply to change the lives of individuals? What kind of group is created? How does such a group relate to the structure of society?

The Jewish salvation of Jews and gentiles

In assuming that Holconius is a Christian, we must allow him some knowledge of Judaism. Apart from anything, he would presumably know Christian Jews, such as those mentioned in Romans 16. He would also probably have some knowledge from encountering Jews more generally, especially if he lived in the Transtiberim area of Rome. He would also have knowledge from general hearsay. Even if Paul is, in some sense, introducing the Jewish nature of Christianity to gentiles (the hypothesis whose testing we are effectively contributing towards), he does assume some knowledge. For example, David is mentioned in 1.3 without a gloss describing him as a king of Israel. If Paul is putting across to a gentile audience something about Judaism, it is not basic information but something that involves persuasion. Let us consider what would be the main points about the Jewish nature of salvation that a gentile such as Holconius might be expected to pick up from the letter.

Romans 1—4

After Paul's initial introduction of himself, the first points in the letter are that the gospel is scriptural and that Jesus was from the Jewish royal line (1.2–3). Holconius can be in no doubt that the gospel is a Jewish message about a Jewish saviour. However, the Jewishness of this declaration is inherently qualified. The gospel is not described as being declared by the prophets but 'promised beforehand' by them: their message points forward to a clearer one. Similarly, the Jewish royal identity of Jesus is κατὰ σάρκα, 'according to flesh'. Again, this identity is clearly not the whole story. Being a Davidic messianic figure is not enough. More comes later, as is explained in v. 4.

The way Paul describes his commission in v. 5 sounds like a piece of Jewish imperialism. To a Roman such as Holconius, it would sound rather topsy-turvy for a Jew to talk of going about bringing the nations to obedience. This was more what Rome did. Paul was bringing non-Jews to obedience to a Jewish faith. Verse 7 then describes the gentile hearers in rather Jewish terms: 'beloved by God, called to be holy ones'. Holconius was being given a rather Jewish identity. However, the converse effect of this ascription of identity would also be significant to Holconius: these Jewish identity terms were being used of gentile Christians, without them having adopted full Jewish practice. They were described in Jewish terms but they were not Jews in the sense that most Jews would have acknowledged.

At v. 16, Paul moves into the body of the letter. He begins this with a statement about the gospel being God's power for salvation for all who believe: Jew first, then Greek. In bringing good things, the gospel gives priority to Jews over gentiles. This would probably seem reasonable to Holconius. After all, the gospel was a Jewish message with a Jewish origin. However (to stray into the history of Judaism and Christianity in Rome), it might also strike him as odd because he would have known that most people who believed this message in Rome were gentile. Most Jews would have nothing to do with it. Holconius might also notice that again, despite the apparently pro-Jewish nature of 1.16, it suggested an incompleteness about traditional Judaism that required the gospel to set it right. Holconius would be rather relieved to note that 1.16 did preserve two distinct identity categories: Jew and Greek (meaning non-Jews). Although Holconius was taking on many aspects of Jewish identity (1.7), gentile and Jewish identities were not ultimately being merged.

The wrath of the gods (cf. 1.18) would be a familiar idea to Holconius. It was a common subject of Pompeian wall paintings. The House of the Menander includes the scene of the death of Actaeon, turned into a stag and torn to pieces by his dogs after spotting Diana bathing. In the House of the Cabinet-Maker itself, the Fall of Icarus represents a kind of divine wrath against hubris, while Paris's judging between the goddesses resulted in wrath and enmity from the ones he did not favour (which ultimately results in the scenes of the fall of Troy, depicted in the House of the Menander, next door). However, the representation of creation, the specific reason for divine wrath, and the specific mode of wrath would have seemed to Holconius to be very Jewish. There was just one God, who was essentially invisible and was made known through the created order (1.19–20). Although the general sin of not acknowledging God, not properly thanking and glorifying him (1.18, 21), would fit well into Graeco-Roman myths, the specific expression of the sin – construction of images to worship (1.23) – was a key virtuous act in Graeco-Roman religious practice. Similarly, although the general mode of God's wrath – transformation of the sinner in a way appropriate to the crime – was familiar from Graeco-Roman stories (such as the transformation of Narcissus and

153

others in Ovid's *Metamorphoses*), the specific transformation – to engagement in shameful behaviour – would presumably be seen by Holconius as something new to him, and Jewish. This was particularly so because the main point that Paul picked on, same-sex relationships, was a common part of Holconius's cultural reference pool, as represented in Pompeian wall-painting.

In 2.6–16, Paul explains judgement and salvation by works, for Jew first, then Greek (2.9–10). He emphasizes that God shows no favouritism between the two (2.11). The 'law' is a key basis for judgement. This is clearly the Jewish Law, because Paul describes gentiles as 'not possessing law' (2.14), a point that a Roman might have heard with a wry smile, living in a society enmeshed in laws and lawyers! However, even those without Jewish Law were subject to judgement according to some law that they inherently had as an equivalent (2.14–15).

Holconius might well have been surprised by Paul's attack on Jewish behaviour in 2.17–24. However, if he lived in Transtiberim (which he did, having the magical ability to fly from Pompeii to Rome whenever my argument needs it), there were no doubt members of every ethnic group who participated in the endemically shady life of the narrow streets, in ways that must quite often have transgressed any formal moral system. The Jewish communities in the Diaspora were doubtless no different from those in Judaea in having the usual share of criminals. However, one difference of Jews living 'among the gentiles' was that such criminality cast a slur on God's reputation (2.24). A Roman from whom a Jew stole would think badly of Jewish religion. Paul effectively brings this argument back round to the point that keeping the law is what counts, not just hearing it (2.25–26; cf. 2.13–14). However, he takes this further by internalizing the key Jewish identity marker of circumcision. He is adamant. Circumcision is not an act done to the flesh (2.28). It is done to the heart (2.29). Lawkeeping without circumcision counts as circumcision (2.26). Holconius would suspect that he was being given some kind of Jewish identity. Given his cultural disdain for Judaism, this might disturb him. However, any such Jewish identity is so radically redefined that he might be reassured that it was not, culturally, making him substantively Jewish. He would certainly be relieved that Paul was implicitly ruling out the need for physical circumcision.

It may have seemed odd to Paul's hearers that he was running down his fellow-Jews and circumcision. The corrective sentence that follows would then seem a natural move. Judaism was indeed of value – as even (Christian) gentiles would acknowledge, given that Jews were the recipients of the oracles that 'promised the gospel beforehand' (cf. 1.2). Incidentally, Holconius might be struck by how dubious a privilege this could be. The Pythia, who was the recipient of the world's most famous oracles, at Delphi, led a risky existence for the sake of being Apollo's mouthpiece.[2] Paul almost immediately switches from defending Judaism to tackling the theological problem of some Jews not believing (3.3), which leads Paul to points about God's judgement (3.4–7) and to a self-defensive exclamation (3.8). He ends up back with Jews and gentiles on a level, this time with all facing the verdict of being 'under sin' (3.9). The possibility of a verdict of innocence, implied in chapter 2, has disappeared somehow. Holconius then hears a string of sayings from scripture, backing this up (3.10–18). The conclusion (3.19–20) then expresses what Paul has been driving at: the Jewish Law forms a basis for judgement that shows Jews to be under sin and (somehow) also draws the rest of the world in under that verdict. In a final twist (like a piece of Galatians, suddenly dropped out of the sky), Paul uses this conclusion to condemn the idea that 'all flesh' could be 'justified by works of the Law'. This would, again, probably have reassured Holconius. Gentile Christians were not expected to keep the practices of Jewish Law. All in all, gentile hearers would perceive that Jewish Law was important but that it did not provide the route to salvation.

This point is reinforced by the next verse. God's righteousness was revealed, apart from the Law but testified to by the Law – drawing the Law into the idea set up in 1.2. Holconius would hear the repeated 'all's, in 3.22–23 and implicitly in 3.24, and apply them to both Jews and gentiles. Redemption (3.24) was a soteriological concept that might surprise him slightly, as he would have lacked knowledge of the scriptural history of the concept. However, it did make sense in a broader cultural framework, where salvation as a setting free from something must have been a fairly universal idea. He was more likely to know that Jesus' death was interpreted in relation to Israelite sacrifices. However, he might still be more likely to hear the specific term ἱλαστήριον (3.25) in relation to Graeco-Roman stories about sacrifices (such as that of Iphigenia) that turned away the wrath of gods (i.e. as 'propitiation') rather than as the cover of the ark of the covenant (for which the word was used in the Septuagint Greek translation of Leviticus 16). Holconius would, without doubt, rejoice at Paul's emphatic declaration that God was the God of gentiles as well as Jews and would justify both (3.29–30). Holconius would also

---

[2] Plutarch, *Moralia* 438, describes the fairly recent death of one prophetess during an oracular consultation that was wrongly conducted.

have noted that Paul had again slipped in a point about being justified without works of the Law (3.28).

Holconius would then hear this point defended at some length in chapter 4, while also coming to understand something of what Paul meant when he asserted that the gospel was testified to by scripture. Holconius would learn quite a lot about scripture, much of it very surprising to him. He discovered that scripture itself testified to justification by faith, without works (4.2–8). He learned that Abraham had, astonishingly, not been circumcised at birth (4.10). He learned that God promised Abraham that he would become the ancestor of many nations (4.18), not only Jews. He found out that scripture held a basis for even the idea of justification through faith in life from the dead, exemplified in the promise of a child to the aged Abraham and Sarah (4.19–22). Finally, Holconius discovered that scripture was written to apply to his situation, not just that of ancient people (4.24).

Romans 5—8

Holconius was very surprised by the assertion, in 5.20, that 'Law came in so that the act of disobedience might increase'. He would have expected a Jewish writer to say that the Law limited sin, rather than increased it. Similarly, Holconius was surprised that Paul wrote, 'sin will not rule you, for you are not under law but under grace' (6.14). Holconius would have expected a Jewish writer to link 'being under law' with 'sin not ruling you', rather than seeing sin's rule as being inoperative because a person is not actually under law. There was nothing in these two chapters that enabled Holconius to resolve these questions.

However, chapter 7 seemed likely to tackle them. He was again rather surprised to be addressed as someone who knew the Law (7.1), although he supposed that he had learned a reasonable amount about Jewish Law through Christian teaching. In fact, he then felt that Paul's examples in the passage could be drawn from law in general, rather than specifically Jewish Law. Death ends the control of law (7.1). A woman does not commit adultery if she sleeps with another man after her husband has died (7.2–3). However, this broke down when Paul applied it to his hearers' situation in 7.4. Holconius now became really confused. Paul described his hearers as having 'died to the Law through the body of Christ'. At the beginning of the letter, Paul had addressed his hearers as gentiles. In what sense had they ever belonged to the Law and had now died to it through Christ? Unless Paul was suddenly addressing only Jewish Christians – which seemed unlikely – the only solution that would present itself to a gentile such as Holconius seems likely to relate to the universal role of the Law in 3.19–20, which may also be suggested in 2.14–15. Although the Law speaks to those 'in the Law' (3.19), presumably Jews, this somehow results in 'the whole world' being 'accountable to God' (3.19). In some sense, maybe the Law had a kind of hold over the whole world, even though it was only heard by the Jews.

Near the end of 7.4, Paul switches from the second-person plural to the first-person plural. However, the links between 'we shall bear fruit' and the rest of the verse, and between v. 5 and v. 4, are so strong that Holconius would probably hear Paul's 'we' as encompassing him and his hearers (and maybe all Christians), rather than as distinguishing between, say, 'we' Jewish Christians and 'you' gentile Christians. However, this ex-acerbated Holconius's confusion because Paul now wrote of 'the sinful passions that the Law produced in the parts of our bodies' (7.5). Since Holconius had been unaware of Jewish Law before he was a Christian, how could it have been at work in his members? Maybe it was at work in the secondary sense of 2.14–15: in being 'a law for themselves' (2.14), with the law evidently 'written on their hearts' (2.15), they had been subject to the same negative effects that Paul evidently (and surprisingly) saw Jews as having been subject to. Holconius might also again try con-sidering whether Paul could be talking about law in general. However, a craftworker's experience of Roman law would be mainly as dealing with issues such as enforcement of contracts, rather than as a holistic body of moral instructions that could be seen as inflaming passions and so on (although he might toy with the idea that some subtleties of Roman divorce law or inheritance law could incite someone to sexual immor-ality for pecuniary gain).[3] Whatever the logic of Paul's apparent linking of the pre-Christian Holconius to the Jewish Law, Holconius would be relieved by Paul's restatement, in 7.6, of the idea that Holconius was now free of the link to this force that had somehow bound him.

It also came as something of a relief to Holconius that, in 7.7, Paul started writing in more of a way that Holconius expected of a Jewish writer. Having presented the Law in a surprisingly negative way, Paul now starts defending it. 'Is the Law sin? Certainly not!' (7.7). Holconius could understand the next point, that the Law enabled Paul to know what sin was (7.7). The example he then used was also comprehensible, although

---

[3] As has been suggested for the case of incest in 1 Corinthians 5 by John K. Chow, *Patronage and Power: A Study of Social Networks in Corinth* (JSNTSup 75; Sheffield: Sheffield Academic Press, 1992), pp. 130–40.

surprising. Holconius could even see how it would work for gentiles, as a 'law for themselves'. He could sort of see how when, as a child, he came to realize that coveting what other people had might be wrong (7.7–8), that this might have led him to do it all the more. He was not sure in what sense that meant he (or even Paul) 'died' (7.10), although it could be the kind of metaphor that some philosophers might use.[4] The description that follows, of tension between right desires and wrong actions (7.14–25), might well seem the kind of thing that Holconius would see philosophers as talking about. Although he would not have had a philosophical education, his education may well have taken him to a level where he would have heard, and possibly memorized, some maxims of somewhat philosophical writers such as Cicero. He may also have heard itinerant philosophers in the Forum. Holconius would probably see this tension as a dilemma that all people faced (again seeing this as an instance where God's law came to the gentiles who were 'a law for themselves'). Paul saw Christ as freeing Holconius from that dilemma.

Holconius differed from Iris in his hearing of the chapter. He took the tension to be a general human one. She took it as being particularly relevant to her situation. For him, being a Christian provided a resolution to the problem. For her, being a Christian made the tension more acute. One way of reading chapter 7 that would have been very unlikely for Holconius is to see Paul as recounting some sort of history of Israel. Holconius would not have the cultural reference points to identify such a subtle presentation of this. Of course, he could have viewed Paul's discussion as autobiographical, given the use of the first-person singular from v. 7 onwards. However, vv. 1–6 had already drawn Holconius into seeing himself in relation to the issue of law, so he would seem likely to continue to see Paul's rhetoric as having a general applicability, as it continued to deal with law from v. 7 to the end of the chapter.

There are rather a lot of 'laws' in 7.25—8.4. 'Law of God' in 7.25 is fairly clear. Since Paul so emphatically declared the Law not to be sin in 7.7, it seems unlikely that a gentile craftworker would take 'law of sin' in 7.25 to refer to Jewish Law. The sense of the terms would appear too subtle. Instead, Holconius would probably take the phrase to refer to some ruling force of sin. The same would then probably be true of 'the law of the spirit of life' and 'the law of sin and death' in 8.2. In 8.3, the unqualified term, 'the law', and the point about inability and flesh, would

---

[4] Cf. Emma Wasserman, *The Death of the Soul in Romans 7: Sin, Death and the Law in Light of Hellenistic Moral Psychology* (WUNT 2.256; Tübingen: Mohr Siebeck, 2008).

seem likely to take even a gentile back to thinking about Jewish Law. The explanation here would probably seem to a gentile Christian to be a rather natural piece of Jewish Christian rhetoric: it was not the Law that was bad; it was that our flesh weakened its capabilities so far that God had to intervene through Christ. Verse 4 accorded with Holconius's experience. Even though gentile Christians had not adopted Jewish Law as such, their Spirit-filled life involved behaviour that was far closer to the ethical ideals of Jewish Law than it was to the typical patterns of their previous gentile behaviour.

Romans 9—11

The change of topic at the beginning of chapter 9 initially came as a surprise to Holconius. However, once he had grasped what Paul was going to talk about, it again seemed a natural topic for Jewish Christian rhetoric. Here they were, facing a situation where most Jews had rejected the message of the Jewish Christians, who had ended up as a minority in an essentially Jewish religious movement that was now numerically dominated, in Rome and many other cities, by gentiles. Jewish rejection was bound to cause anguish for Jewish Christians. Paul expressed that anguish with his usual eloquence.

Holconius noticed that Paul ascribed to the Jews various characteristics that he had also ascribed to Christians, particularly 'adoption' (9.4). Holconius recognized the theological problem about the success or otherwise of God's word (9.6). However, Holconius was unclear about the distinctions that Paul started drawing between 'Israel' and 'those of Israel' (9.6), and between Abraham's 'seed' and his 'children'. As with chapter 4, Holconius learned some surprising facts about scripture. It was also unexpected when gentiles came into the equation in 9.24. They were then featured in a couple of verses before Paul reverted to the key concern of the chapter by citing prophecies about Israel being reduced to a remnant (9.27–29). Paul then put Jewish failure to 'attain the Law' down to pursuing it 'as if by works' (9.32). 'Works' were being seen by Paul as a problem for Jews, rather than just something that gentile Christians should avoid. From 10.4, Holconius gathered that the ending of the Law's role as a route to righteousness was not just an individual matter, as one might have inferred from 7.1–7, in which the Law's role ended as each person died to it. Instead, Christ's arrival put a definitive end to this role for the Law, whether for gentiles or Jews. The new righteousness was through faith in Christ (10.5–11) and, in that new righteousness, there was no difference between Jew and Greek (10.12).

A new note entered at 10.19. Gentiles such as Holconius were pro-phesied by Moses as making Jews jealous, as enraging them. Holconius had experience of the latter but maybe not in the sense that Paul in-tended. In 10.21, the situation of the Jewish Christians is prophesied in terms of God's action: holding out his hands to a disobedient people. The idea of the remnant recurs in chapter 11. Paul himself is a member of this (11.1). A further scriptural quotation supports it (11.2–5). Paul yet again brings the issue of 'works' into his discourse (11.6). He then portrays other Jews as having been 'hardened' by God (11.7–10). Holconius would prob-ably think he knew where this argument was going: the remnant would be saved, the others damned. But now the argument twists sharply. The other Jews have not 'stumbled so as to fall' (11.11). They have 'transgressed' in a way that brings salvation to the gentiles. This, in turn, will make the other Jews jealous (11.11). Paul looks forward to their full inclusion (11.12). As Holconius is still coming to terms with this, Paul turns and directly addresses him and the other gentiles: 'I say to you gentiles' (11.13). Even his talking about his ministry to them is intended to make his fellow-Jews jealous and thus save some of them (11.14). (Holconius might wonder about how the 'some' here relates to the apparently complete group mentioned elsewhere.) Holconius then hears gentile Christians likened to a wild olive, grafted onto a Jewish root stock, after some natural branches have been removed (11.17). He is urged not to boast over the non-Christian Jews who have been removed from the olive tree (11.18). He should not be proud, but fearful, because ingrafted branches can easily be removed and natural ones reattached if the non-Christian Jews do not persist in their lack of faith (11.19–24). In fact, the partial hardening of Israel will only last until the full number of gentiles have entered (entered Israel, in some sense?) and, in this way, 'all Israel will be saved' (11.25–26). Although, 'in relation to the gospel', non-Christian Jews are 'enemies' on account of Holconius and the other gentile Christians, 'in relation to election' they are 'beloved on account of the ancestors' (11.28). Jewish disobedience was for the sake of mercy to the gentiles, so that Jews too would receive mercy (11.31). Finally, and most comprehensively of all, 'God bound everyone into disobedience so that he would have mercy on everyone' (11.32).

This all made Holconius reconceptualize the world around him in Transtiberim. He had thought of his gentile house church as a bright light (hidden from view by the workshop shutters) in a dark, largely irredeemable society, Jew and gentile, from which a few people escaped into the light. Paul called him, instead, to see the Jews around him as still part of God's redemptive future, and to see every single person as, in some sense, an intended object of God's mercy.

Romans 12—15

Paul then turned to direct instruction to the community. Holconius noticed that Paul did not generally present this as being instruction from the precepts of Jewish Law (12.1–18). Instead, Paul viewed his commission to the gentiles as authority to instruct them (12.3). Scripture was eventually cited to back up, and expand upon, an instruction not to take revenge (12.17–21). The instruction about obedience to authorities clearly had some theological basis (13.1–2, 4–6) but no scripture was cited in support. In fact, when the Jewish Law was cited, it was used in the opposite way from what Holconius might have expected. 'Do not commit adultery' and so on (13.9) were not quoted as instructions to Christians. They were quoted as examples of the way in which Christian behaviour, based on love, fulfilled such commands anyway (13.8–10). Holconius heard Christian eschatology, which he knew to be a form of Jewish eschatology, in 13.11–12. Unlike Graeco-Roman ideas of cycles of history, golden ages and so on, Jews saw time as heading towards the judgement and salvation of God.

When Paul began discussing those who were 'weak in the faith' (14.1), Holconius initially thought about people at the fringes of the house churches: people whose commitment was not clear and whose behaviour sometimes fell short of group norms. He was very surprised when Paul began unpacking the 'weakness' in terms of vegetarianism (14.2). Holconius knew of some philosophical or religious groups that were vegetarian, such as Pythagoreans,[5] but none of them belonged to any house churches that he knew of. Paul's next example was 'considering one day more significant than another' (14.5). Holconius presumed that this was to do with either Graeco-Roman religious festivals or the Jewish sabbath. Neither could easily be ruled out. Everyone in the churches was faced with the issue of whether to act in special ways on days that society in Rome generally treated as special, such as Saturnalia, when slaves and owners exchanged roles, or the festival of the spirits of the dead, when various rituals were performed to placate them, or the emperor's birthday, when celebrations happened publicly and in many households.[6] Every Christian at least had to go along with giving slaves holidays on

---

[5] Mary Beard, John North and Simon Price, *Religions of Rome. Volume I: A History* (Cambridge: Cambridge University Press, 1998), p. 229.
[6] Beard, North and Price, *Religions of Rome*, pp. 50, 207, 325.

the expected days. What further they might do was probably the subject of disagreement from fairly early on. It is certainly a key concern for Tertullian, at the end of the second century.[7] The Jewish sabbath was also a potentially controversial issue for early house churches. Writing at the same time as Paul, Seneca sees its observance as the most visible indicator of Jewish culture, especially in the lighting of lamps.[8] Jewish Christians would presumably continue observing the sabbath. As can be seen from Seneca's disdain, there would be high cultural barriers to a gentile such as Holconius taking on the practice. It meant identifying oneself, culturally, with Jews. Many gentile Christians were probably reluctant to do this.

By the time he heard 14.13, Holconius would understand that, whatever practices Paul was referring to, he expected Christians to accept each other without criticizing the diversity of how they acted. In 14.14–15, Paul's language about what was or was not κοινόν, 'common' with a probable implication of 'defiled', especially in relation to food, would seem likely to make Holconius think he was referring to Jewish food laws. This would retrospectively make some sense of the issues that Paul had discussed earlier. Even limiting oneself to vegetables could be a strategy for a Jew to avoid eating defiled food in a gentile environment.[9] Paul was now going beyond the issue of not judging each other to arguing that Christians ought to accommodate their behaviour to each other's beliefs about food, and so on (14.13–21). As a gentile Christian, this might rather annoy Holconius. It was clear from earlier in the letter that Paul did not expect gentiles to take on the practice of the Jewish Law. However, now he was expecting them to adapt their eating habits to the scruples of any Law-observant Jewish Christians with whom they came into contact. This might not be much of an issue in the all-gentile house church that we are imagining for Holconius, but he might still worry that the presence of Law-observant Jews in some house churches could mean that Paul's prescription would lead to house-church life taking on an increasingly Jewish nature. Holconius's conclusion that the key issues were about relations between gentiles and Jews was confirmed by Paul ending the section with a call to mutual acceptance that was all about Jews and gentiles (15.7–12).

---

[7] For discussion of this and related issues see Tertullian, *De corona*.

[8] Seneca, *Letters* 95.

[9] As classically represented in Daniel 1.

As the final section of the letter was read aloud, Holconius first heard a validation of the identity and abilities of the gentile addressees (15.14). Then he heard the nature of gentile Christians described in terms of actions in a temple. Using a pattern that related slightly more closely to Graeco-Roman religious practice than to Jewish practice, Paul says he has been appointed to exercise a λειτουργία, a 'ministry', in which he has become a priest who is carrying the gentiles to God as a sacred offering (15.15–16). Although much of this could fit Jewish practice, their priesthood was hereditary rather than an office to which someone was appointed. Paul then talks of his evangelistic ministry bringing about the 'obedience of the gentiles' (15.17–21). He also talks about the collection for Jerusalem and argues that the way in which the 'spiritual things' of the 'holy ones in Jerusalem' have been shared by the gentiles lays an obligation on the gentiles to reciprocate materially (15.27). Any economic concerns that Holconius might have had about this obligation would have been softened by the fact that Paul was not expecting the Roman Christians actually to contribute to the collection.

The creation of a holy people

Finally, we will consider how Paul's ideas of salvation in Romans would appear to Holconius as house-church host, concerned to understand the nature of the group that is meeting in his workshop.

One of the key ideas that Paul presents about the group is that they are 'holy'. For most Westerners, this is a problematic concept. We tend not to use anything like 'sacredness' as a basis for categorizing the people or objects we encounter. The way in which particular religious groups relate persons or objects to the divine is not viewed by most other people as according an objective sacredness to the persons or objects. Even among Christians, many are reluctant to accord any religious special-ness to things or people. In common parlance, the term 'holy' is most commonly heard in expressions such as 'holier than thou', denoting an attitude of (usually unjustified) self-righteousness, coupled with a lack of love and understanding towards others.

In Paul's world, as in much of the non-Western world today, the concept of the sacred was a very strong one. All sorts of people, objects and places were regarded by various groups as sacred. In a generally polytheistic world, there was considerable overlap between groups as to what was considered sacred. It was not only the particular devotees of Isis who would have regarded a temple of hers as being sacred. The population as a whole would have ascribed some sacredness to it.

Paul calls his addressees ἅγιοι, 'holy ones' (1.7; 8.27; 16.2, 15; cf. 12.13; 15.25, 26, 31). As I have argued elsewhere, Paul uses this term here in accordance with a bipolar model of holiness: a world divided between a sphere of the holy and the broader realm of the ordinary, outside that sphere. Such a bipolar model implies that holiness can be indicated either as closeness to the divine (the archetypally holy) or separation from the ordinary. Gentile Christians gain the status of holiness (in this sense) at conversion (Rom. 15.13–19; cf. 1 Cor. 1.2; 6.11).[10] Paul can also use holiness language in other senses (e.g. Rom. 6.19, 22; 1 Thess. 5.23). In entitling this section 'The creation of a holy people', I am focusing on the religious specialness of the group identity that Paul presents for his addressees, an identity which puts them close to the divine and distinct from the ordinary. Holconius reflects on Paul's presentation of salvation as the creation of such a group, instantiated in the house church of which Holconius is the host.

The house-church members in the cabinet-maker's workshop are 'called by Jesus Christ',[11] 'loved by God', 'called as holy ones' (Rom. 1.6–7). Calling is both a drawing out from the realm of the ordinary and a drawing towards Christ who calls. Love from God means a close connection with him. Holiness means being part of the sphere of specialness in close proximity to the divine. Holconius would probably find this marvellous but quite difficult to get his head around, given the people it was supposed to apply to. Religiously special groups in Rome tended to be more obvious than this: emperors and their families; groups of priests; the Vestal Virgins. Instead, this was a ragbag of craftworkers, slaves, men, women, children, young, old, modestly well off, destitute. It included Holconius himself, who would be aware that even he was far from having the dignity and distinction associated with most of Rome's sacred people. He would also be aware that neither he nor the others in the house church followed the radically set-apart lives of those such as the Vestal Virgins, or of other sacred people of lower social status, such as slave girls who were full-time oracles. The lives of the house-church members seemed too ordinary to be special.

---

[10] Peter Oakes, 'Made Holy by the Holy Spirit: Holiness and Ecclesiology in Romans', in Kent E. Brower and Andy Johnson (eds), *Holiness and Ecclesiology in the New Testament* (Grand Rapids: Eerdmans, 2007), pp. 167–70.

[11] Peter Stuhlmacher, *Paul's Letter to the Romans: A Commentary*, tr. S. J. Hafemann (Edinburgh: T. & T. Clark, 1994), p. 18. See Oakes, 'Made Holy by the Holy Spirit', p. 172, n. 9.

This introductory characterization of the addressees leads into a letter which gives a multi-faceted depiction of the new people that God has brought into existence through the gospel. That depiction is staggering. To give an overall sense of the depiction we will draw together some elements of it, before considering how it might sound to a house-church host such as Holconius.

Jesus is the beginning of a new family of God. He is the first-born among many brothers and sisters (8.29). This creates a new people. Paul describes the identity of this new people in various ways. Philip Esler argues that the social identity of a group is represented in the whole trajectory of the group through time: the narrative of the past, the description of the present, and the prospect of the future. All contribute to the group's current identity.[12] Esler's approach helps us to be aware of the relevance to group identity of a much wider range of material in Romans than scholars have generally drawn on. In order to bring out the past, present and future dimensions of some key material, Table 6.1 uses these dimensions to set out material in the letter that is particularly relevant to the identity of the group that is created by the salvation described in Romans.

Holconius ought to have been staggered. If someone such as Holconius had been asked to picture a group of people answering to the description that Paul gives in Romans, the picture would not look like that group in the workshop, including his own slaves and children, the pair of stoneworkers who were scrabbling for subsistence, and the rather dubious serving girl from the bar down the street. Surely the Spirit-filled children of God ought to be a carefully selected group living a contemplative life in a temple on an island somewhere? Paul said that the Christians were indeed carefully chosen – but they turned out to be this lot!

If Holconius considered first the past events that were supposed to have happened to the group, various points might strike him. The key one was that all of these were supposed to have happened to all of them. They had all been baptized, so they were all taken to have died with Christ and gained new life with him. This brought in other concepts such as being justified and redeemed. All this had happened to each person. This was hard for Holconius to grasp. In Graeco-Roman society, the status of the members of his family depended on what happened to him. If, after receiving an

---

[12] Philip F. Esler, *Conflict and Identity in Romans: The Social Setting of Paul's Letter* (Minneapolis: Fortress, 2003), pp. 22–4, 252–67, citing the work of Susan Condor, 'Social Identity and Time', in P. Robinson (ed.), *Social Groups and Identities: Developing the Legacy of Henri Tajfel* (Oxford: Butterworth Heinemann, 1996), pp. 285–315.

Table 6.1 Characteristics of the Christian group according to Romans, roughly categorized as past, present or future

Past	Present	Future
Called by Jesus Christ (1.6)		
	Beloved by God (1.7; 9.25)	
	Called as holy ones (1.7; 16.2, 15)	
	Objects of the righteousness of God (3.22)	
Freely justified (3.24; 5.1, 9, 17–19)		
Redeemed (3.24)		
Forgiven (4.7)		
	Children of Abraham (4.11, 17)	
	At peace with God (5.1, 10, 11)	
	Having been given access to a current state of grace (5.2)	
		With hope of the glory of God (5.2)
	Suffering (5.3; 8.17–18; 12.12)	
With the love of God poured into their hearts through the Holy Spirit given to them (5.5)		
		Heading for salvation from God's wrath (5.9; cf. 10.9–10, 13)
		Will reign 'in life' (5.17)
'The many' made righteous (5.19)		
	Still needing to make moral decisions about sin and new life (6.1–23)	

Table 6.1 (*cont'd*)

Past	Present	Future
Having died to sin (6.2, 6–7, 11)		
Having, in baptism, shared in Christ's death (6.3–5, 8)		
		Will share in Christ's resurrection (6.5) and live with him (6.8)
Freed from sin's rule, enslaved to righteousness and God (6.14, 17–18, 22; cf. 7.6)		
	Still with 'weakness of flesh' (6.19)	
	Having 'fruit producing sanctification' (6.22)	
		Heading for eternal life (6.22–23; cf. 5.21)
Having died to the Law (7.4)		
	Belonging to Christ (7.4; 8.9; 14.8)	
No longer 'in flesh' (7.5; 8.9; cf. 6.19?)		
	Serving 'in newness of Spirit' (7.5)	
	Uncondemned people in Christ (8.1)	
Freed from the 'law of sin and death' (8.2)		
	Living according to the Spirit, not the flesh (8.4)	
	Fulfilling 'the righteous requirement of the Law' (8.4)	
	With a mind of life and peace (8.6)	

Table 6.1 (*cont'd*)

Past	Present	Future
	In the Spirit/with the Spirit of God living in them/having the spirit of Christ (8.9, 11)	
	With Christ in them (8.10)	
	With the body being dead but the Spirit being life and with life promised to mortal bodies (8.11)	
	Led by the Spirit (8.14)	
	Sons (and daughters) of God (8.14–17, 19; 9.26)	
Adopted by God (8.15)		
	Crying out to God as father, by means of the Spirit (8.15–16)	
		Fellow-heirs with Christ (8.17)
	Suffering with Christ (8.17)	
		If so, heading for glory with Christ (8.17, 18)
		A people to be revealed ultimately to all . . .
	. . . an event eagerly awaited by all creation (8.19)	
		Creation's own redemption will be a sharing in theirs (8.21)
	Having the first-fruits of the Spirit (8.23)	
	Still groaning, awaiting . . .	
		. . . adoption (cf. 8.15?), the redemption of bodies (8.23)

Table 6.1 (*cont'd*)

Past	Present	Future
	Waiting, with endurance, for an unseen hope (8.25)	
	Not knowing how to pray (8.26)	
	But with the Spirit helping, interceding with inexpressible groans (8.26–27)	
	Those who love God (8.28)	
	People for whom all things work together for good (8.28)	
Foreknown, predestined, called, justified, glorified (8.28–30)		
Predestined to be like Christ (8.29)		
	Brothers and sisters of Christ in the family initiated by him (8.29)	
	With God for them (8.31)	
		Due to be given all things with Christ (8.32)
Chosen by God (8.33)		
	Not subject to accusation or condemnation (8.33–34)	
	With Christ interceding for them at the right hand of God (8.34)	
	Facing suffering, persecution and death (8.35–36)	

Table 6.1 (*cont'd*)

Past	Present	Future
		But unable to be separated from Christ's love (8.35–39)
		'Vessels of mercy', prepared beforehand for glory (9.23)
Called from among Jews and gentiles (9.24)		
	God's people, even those who previously were not (9.25–26)	
Having attained righteousness by faith (9.30)		
Having believed in their heart and acknowledged the Lord Jesus verbally (10.9)		
	Saved to make Israel jealous (11.11)	
Grafted onto the root, Israel (11.17–18)		
	In danger of being cut off if they do not remain in God's kindness (11.22)	
	If transformed, will be able to discern God's will (12.2)	
	One body in Christ (12.4)	
	Equipped with diverse gifts (12.4–8)	
	Members of one another (12.5)	
	Facing various moral imperatives, to love etc. (12.9—15.7)	

Table 6.1 (*cont'd*)

Past	Present	Future
	To be obedient citizens (13.1–7) Fulfilling the Law through love (13.8–10)	
		With a final salvation about to arrive (13.11–12)
	With a need to 'put on' the Lord Jesus Christ (13.14) Including both 'weak' and 'strong' (14.1) Accepted by God in their diversity (14.3) Enabled to stand (14.4)	
		Belonging to Christ, whether alive or dead (14.8)
	Not to judge each other (14.10)	
		Will all stand before God's judgement seat (14.10)
	In danger of destroying each other (14.15, 20) Part of God's kingdom of righteousness, peace and joy in the Holy Spirit (14.17)	
		Gentiles will praise with God's own people (15.10)
	Full of goodness and knowledge (15.14)	
		An offering to be made to God by Paul (15.16)
Made holy by means of the Holy Spirit (15.16)		

unexpected vast legacy, he were elected as a magistrate, the status of his family – especially his wife and children – would rise dramatically. It was not necessary for each of them to be elected as magistrate. It just had to happen to him. In the Christian group, all were justified and made children of God. The status of each person depended on what had happened to him or to her, not to anyone else on their behalf. This was a very radical idea.

Moreover, the same things had happened to all of them. There wasn't a first-class divine sonship given to him and a third-class one given to the slave who cleaned out the latrine. Even in an association that allowed in members of a range of statuses, the best honours would be kept for the wealthier members. This was inherent in the system because such honours tended to depend on making donations to defray the costs of the association.[12] Holconius might well also think that some of the things that had happened to all were rather risky to apply to some people. The idea that Christian slaves had been 'redeemed' – set free – was an obvious case in point. Would they think that they were less under the authority of their owners? More generally, the idea that slaves could be 'justified' might be worrying. Slaves were frequently stereotyped in Graeco-Roman culture, such as popular theatre, as being inherently unreliable and prone to theft. The viewing of them as permanently guilty could well have legitimated a range of oppressive controls. Viewing them instead as justified and forgiven could disrupt Holconius's normal basis for handling them.

The point goes further still. Both Paul's language of justification and his rhetoric of moral choice construct the hearers as being in good moral standing with God and as being morally responsible. To varying degrees, Holconius, his peers and his social superiors would have denied these qualities not only to slaves but to children, women and the poor in general. Children were subject to harsh control. Women were often stereotyped as flighty and irresponsible.[13] The attitude to the poor can be seen in legislation that gave preference to the testimony of the wealthy, as the poor could not be trusted because their poverty made them open to bribery.[14]

---

[12] Richard S. Ascough, *Paul's Macedonian Associations* (WUNT 2.161; Tübingen: Mohr Siebeck, 2003), pp. 61–3.

[13] For a discussion of this in relation to legal issues see Suzanne Dixon, 'Womanly Weakness in Roman Law', in Suzanne Dixon, *Reading Roman Women: Sources, Genres and Real Life* (London: Duckworth, 2001), pp. 73–88.

[14] Peter Garnsey, *Social Status and Legal Privilege in the Roman Empire* (Oxford: Clarendon Press, 1970), pp. 211–12.

In terms of the group's present existence, Holconius would note the combination of high privileges and present struggle. Again, it is significant that the combination happens to everyone. That might seem a truism but it actually cuts across the general shape of experience in society. In the first century, the privileges went to those of high status and, although everyone suffered to some extent, suffering was much greater among the poor. Primus sweated away stoking the heater, getting the occasional burn and getting beaten if the overseer thought that more work could be got out of him that way. Primus's owner enjoyed the bath.

All were holy. This was a group in which each should have considerable self-respect. Conversely, this status carried expectations about behaviour. Each person was both valuable and responsible. The actions expected of these holy people were not the performance of elaborate ceremonies, as the Graeco-Roman priests would do on festival days. The duties commensurate with holiness were those of day-to-day love, of building up the life of the community.

The community had helpers too. The indwelling Spirit led each person, provided the means to pray and brought an awareness that the person was a child of God. Jesus, having provided the basis for renewed existence, now sat with God in authority, and used that position to make requests on behalf of his people. God himself was on their side. Holconius was used to the self-sufficiency of a craftworking family in a society where external help was scarce and unreliable. Here was the promise of substantive help for the group from beings with unlimited resources.

Finally, Holconius looked at the group's future, as presented by Paul. The most striking promise was that of 'reigning in life' (5.17). No one in the house church except for the handful of householders had ever exercised any authority at all. Even he and the other householders were immeasurably far from anything that could be described as 'reigning'. The emperor ruled. Under him, Holconius would see the Senate as also ruling, to quite an extent. He would presumably envisage Paul's promise of Christians ruling corporately as something like the Senate. To put the house-church members in such a situation violated the expectations of birth, wealth, gender and servitude. It went beyond ascribing moral responsibility to slaves and others. It ascribed to them the capacity to govern. One wonders if Holconius might see the seed of such capacity developing in the unexpected rulers-to-be in the house church, as God distributed gifts for the operation of the house church (12.5–8).

The people in the house church were children of God, to be revealed to the world (8.18). Holconius must have been tempted to feel ashamed of the group who met in his workshop. He was welcoming some people whom his peers would have expected him not to associate with, especially eat with. If Holconius followed something like Paul's instructions in Romans 12, he was interacting with them in ways that strongly contravened social norms. He may often have been glad if the workshop shutters generally kept the poorer people in the church out of sight of passers-by. Yet these people, of whom it was easy for Holconius to be ashamed, were to be revealed to the world in a blaze of glory. Not only that, but this revealing would bring redemption to the universe (8.19–21). The glory of the group was beyond comprehension.

A socially diverse church today is a sharp challenge to our social expectations and typical behaviour. C. S. Lewis's Screwtape advised a more junior devil to attack a new Christian convert by getting him to look around at the other people in church and compare them with New Testament rhetoric about the high nature and destiny of the Church.[15] If Paul's ideas of salvation have force, they give a holy identity to every church member. There is no scope for Holconius, or for us, to be ashamed of associating with fellow-Christians, however much they differ from us.

---

[15] C. S. Lewis, *The Screwtape Letters* (London: Fontana Books, 1955), pp. 15–16.

7

Reading Romans in view of first-century social diversity

The reader will have to decide whether our various exercises in seeking to hear Romans in relation to a diverse first-century audience have yielded results of interest and value. In any case, these exercises are clearly very basic and approximate. I am particularly aware that, in touching lightly on a wide range of scholarly issues, I have repeatedly entered areas that others could have dealt with far more effectively. However, it seemed important to put all these points together, even though my handling of them could undoubtedly be improved on.

Some readers may fear that our method turns the text into a mirror, simply reflecting whatever colour light is shone on it. We look in the text for justice and find it. We look for survival and find it. If we looked for coffee-advertising, maybe we would find that too (13.11: 'the time has come for you to wake up from sleep'?). In fact, what happened in the research process is that Romans was investigated in relation to a number of social types. Complex, overlapping sets of results were produced, many of them relatively insignificant: for instance, where one isolated verse happened to address an issue relevant to one of the types. What are presented above are results that looked sufficiently substantive to be worth considering seriously. Also, the overlaps between the results for the various social types have been removed, to leave an analysis that is simplified so as to make its case clearly. Readers may also wish to consider what would happen if we looked at other Pauline texts in relation to our four social types. It is clear that each of the readings would be very different from those based on Romans. There would be some common motifs, such as life after death, but even those would recur in rather different forms.

When I was working on Romans 12, I had expected to be constantly interacting with commentators' alternative views of what Paul's various specific instructions might mean in practice in a first-century context. I was repeatedly surprised by how little attention they tended to give this. Commentators preferred to consider the structure of the passage, possible sources or literary parallels. These topics are important, especially the question of the extent to which the sayings of Jesus are a source.[1] However, I was surprised that they consistently found these matters more important than elucidating what these practical instructions meant. For instance, commentators were more interested in exploring which biblical texts Paul was citing in his instructions about revenge than in exploring what, in a first-century context, not taking revenge involved. Where commentators did make a practical comment on the chapter, it was generally to suggest a link to the tensions of chapters 14—15 but, even then, there was rarely any serious engagement with how, in practice, these particular instructions would contribute to the easing of those tensions. Whatever the merits of our particular reading of Romans 12, a general point is that, if the content of a text is practical instruction, surely the primary task of the commentator is to investigate what the instructions would have meant in practice? This could be done in many ways other than our use of a model house church, but it does require study that relates the text to a fairly detailed examination of its socio-cultural context.

A second surprise was the way in which an attempt to read Romans from the viewpoint of a first-century slave demanded that God's judgement should be seen as part of the gospel. This reversed many years of my own reading of Romans, in which the news of God's wrath and justice in 1.18—3.20 was simply seen as setting up the need for the redemption of 3.21 onwards. Of course, redemption is still needed, because Paul catches even Primus in his net: 'all have sinned' (3.23). However, 1.18—3.20 also carries a positive message of its own, which is summed up in 2.16, 'on the day when God will judge the secret things of people, in accordance with my gospel, through Christ Jesus'.

Commentators are rather shy of discussing what it means for this judgement to be part of Paul's gospel. A link between the gospel and judgement must be there, however we see the parts of the sentence as fitting together. Dunn is probably incorrect in seeing the verse as asserting that Paul's gospel is the criterion for judgement.[2] Other uses of κατά with εὐαγγέλιον (Rom. 11.28; 16.25; 1 Tim. 1.11; 2 Tim. 2.8) suggest that the NRSV is more likely to be correct in rendering the verse as, 'on the day when, according to my gospel, God, through Jesus Christ, will judge the secret thoughts of all'. Jewett objects that, 'since it was widely believed that God judges secretive thoughts and behaviour, this could not be

---

[1] On which, see especially Michael B. Thompson, *Clothed with Christ: The Example and Teaching of Jesus in Romans 12.1—15.13* (JSNTSup 59; Sheffield: Sheffield Academic Press, 1991).

[2] James D. G. Dunn, *Romans 1—8* (Dallas: Word, 1988), p. 103.

presented as a distinctive aspect of Paul's gospel'.[3] However, there is no need for 'my gospel' to imply that this was distinctive to Paul. When 2 Timothy 2.8 says, 'Remember Jesus Christ, raised from the dead, of the seed of David, according to my gospel', it is not asserting that the author was the only person to teach this. In Romans Paul emphasizes that he brings the gospel to gentiles. The news that God was just and would judge the world, setting it to rights, was a wonderful Jewish message to the gentiles, now seen by Paul as being put into action through Jesus Christ.

One scholar who does emphasize the good news of such justice is N. T. Wright. He discusses translation of the phrase δικαιοσύνη θεοῦ ('righteousness of God') and stresses the importance of 'justice' as a key element of a good translation:

> The word 'justice' itself evokes that element of what Paul, and the texts on which he drew, was talking about which is all too often forgotten today, namely that because God is the creator he has the obligation to put the world to rights once and for all[. . .][4]

He sees this in relation to covenant faithfulness[5] and in contrast to the Augustan imperial ideology of justice, *iustitia*.[6] He compares Romans 2.16 to Paul's proclamation of God's justice in the Acts 17 account of his Areopagus speech.[7] The possible relationship to Augustan *iustitia* language is hard to gauge. However, a point in favour is that *iustitia* is a term that was very central to Roman imperial ideology, unlike terms such as παρουσία (arrival), for which similar arguments have been made.[8] In any case, Wright's argument about Paul's Jewish message of God's justice is surely an important corrective to scholarship that has consistently under-played this theme.

Another surprise was that Romans appeared to speak so eloquently to the situation of someone whose life was characterized by tension related to bodily experience. This made the text particularly relevant to the situation of Iris, the slave barmaid. Romans clearly does not engage the situation of a sexually exploited slave specifically enough for us to infer

---

[3] Robert Jewett, *Romans: A Commentary* (Hermeneia; Minneapolis: Fortress, 2007), p. 218.

[4] N. T. Wright, *Paul: Fresh Perspectives* (London: SPCK, 2005), pp. 25–6.

[5] Wright, *Paul*, p. 25.

[6] Wright, *Paul*, pp. 63, 77.

[7] Wright, *Paul*, p. 105.

[8] Peter Oakes, 'Re-mapping the Universe: Paul and the Emperor in 1 Thessalonians and Philippians', *JSNT* 27 (2005), pp. 316–17, responding to J. R. Harrison, 'Paul and the Imperial Gospel at Thessaloniki', *JSNT* 25 (2002), pp. 82–92.

directly from the text whether such people were or were not among the expected hearers. However, the prevalence of such exploitation of slaves and the almost certain inclusion of slaves among the expected hearers does indirectly suggest that Paul would be expecting such hearers. Oddly, a possible effect of this could be to turn what might be perceived as a weakness in the letter – the somewhat irreducible complexity of its teaching about bodies – into a kind of strength. The combination of a complex picture of present existence with a promise of final resolution of tension could be seen as creating the kind of conceptual space that someone such as Iris might be able to inhabit. There is also a broader methodological point here. Slave women were certainly part of early Christian groups. Slave women were typically sexually exploited. It is therefore an important exegetical enterprise to ask how NT texts would have sounded to such people – as also to various other social types. Scholars cannot avoid this task simply on the grounds that the texts do not mention such people. An author's likely expectation that the text would be received by such people is part of the nature of the text in its context.

A fourth surprise was how interesting an exercise it was to attempt to read the Jewish material in Romans from the viewpoint of a first-century gentile who had no great interest in Judaism and was rather embarrassed by the fact that Christian life has a Jewish basis. It is a very common view in scholarship that the amount of Jewish material in Romans implies that the addressees must be interested in, and knowledgeable about, Judaism. The only reason I tried out the opposite scenario was because that was all the Pompeian material gave me: ordinary gentiles with Graeco-Roman cultural reference points. But it seemed to work. Wiefel's argument that Paul's building up of Israel in Romans 11 seems aimed at anti-Jewish gentiles looks rather plausible for the letter as a whole. Paul's rhetoric seems to work well as including a substantial element of introducing, to the relatively ignorant gentile, key aspects of Israel and its situation since the advent of Christ. The points about the scriptures that Paul assumes hearers already know seem easily within the scope of biblical instruction within the house churches.

Finally, Sabina's reading surprised me in revealing two significant aspects of Romans that I had not appreciated before. The first is the curiously prominent minor motif of endurance. Why is endurance involved in Paul's first description of the criterion for eternal life: 'endurance in good work' rather than simply 'doing good work'? Why the strange double reference to endurance in 15.4–5? Why is endurance and hope so central to the culmination of the instructions in chapters 14—15 and, indeed, of the body of the letter as a whole? Endurance is a factor that writers of commentaries on Romans probably need to integrate more effectively into their reading of the letter.

The second aspect is the more substantial one of the letter's major motif of eternal life. There is a great deal of material and it occupies several key locations in chapters 2—8. I was again struck by how little attention is given to this by commentators. However, just before this volume went to press, a new book by Daniel Kirk arrived on my desk. He suggests that resurrection is actually the key to the argument of Romans, a case that he particularly makes by studying second-temple Jewish texts in which resurrection functions as a way of enabling God to be vindicated despite the apparent hopelessness of present situations.[9] To take the resurrection texts in Romans as functioning in this way is an interesting and attractive idea. It is, like most scholarly theories, quite a high-level conceptual idea. Our interests in this study have been elsewhere, with Sabina, struggling in poverty, worrying about survival. She would no doubt have been interested in the vindication of her God. However, the main message that she would surely have heard in the resurrection texts in Romans was that they promised her life after death.

I was once in a class taught by the missiologist Peter Cotterell, who asked us what we saw as being of most value in Christianity. We offered various answers. He said that, in his many years working in Ethiopia, he had discovered that, to people in desperate situations there, overwhelmingly the most valuable promise of Christianity was life after death. To many scholars, this may seem too basic an idea to make much of in the study of a classic text such as Romans. Scholars have always tended to prefer the production of subtle intellectual theories. There is, of course, an important place for theorizing about the many complexities of Paul's greatest letter. However, there is also a place for thinking about how it sounds to people at ground level.

---

[9] J. R. Daniel Kirk, *Unlocking Romans: Resurrection and the Justification of God* (Grand Rapids: Eerdmans, 2008). On resurrection in Romans, see also Peter Head, 'Jesus' Resurrection in Pauline Thought: A Study in Romans', in Peter Head (ed.), *Proclaiming the Resurrection: Papers from the First Oak Hill College Annual School of Theology* (Carlisle: Paternoster, 1998), pp. 58–80; N. T. Wright, *The Resurrection of the Son of God* (London: SPCK; Minneapolis: Fortress, 2003), pp. 241–67.

Bibliography

Alföldy, Geza, *The Social History of Rome* (Totowa, NJ: Barnes & Noble, 1985).

Allison, Penelope M., *The Insula of the Menander at Pompeii. III: The Finds: A Contextual Study* (Oxford: Clarendon Press, 2007).

Allison, Penelope M., *Pompeian Households: An Analysis of the Material Culture* (Monograph 42; Los Angeles: Cotsen Institute of Archaeology at UCLA, 2004).

Ascough, Richard S., *Paul's Macedonian Associations* (WUNT 2.161; Tübingen: Mohr Siebeck, 2003).

Bagnall, Roger S. and Bruce W. Frier, *The Demography of Roman Egypt* (Cambridge: Cambridge University Press, 1994 edn).

Balch, David L., 'Rich Pompeiian Houses, Shops for Rent, and the Huge Apartment Building in Herculaneum as Typical Spaces for Pauline House Churches', *JSNT* 27 (2004), pp. 27–46.

Balch, David L., *Roman Domestic Art and Early House Churches* (WUNT 228; Tübingen: Mohr Siebeck, 2008).

Beard, Mary, John North and Simon Price, *Religions of Rome. Volume I: A History* (Cambridge: Cambridge University Press, 1998).

Bonner, S. F., *Education in Ancient Rome: From the Elder Cato to the Younger Pliny* (London: Methuen, 1977).

Bradley, Keith R., *Discovering the Roman Family* (Oxford: Oxford University Press, 1991).

Bradley, Keith R., *Slavery and Society at Rome* (Cambridge: Cambridge University Press, 1994).

Byron, John, *Slavery Metaphors in Early Judaism and Pauline Christianity* (WUNT 2.162; Tübingen: Mohr Siebeck, 2003).

Chow, John K., *Patronage and Power: A Study of Social Networks in Corinth* (JSNTSup 75; Sheffield: Sheffield Academic Press, 1992).

Clarke, A. D., *Secular and Christian Leadership in Corinth: A Socio-Historical and Exegetical Study of 1 Corinthians 1—6* (Leiden: Brill, 1993).

Clarke, John R., *The Houses of Roman Italy, 100 BC–AD 250: Ritual, Space, and Decoration* (Berkeley: University of California Press, 1991).

Condor, Susan, 'Social Identity and Time', in P. Robinson (ed.), *Social Groups and Identities: Developing the Legacy of Henri Tajfel* (Oxford: Butterworth Heinemann, 1996), pp. 285–315.

Cranfield, C. E. B., *A Critical and Exegetical Commentary on the Epistle to the Romans. Vol. I: Romans I—VIII* (ICC; Edinburgh: T. & T. Clark, 1975).

Cranfield, C. E. B., *A Critical and Exegetical Commentary on the Epistle to the Romans. Vol. II: Romans IX—XVI* (ICC; Edinburgh: T. & T. Clark, 1975).

Das, A. Andrew, *Solving the Romans Debate* (Minneapolis: Fortress, 2007).

Della Corte, M., *Case ed abitanti di Pompei* (Naples: Faustino Fiorentino, 3rd edn, 1965).

Della Corte, M., 'Epigrafi della via fra le Isole VI e X della Reg. I', *Notizie degli scavi* (1929), pp. 455–76.

Della Corte, M., 'Pompei: Iscrizioni dell'Isola X della Regione I', *Notizie degli scavi* (1933), pp. 277–331.

Della Corte, M. (ed.), *Corpus Inscriptionum Latinarum* (Berlin: Königlich Preussische Akademie der Wissenschaften zu Berlin, 1952), IV.3.I.

Dixon, Suzanne, *The Roman Family* (Baltimore: Johns Hopkins University Press, 1992).

Dixon, Suzanne, 'Womanly Weakness in Roman Law', in Suzanne Dixon, *Reading Roman Women: Sources, Genres and Real Life* (London: Duckworth, 2001), pp. 73–88.

Duling, Dennis C., 'Matthew as Marginal Scribe in an Advanced Agrarian Society', *Hervormde Teologiese Studies* 58 (2002), pp. 520–75.

Dunn, James D. G., *Romans 1—8* (Dallas: Word, 1988).

Dunn, James D. G., *Romans 9—16* (Dallas: Word, 1988).

Eisenstadt, S. N. and L. Roniger, *Patrons, Clients and Friends: Interpersonal Relations and the Structure of Trust in Society* (Cambridge: Cambridge University Press, 1984).

Elia, Olga, 'Pompei: Relazione sullo scavo dell'Insula X della Regio I', *Notizie degli scavi* XII (1934), pp. 264–344.

Elliott, John H., *Social-Scientific Criticism of the New Testament* (London: SPCK, 1995).

Elliott, Neil, *Liberating Paul: The Justice of God and the Politics of the Apostle* (Sheffield: Sheffield Academic Press, 1995; Minneapolis: Fortress Press edition, 2006).

Elliott, Neil, *The Rhetoric of Romans: Argumentative Constraint and Strategy and Paul's Dialogue with Judaism* (JSNTSup 45; Sheffield: Sheffield Academic Press, 1990; Minneapolis: Fortress, 2005).

Esler, Philip F., *Conflict and Identity in Romans: The Social Setting of Paul's Letter* (Minneapolis: Fortress; London: SPCK, 2003).

Festinger, Leon, *A Theory of Cognitive Dissonance* (Stanford: Stanford University Press, 1962).

Filson, Floyd, 'The Significance of Early House Churches', *JBL* 58 (1939), pp. 105–11.

Finger, Reta Haltemann, *Paul and the Roman House Churches: A Simulation* (Scottdale, Penn.: Herald Press, 1993).

Friesen, Steven J., 'Poverty in Pauline Studies: Beyond the So-called New Consensus', *JSNT* 26 (2004), pp. 323–61.

Garnsey, Peter, *Social Status and Legal Privilege in the Roman Empire* (Oxford: Clarendon Press, 1970).

Garnsey, Peter and Richard Saller, *The Roman Empire: Economy, Society and Culture* (London: Duckworth, 1987).

Gaston, Lloyd, 'Faith in Romans 12 in the Light of the Common Life of the Roman Church', in Julian V. Hills (ed.), *Common Life in the Early Church: Essays Honoring Graydon F. Snyder* (Harrisburg, Penn.: Trinity Press International, 1998), pp. 258–64.

Geertz, Clifford, 'Thick Description: Toward an Interpretive Theory of Culture', in Clifford Geertz, *The Interpretation of Cultures: Selected Essays* (New York: Basic Books, 1973), pp. 3–30.

Gehring, Roger W., *House Church and Mission* (Peabody, Mass.: Hendrickson, 2004), ET of Roger W. Gehring, *Hausgemeinde und Mission* (Bibelwissenschaftliche Monographien 9; Giessen: Brunnen Verlag, 2000).

George, Michele, '*Servus* and *domus*: The Slave in the Roman House', in R. Laurence and A. Wallace-Hadrill (eds), *Domestic Space in the Roman World: Pompeii and Beyond* (JRASup 22; Portsmouth, RI: Journal of Roman Archaeology, 1997), pp. 15–24.

Glancy, Jennifer A., *Slavery in Early Christianity* (Oxford: Oxford University Press, 2002; paperback edn Minneapolis: Fortress, 2006).

Harland, Philip A., *Associations, Synagogues and Congregations: Claiming a Place in Ancient Mediterranean Society* (Minneapolis: Fortress, 2003).

Harrill, J. Albert, *The Manumission of Slaves in Early Christianity* (Hermeneutische Untersuchungen zur Theologie 32; Tübingen: Mohr Siebeck, 1995).

Harrill, J. Albert, *Slaves in the New Testament: Literary, Social and Moral Dimensions* (Minneapolis: Fortress, 2006).

Harrison, J. R., 'Paul and the Imperial Gospel at Thessaloniki', *JSNT* 25 (2002), pp. 71–96.

Head, Peter, 'Jesus' Resurrection in Pauline Thought: A Study in Romans', in Peter Head (ed.), *Proclaiming the Resurrection: Papers from the First Oak Hill College Annual School of Theology* (Carlisle: Paternoster, 1998), pp. 58–80.

Hoepfner, W. and E.-L. Schwander, *Haus und Stadt in klassischen Griechenland* (Munich: Deutscher Kunstverlag, 1986).

Horrell, David G., 'Domestic Space and Christian Meetings at Corinth: Imagining New Contexts and the Buildings East of the Theatre', *New Testament Studies* 50 (2004), pp. 349–69.

Jewett, Robert, *Romans: A Commentary* (Hermeneia; Minneapolis: Fortress, 2007).

Jongman, Willem M., 'The Loss of Innocence: Pompeian Economy and Society between Past and Present', in John J. Dobbins and Pedar W. Foss (eds), *The World of Pompeii* (London: Routledge, 2007), pp. 499–517.

Jongman, Willem M., *The Economy and Society of Pompeii* (Dutch Monographs on Ancient History and Archaeology 4; Amsterdam: Gieben, 1988).

Kirk, J. R. Daniel, *Unlocking Romans: Resurrection and the Justification of God* (Grand Rapids: Eerdmans, 2008).

Klauck, Hans-Josef, *Hausgemeinde und Hauskirche im frühen Christentum* (Stuttgarter Bibelstudien 103; Stuttgart: Verlag Katholisches Bibelwerk, 1981).

Klutz, Todd, *The Exorcism Stories in Luke–Acts: A Sociostylistic Reading* (SNTSMS 129; Cambridge: Cambridge University Press, 2004).

Lampe, Peter, *From Paul to Valentinus: Christians at Rome in the First Two Centuries*, ed. M. D. Johnson, tr. M. Steinhauser (Minneapolis: Fortress; London: T. & T. Clark, 2003).

Lawrence, Louise J., *An Ethnography of the Gospel of Matthew: A Critical Assessment of the Use of the Honour and Shame Model in Biblical Studies* (WUNT 2.165; Tübingen: Mohr Siebeck, 2003).

Lenski, Gerhard, *Power and Privilege: A Theory of Social Stratification* (New York: McGraw-Hill, 1966).

Lewis, C. S., *The Screwtape Letters* (London: Fontana Books, 1955).

Lewis, N. and M. Reinhold, *Roman Civilization, Selected Readings. II: The Empire* (New York: Columbia University Press, 3rd edn, 1990).

Ling, Roger, *The Insula of the Menander at Pompeii. I: The Structures* (Oxford: Clarendon Press, 1997).

Ling, Roger, 'Working Practice', in Roger Ling (ed.), *Making Classical Art: Process and Practice* (Stroud: Tempus, 2000), pp. 91–107.

Ling, Roger and Lesley Ling, *The Insula of the Menander at Pompeii. II: The Decorations* (Oxford: Clarendon Press, 2004).

McGinn, Thomas A. J., 'The Legal Definition of Prostitute in Late Antiquity', in Malcolm Bell III and Caroline Bruzelius (eds), *Memoirs of the American Academy in Rome* 42 (Washington, DC: American Academy in Rome, 1997), pp. 73–116.

McGinn, Thomas A. J., *Prostitution, Sexuality and Law in Ancient Rome* (New York: Oxford University Press, 1998).

MacMullen, Ramsay, *Roman Social Relations: 50 BC to AD 284* (New Haven: Yale University Press, 1974).

Maiuri, Amadeo, *La Casa del Menandro e il suo tesoro di argenteria* (Rome: La Libreria dello Stato, 1933).

Malina, Bruce J., *The New Testament World: Insights from Cultural Anthropology* (London: SCM Press, 1983).

Malina, Bruce J. and John J. Pilch, *Social Science Commentary on the Letters of Paul* (Minneapolis: Fortress, 2006).

Manson, T. W., 'St. Paul's Letter to the Romans – and Others', in M. Black (ed.), *Studies in the Gospels and Epistles* (Manchester: Manchester University Press, 1962), pp. 225–41.

Martin, Dale B., *Slavery as Salvation: The Metaphor of Slavery in Pauline Christianity* (New Haven: Yale University Press, 1990).

Meeks, Wayne A., *The First Urban Christians: The Social World of the Apostle Paul* (New Haven: Yale University Press, 1983).

Meggitt, Justin J., *Paul, Poverty and Survival* (Edinburgh: T. & T. Clark, 1998).

Meyer, Marvin W. and Richard Smith, *Ancient Christian Magic: Coptic Texts of Ritual Power* (Princeton: Princeton University Press, 1999).

Mitchell, Alan C., 'The Social Function of Friendship in Acts 2:44–47 and 4:32–37', *JBL* 3 (1992), pp. 255–72.

Mosco, Maisie, *Almonds and Raisins* (London: New English Library, 1979).

Moxnes, Halvor, 'Honour and Righteousness in Romans', *JSNT* 32 (1988), pp. 61–77.

Mullins, T. Y., 'Greetings as a New Testament Form', *JBL* 88 (1968), pp. 418–26.

Murphy-O'Connor, Jerome, 'Prisca and Aquila: Traveling Tentmakers and Church Builders', *Bible Review* 8.6 (1992), pp. 40–51, 62.

Murphy-O'Connor, Jerome, *St. Paul's Corinth: Texts and Archaeology* (Good News Studies 6; Wilmington, Del.: Glazier, 1983).

Muscettola, Adamo, 'Le ciste di piombo decorate', in Università di Napoli, *La regione sotterrata del Vesuvio: studi e prospettive* (Naples: Università degli studi di Napoli, 1982), pp. 701–34.

Nanos, Mark, *The Mystery of Romans* (Minneapolis: Fortress, 1996).

Oakes, Peter, 'Constructing Poverty Scales for Graeco-Roman Society: A Response to Steven Friesen's "Poverty in Pauline Studies"', *JSNT* 26 (2004), pp. 367–71.

Oakes, Peter, 'Contours of the Urban Environment', in Todd Still and David Horrell (eds), *After the First Urban Christians* (London: T. & T. Clark, 2009).

Oakes, Peter, 'Jason and Penelope Hear Philippians 1:1–11', in C. Fletcher-Louis and C. Rowland (eds), *Understanding, Study and Reading: Essays in Honour of John Ashton* (JSNTSup 153; Sheffield: Sheffield Academic Press, 1998), pp. 199–212.

Oakes, Peter, 'Made Holy by the Holy Spirit: Holiness and Ecclesiology in Romans', in Kent E. Brower and Andy Johnson (eds), *Holiness and Ecclesiology in the New Testament* (Grand Rapids: Eerdmans, 2007), pp. 167–83.

Oakes, Peter, *Philippians: From People to Letter* (SNTSMS 110; Cambridge: Cambridge University Press, 2001).

Oakes, Peter, 'Re-mapping the Universe: Paul and the Emperor in 1 Thessalonians and Philippians', *JSNT* 27 (2005), pp. 301–22.

Osiek, Carolyn and David L. Balch, *Families in the New Testament World: Households and House Churches* (Louisville: Westminster John Knox, 1997).

Osiek, Carolyn and Margaret Y. MacDonald with Janet H. Tulloch, *A Woman's Place: House Churches in Earliest Christianity* (Minneapolis: Fortress, 2006).

Packer, James E., *The Insulae of Imperial Ostia* (American Academy in Rome Memoirs 31; Rome: American Academy in Rome, 1971).

Painter, Kenneth S., *The Insula of the Menander at Pompeii. IV: The Silver Treasure* (Oxford: Clarendon Press, 2001).

Parkin, Tim G., *Demography and Roman Society* (Baltimore: Johns Hopkins University Press, 1992).

Pilhofer, Peter, *Philippi II: Katalog der Inschriften von Philippi* (WUNT 119; Tübingen: Mohr Siebeck, 2000).

Portefaix, Lilian, *Sisters Rejoice: Paul's Letter to the Philippians and Luke–Acts as Received by First Century Philippian Women* (Coniectanea Biblica NT Series 20; Uppsala and Stockholm: Almqvist and Wiksell International, 1988).

Pudsey, April, 'Sex, Statistics and Soldiers: New Approaches to the Demography of Roman Egypt', *28 BC–259 AD* (Manchester: unpublished PhD thesis, 2007).

Purcell, Nicholas, 'vigiles', in *Oxford Classical Dictionary*, ed. S. Hornblower and A. Spawforth (Oxford: Oxford University Press, 3rd edn, 1996), p. 1598.

Rodger, A. F., 'peculium', in *Oxford Classical Dictionary*, ed. S. Hornblower and A. Spawforth (Oxford: Oxford University Press, 3rd edn, 1996), p. 1130.

Scheid, John, 'Saturnus, Saturnalia', in *Oxford Classical Dictionary*, ed. S. Hornblower and A. Spawforth (Oxford: Oxford University Press, 3rd edn, 1996), pp. 1360–1.

Shelton, Jo-Ann, *As the Romans Did: A Sourcebook in Roman Social History* (New York: Oxford University Press, 2nd edn, 1998).

Sherwin-White, A. N., A. H. M. Jones and T. Honoré, 'decuriones', in *Oxford Classical Dictionary*, ed. S. Hornblower and A. Spawforth (Oxford: Oxford University Press, 3rd edn, 1996), pp. 437–8.

Stegemann, Ekkehard W. and Wolfgang Stegemann, *The Jesus Movement: A Social History of its First Century*, tr. O. C. Dean Jr (Minneapolis: Fortress, 1999).

Stendahl, Krister, 'The Apostle Paul and the Introspective Conscience of the West', *Paul Among Jews and Gentiles* (Philadelphia: Fortress, 1976), pp. 78–96.

Stevenson, G. H. and A. W. Lintott, 'clubs, Roman', in *Oxford Classical Dictionary*, ed. S. Hornblower and A. Spawforth (Oxford: Oxford University Press, 3rd edn, 1996), pp. 352–3.

Stowers, Stanley K., *A Rereading of Romans: Justice, Jews, and Gentiles* (New Haven: Yale University Press, 1994).

Stuhlmacher, Peter, *Paul's Letter to the Romans: A Commentary*, tr. S. J. Hafemann (Edinburgh: T. & T. Clark, 1994).

Theissen, Gerd, *The Social Setting of Pauline Christianity: Essays on Corinth* (Edinburgh and Philadelphia: T. & T. Clark and Fortress, 1982).

Thompson, Michael B., *Clothed with Christ: The Example and Teaching of Jesus in Romans 12.1—15.13* (JSNTSup 59; Sheffield: Sheffield Academic Press, 1991).

Thorsteinsson, Runar M., *Paul's Interlocutor in Romans 2: Function and Identity in the Context of Ancient Epistolography* (Coniectanea Biblica NT Series 40; Stockholm: Almqvist and Wiksell, 2003).

Wallace-Hadrill, Andrew, '*Domus* and *Insulae* in Rome: Families and Housefuls', in David Balch and Carolyn Osiek (eds), *Early Christian Families in Context: An Interdisciplinary Dialogue* (Grand Rapids: Eerdmans, 2003), pp. 3–18.

Wallace-Hadrill, Andrew, *Houses and Society in Pompeii and Herculaneum* (Princeton: Princeton University Press, 1994).

Wasserman, Emma, *The Death of the Soul in Romans 7: Sin, Death, and the Law in Light of Hellenistic Moral Psychology* (WUNT 2.256; Tübingen: Mohr Siebeck, 2008).

Weiser, Anton, 'Evangelisierung im Haus', *BZ* 34 (1990), pp. 64–77.

Wengst, Klaus, *Humility: Solidarity of the Humiliated. The Transformation of an Attitude and its Social Relevance in Graeco-Roman, Old Testament-Jewish and Early Christian Tradition*, tr. J. Bowden (London: SCM Press, 1988).

White, L. M., *Building God's House in the Roman World: Architectural Adaptation among Pagans, Jews and Christians* (Baltimore: Johns Hopkins University, 1990).

Whittaker, C. R., 'The Poor in the City of Rome', in C. R. Whittaker, *Land, City and Trade in the Roman Empire* (Variorum; Aldershot: Ashgate, 1993).

Wiefel, Wolfgang, 'The Jewish Community in Ancient Rome and the Origins of Roman Christianity', in K. P. Donfried (ed.), *The Romans Debate* (Peabody, Mass.: Hendrickson, 1991 edn), pp. 85–101.

Witherington, Ben, III with Darlene Hyatt, *Paul's Letter to the Romans: A Socio-Rhetorical Commentary* (Grand Rapids: Eerdmans, 2004).

Wright, N. T., *Paul: Fresh Perspectives* (London: SPCK, 2005).

Wright, N. T., *The Resurrection of the Son of God* (London: SPCK; Minneapolis: Fortress, 2003).

Zanker, Paul, *Pompeii: Public and Private Life*, tr. D. L. Schneider (Cambridge, Mass.: Harvard University Press, 1998).

Index of biblical references

Index of modern authors

Index of subjects